Series authors:
Malcolm Mann
Steve Taylore-Knowles

Laser B1+

Teacher's Book

MACMILLAN

Macmillan Education
4 Crinan Street
London N1 9XW
A division of Macmillan Publishers Limited
Companies and representatives throughout the world

ISBN 978-0-230-43374-8

Series authors: Malcolm Mann & Steve Taylore-Knowles

This edition published 2013
Second edition published 2008
First edition published 2004

Original design by Peter Burgess
Page make-up by Expo Holdings, Malaysia
Cover design by Peter Burgess

Teacher's DVD-ROM

ISBN 978-0-230-43379-3

Series authors: Malcolm Mann & Steve Taylore-Knowles

Software developed by MPS Limited

The authors and publishers would like to thank the following for permission to reproduce their photographs:
Alamy; Corbis; Getty Images; Macmillan New Zealand

Audio produced and recorded by James Richardson Ltd

For technical support, please visit help.macmillan.com

Printed and bound in Thailand

2017 2016 2015
11 10 9 8 7 6 5

Contents

Introduction: Welcome to *Laser B1+*!

Laser B1+ is designed to make your job as easy and stress-free as possible. To this end, it's worth spending a few minutes reading this introduction to see how the course is structured and what it provides you with in terms of materials.

We hope this Teacher's Book will be a useful tool for you throughout the teaching year. The more familiar you are with the various features that are included in the book, the more useful we think you will find it.

Components
A number of different components make up the *Laser B1+* course:

- *Laser B1+* **Student's Book** with Student's **CD-ROM**
- *Laser B1+* Student's Book **Class Audio CDs**
- *Laser B1+* **Workbook** (with and without key versions) with **Audio CD**
- *Laser B1+* **Teacher's Book**
- *Laser B1+* **Teacher's DVD-ROM** (packaged with the Teacher's Book)
- *Laser B1+* **Digibook** (packaged with the Teacher's Book)

Let's look at each of them in turn.

Laser B1+ Student's Book

There are 16 topic-based units. Each unit contains the following sections:

- **Start thinking!**, a short warm-up and lead-in to the topic
- **Reading**, developing key reading skills through the presentation of an attractively illustrated text
- **WORD BOX**, focusing on topic-based lexis and lexico-grammar from the Reading section, this section seeks to build up students' lexical knowledge
- **Have your say!**, an opportunity for students to give their own opinions
- **Grammar clinic**, focusing on one key grammar point (which has been exemplified in the preceding Reading text), this section presents the grammar point and is followed by exercises for consolidation
- **Vocabulary builder**, focusing on topic-based phrasal verbs, word formation, patterns, collocations, etc, again aimed at building up students' lexical repertoire
- **Listening**, developing key listening skills through a variety of exercise types
- **Soundbite**, focusing on the production and reception of key phonetic areas that may prove problematic for students
- **Speaking**, developing key speaking skills based on a variety of scenarios that are relevant to both the students' lives and the requirements of exams
- **Use of English**, revising, consolidating and building on language from the unit within exam-style contexts
- **Writing**, developing key writing skills through the study of model writing tasks and related exercises and working towards the production of a piece of writing

After every two units, there is a two-page **Revision** section, revising and consolidating the grammar and vocabulary from the preceding two units.

At the back of the book, there is:

- a **Writing database**, with key information about each writing type students are expected to produce in *Laser B1+*
- a set of 16 **Writing Planners** (one for each unit)
- a **Word pattern database**, with word patterns appearing in the course
- an alphabetical **Phrasal verb database**, with phrasal verbs appearing in the course with definitions
- a **Speaking database** arranged by function, providing examples of all the key language required for the Speaking sections
- a 31-page **Grammar database**, containing additional information for each grammar point covered in the Student's Book, plus a **Quick Check** task for each grammar point.
- an **Alphabetical index of Grammar database points** for students' reference
- a **Webquests** section, containing Webquests for students to complete every two units

Laser B1+ Student's CD-ROM

Every Student's Book includes a CD-ROM which gives students the opportunity to practise and develop their language learning in a motivating and enjoyable way. It contains nine additional revision and consolidation tasks for each unit:
- three of these tasks focus on **vocabulary**
- three of these tasks focus on **grammar**
- three of these tasks focus on grammar and/or vocabulary within an exam-style task

One or two of the above tasks in each unit require the students to carry out some form of **listening** activity.

The Student's CD-ROM provides the opportunity for extra practice and consolidation of the structures and lexical items learned in the Student's Book units. It is a flexible component in that it can be used in class as an integrated part of the lesson, or can be used by students independently outside the classroom, either as a homework task or as an extra option to support their learning.

Laser B1+ Student's Book Class Audio CD

This contains all the recorded material for the Reading, Listening and Soundbite sections of the Student's Book.

The CD track references for this audio material are provided in the Teacher's Book.

Laser B1+ Workbook

There are two versions of the Workbook: one with answer key and one without.

The Workbook revises and consolidates the work done in the Student's Book, and at times extends it further too.

All Workbook exercises are designed so that they can be assigned for homework.

Each unit of the Workbook contains the following sections:
- **Reading**, consolidating and extending the work done in the Student's Book Reading section, using a variety of text types and exercises
- **Vocabulary**, revising and consolidating the work done in the Student's Book **WORD BOX** section
- **Grammar 1**, revising and consolidating the work done in the Student's Book Grammar clinic section
- **Vocabulary builder**, revising and consolidating the work done in the Student's Book Vocabulary builder section
- **Grammar 2**, revising and consolidating the grammar work done in the Student's Book Use of English section
- **Use of English**, revising and consolidating the vocabulary and grammar work done throughout the unit
- **Writing**, revising, consolidating and extending the work done in the Student's Book Writing section
- **Listening**, consolidating and extending the work done in the Student's Book Listening section, using a variety of listening situations and a range of speakers

The Workbook also contains ten two-page **Check your progress!** tests for units 1–2, 3–4, 5–6, 7–8, 1–8, 9–10, 11–12, 13–14, 15–16 and 9–16.

The **Workbook Audio CD** contains all the recorded material for the Listening sections.

Laser B1+ Teacher's Book

As we said earlier, this Teacher's Book has been specially written in order to make your life as a teacher easier. We have tried to include a range of useful information along with detailed teacher's notes for every Student's Book task. Once you have familiarised yourself with the Teacher's Book and you know what information it contains and where that information can be found, we hope you will find it constructive and helpful as you work your way through *Laser B1+* with your students.

The Teacher's Book contains:
- information on the **Target language** for each unit
- information on the **Aim** of each task and section
- detailed guidelines for teachers on how to use the material in the Student's Book most effectively, including what to write on the board in **On the Board** sections
- an **Answer key** to all exercises with additional explanation of answers where appropriate
- **Additional Task** boxes, containing suggestions for supplementary activities
- A **CD Track reference** for each listening activity
- **Suggested homework** sections indicating when and which Workbook exercises should be assigned
- The **audioscripts** for all listening activities in the Student's Book where the complete script does not appear on the Student's Book page
- References to additional tasks and tests on the **Student's CD-ROM** and the **Teacher's DVD-ROM**

We recommend that, irrespective of whether you're a new or highly experienced teacher, you make the most of the material provided in the Teacher's Book both during the planning of a lesson and, if appropriate, during the lesson itself.

However, we do not want you to feel restrained by the notes and guidance in the Teacher's Book. You may wish to omit certain parts of an activity, or extend an activity further, or carry out an activity in a different way to the way suggested. You know your students and their needs best, and you know what the time constraints are. The aim of the Teacher's Book is to help you, not hinder you, in your teaching.

Laser B1+ Teacher's DVD-ROM

This is packaged with the Teacher's Book and contains several extra resources which we hope you will find useful.

There are three sections on the DVD-ROM:
Tests, Test Generator and **Teacher's support videos.**

The **Tests** section contains:
- 16 **Unit Tests**, focusing on reading, listening, grammar, vocabulary and writing
- three **Term Tests**, covering units 1–5, 6–10 and 11–16
- one complete **FCE (Lite) Practice Test** (a version of the FCE exam which has been made more appropriate for students at this level)
- the **Answer key** for these tests

All the tests are available as either editable Word documents or as PDFs. If you opt for the Word documents, you can change or add to the material as many times as you like in order to make it suitable for your particular student group. If you opt for the PDFs, the tests are formatted and ready for you to print and use immediately. But you won't be able to edit the tests in PDF format.

The **Test Generator** section allows you to produce custom-made tests, and contains the following elements for each unit:
- six **Vocabulary** tasks
- six **Grammar** tasks
- four **Reading** tasks
- three **Speaking** tasks
- four **Listening** tasks
- the **Answer key** for these tasks

The **Test Generator** enables you to select the specific skills you wish to test, choosing as few or as many as you like. It also enables you to choose which unit or units you would like to test at any one time.

Approximately half of the **Test Generator** tasks in each unit are labelled as being **less challenging** and the other half as **more challenging**, allowing you to choose appropriate tasks for particular students or groups of students depending on their level and ability.

Many of the tasks included in the bank of **Test Generator** material are the same as or similar to exam-style tasks.

The **Teacher's support videos** section of the DVD-ROM contains a series of short videos featuring both the *Laser* authors (Malcolm Mann and Steve Taylore-Knowles).

The aim of the videos is to provide teachers with a range of suggestions and ideas about how to use the material in *Laser B1+*.

The topics covered in *Laser B1+* **Teacher's support videos** are:
- **Introduction**
- **Reading:** Developing reading skills
- **Writing:** Using the writer's database
- **Listening:** Varying the second listening task
- **Speaking:** Using class discussions
- **Vocabulary:** Magic metaphors
- **Pronunciation and phonetics:** Using Soundbite

In the videos, the authors explain the rationale behind some of the features in *Laser B1+* Student's Book, suggest procedures for working through the *Laser B1+* material or give ideas for more ways of exploiting the Student's Book material.

Each video is between three and four minutes long.

There are also **Extra Reading tasks** on the Teacher's DVD-ROM. New to the third edition, these offer more opportunities for exploitation of the reading texts in each unit of the Student's Book.

Laser B1+ Digibook

The **Digibook** is a page-faithful, digital version of the Student's Book.

The *Laser B1+* **Digibook** is designed for you to use in class. To use the book, you will need a computer connected to a projector, or an interactive white board (IWB). However, for those of you who are not familiar with IWB techniques, it is important to remember that the Digibook is very simple to use and requires no previous IWB experience whatsoever. You will be able to see the relevant icons for audio material, answer keys and links to the grammar database explanations, as well as the zoom feature enabling you to enlarge specific exercises or areas of the Student's Book page.

The **Digibook** contains a full answer key to all tasks. Answers for each individual exercise can be revealed as and when you feel it's appropriate.

The **Audio** section contains all of the audio material featured in the Student's Book, including all listening exercises.

The **Digibook** can provide a visual focal point for your lesson and enable more 'heads-up' learning, where your students are much more engaged and are all focusing on the Student's Book pages as projected at the front of the classroom rather than all working with their heads down, reading the book on their desks. This makes the class more cohesive. You can consolidate new vocabulary, demonstrate exercises, play audio tracks, and check answers to exercises. You can also personalise the content, adapting it to your own teaching style, by writing, highlighting and drawing on the pages using the optional IWB tools provided.

We very much hope you and your students enjoy using *Laser B1+* as much as we enjoyed writing it. If you or your students have any questions about the course, please contact us through the publisher. We would love to hear from you!

Have a great school year!

Malcolm Mann & Steve Taylore-Knowles

Student's Book contents map

Listening	Speaking	Use of English	Writing
predicting, Soundbite: /ɪ/ and /iː/	talking about family	stative verbs, word patterns	selecting correct register, informal letter/email
identifying location, Soundbite: /æ/and /e/	comparing	*would*, *used to*, *be used to*, word patterns	presenting an argument, essay
understanding attitude, Soundbite: /ʌ/	making suggestions	articles, synonyms	awareness of target reader, informal letter/email
listening for specific information, Soundbite: silent letters (1)	expressing uncertainty	comparatives and superlatives	layout and text structure, report
listening for gist, Soundbite: /ɜː/	talking about experiences	countable and uncountable nouns, homonyms	using descriptive language, story
listening for specific information, Soundbite: weak forms (1)	speculating	question tags, connectors	selecting appropriate style, article
identifying roles, Soundbite: /k/, /g/ and /ŋ/	agreeing and disagreeing	indirect questions, prepositions	using prompts, formal letter/email
listening for specific information, Soundbite: /s/ and /z/	giving examples	*prefer*, *would rather*, *had better*, parts of speech	expressing opinion, review

Listening	Speaking	Use of English	Writing
listening for specific information, Soundbite: /s/ and /ʃ/	talking about hopes	*unless, in case, as long as,* word patterns	paragraphing, informal letter/email
predicting, Soundbite: /ə/	expressing attitude and opinion	parts of speech, word formation: prefixes	cohesion, essay
predicting, Soundbite: stress (1)	prioritising	relative pronouns and prepositions, word patterns	selecting correct register, informal letter/email
listening for gist, Soundbite: /ɑː/, /ɔː/ and /uː/	discourse management	infinitives of purpose, word patterns	awareness of purpose, report
identifying relationships, Soundbite: silent letters (2)	talking about interests	gradable and ungradable adjectives and adverbs, synonyms	making recommendations, review
listening for specific information, Soundbite: stress (2)	comparing	the unreal past, common mistakes	selecting correct register, article
understanding purpose, Soundbite: /ɒ/ and /əʊ/	expressing attitude and opinion	transferred negation, word formation	using prompts, formal letter/email
listening for specific information, Soundbite: weak forms (2)	seeking clarification	wishes and regrets, parts of speech	paragraphing, story

1

Family Ties

Target language

Grammar:	present simple and present continuous / stative verbs / word patterns
Lexis:	topic vocabulary / word formation (prefixes) / phrasal verbs with *up* / metaphors (people)
Reading skills:	scanning for specific information
Listening skills:	predicting
Speaking skills:	talking about family
Writing skills:	selecting correct register / informal letter/email
Pronunciation:	/i/ and /iː/

- The phrase *family ties* means close connections or relationships between people within the same family, eg *Family ties have become weaker over the past 50 years.*
- Write the phrase *family ties* on the board.
- Ask students what they think the title refers to.
- Explain the meaning of the phrase *family ties.*
- Write the example sentence given above on the board.
- Elicit suggestions as to what the unit might be about.

ON THE BOARD

family ties
Family ties have become weaker over the past 50 years.

Start thinking!

Aim: to introduce the topic of family life through personal responses

- Ask students to work in pairs to talk about the questions in the Student's Book.
- Go round the class monitoring and helping where necessary.
- If you prefer, conduct a brief discussion involving the whole class by reading the questions and inviting different students to give their answers.

Additional task

- Before students attempt this task, write these phrases on the board: *close family* and *extended family.*
- Elicit from the students which family members they would put into each category. You might need to prompt them by offering a few suggestions, eg brother, cousin, father, grandmother, etc.
(*Close family* refers to those family members to whom you are directly related, for example, a parent, child, brother or sister. *Extended family* refers to those family members outside the close family and includes grandparents, cousins and aunts and uncles.)
- Ask students to write down as many words for members of a family as they can, eg brother, uncle, etc.
- You may wish to set a time limit of one or two minutes for this.
- Ask them to tick those people who belong to their close family and those who belong to their extended family.

Reading CD1, Track 1

1

Aim: to read for gist

- Students are going to read someone's post from a social networking site and the comments left by her friends. Begin by asking if any students are on social networking sites and which ones are most popular. Ask them what kinds of things they post on social networking sites.
- Ask students to read the post and the comments quickly. Remind students that at this stage they do not need to understand all of the vocabulary as items will be covered in the **WORD BOX** section.
- Ask a few students to comment on which family is most like their own. Ask them to say why.

2

Aim: to scan for specific information

- Explain to students that they are going to read statements about the people and decide whether each statement is true, false or not stated in the post and comments. Tell them that they should not read everything in detail, but should scan (move their eyes across the text looking for specific information) until they find the relevant part of the text. They should then look only at that part in detail to do the task.

- Do the first one together. Ask a student to read the statement and say which part of the text will contain the information relevant to that statement (the first paragraph, written by Jenny). Ask the students to quickly scan that paragraph and to say whether it contains information about the size of Jenny's family (no, it doesn't). Elicit the fact that this means that the first statement is 'not stated'.
- Either complete the exercise in the same way as a whole class, or give students some time to complete the exercise. Go over the answers orally.

1 N	3 T	5 F
2 F	4 T	6 N

3

Aim: to scan for specific information

- Ask students to read the questions and explain that again they need to scan the text to find the answers to each one. This time, they need to find a specific word or phrase from the post and the comments that answers each question.
- Explain that often scanning for specific information means that you need to look for things expressed in other words. Ask a student to read the first question and tell students that as they are scanning they may not find the word 'pet', but they may find a word connected to that, such as 'cat', 'dog', etc.
- Ask them to scan and put their hand up when they find the relevant part of the text (the middle of Alicia's comment). Elicit that the answer to the first question is 'Alicia'.
- Either complete the exercise in the same way as a whole class, or give students some time to complete the exercise. Go over the answers orally.

1 Alicia
2 she's older (and works in New York)
3 (a bit) spoilt
4 almost every weekend
5 share a room (with their brother or sister)
6 a project on families (at school)

Additional task

- Ask students to write a short paragraph of 50 words describing what their family is like. Invite students to read their paragraphs to the whole class.

WORD BOX

4

Aim: to introduce new vocabulary

- Before students do this exercise, ask them to read the sentences.
- Remind them of the importance of deciding before they complete the sentences whether they need to look for a noun, adjective or verb in the passage.
- Ask students to work individually or with a partner to do the exercise.
- Elicit answers.
- Ask students if there were any other words in the passage which they didn't know the meaning of.
- Remind them to make a note of the words and to look them up in a dictionary before the start of the next lesson.
- Ask students if they enjoyed reading the article and whether they learned anything from it or not and get them to justify their answers.

1 only child	5 stepsister
2 spoilt	6 loving
3 divorced	7 adopted
4 remarried	8 half brother

Additional task

- Ask students to choose five words or phrases from the **WORD BOX** and to write their own sentences with the word missing.
- Students then swap their sentences with a partner and try to fill in the missing word.

Have your say!

Aim: to give students the opportunity to express their own opinions

- Put the students in pairs and get them to ask each other the questions. Ask them to make brief notes on their partner's answers. When they have finished, invite various students to tell the whole class what they discussed.
- Alternatively, you may like to do the activity as a whole class. Invite various students to give their opinions, encouraging them to agree or disagree with what other students have said. Encourage them to give reasons for their opinions.

Suggested homework

Assign Ex. 1 – Workbook, p.4–5
Ex. 1 – Workbook, p.5

G Grammar clinic

1

Aim: to review present tenses

- Before students do the exercises on this page, ask them to study pages 166–168 of the **Grammar database**, either in class or at home before the lesson starts.
- The first exercise refers back to the reading passage so that students can see the grammar in question being used in context.

- Read the sentences and ask students to tell you which tense is being used in each sentence.
- Ask students to match each sentence to its explanation.

1 d	2 e	3 a	4 c	5 b

Additional task

- Ask students to write five sentences of their own, which can be matched to the list of explanations in a–e.

2

Aim: to practise using present tenses in context

- Students work individually or with a partner to do the exercise.
- Elicit answers, asking students to give reasons for their answers based on the information in the **Grammar database**.

1 goes: a regular habit
2 are staying: a temporary situation
3 doesn't drive: a general ability
4 live: a general truth
5 argue: a regular habit

3

Aim: to practise using present tenses

- First, write this sentence on the board: *I am playing volleyball for my local team.*
- Ask students to explain to you what is wrong with the sentence (The *present simple* is used to talk about habits.).
- Go through the first sentence together.
- Tell them to ignore the missing verb for the moment.
- Ask: *Is this a feeling or an action?* (an action)
- Ask: *Is it a regular habit or a temporary situation?* (a regular habit)
- Ask: *What tense do we use for regular habits?* (*present simple*)
- Remind students to go through this process of asking themselves questions about the sentence before they fill in the gaps.
- Students then work individually or with a partner to do the exercise.
- Elicit answers.

1 go	3 am learning	5 am trying
2 are living	4 don't like	6 see

ON THE BOARD

I am playing volleyball for my local team.

4

Aim: to further practise using present tenses

- First, go through the first one together.
- Tell them to ignore the missing words for the moment.
- Ask: *Is this a feeling or an action?* (an action)
- Ask: *Is it a habit or a temporary situation?* (a habit)
- Ask: *Is it a regular habit or an annoying habit?* (an annoying habit)
- Ask: *What tense do we use for annoying habits?* (*present continuous*)
- Remind students to go through this process of asking themselves questions about the sentence before they write the sentences.
- Students then work individually or with a partner to do the exercise.
- Elicit answers.

1 My brother is always complaining about me to my parents.
2 In our house, we always eat dinner together and I like it.
3 My stepsister plays the piano and she knows hundreds of songs.
4 I think Mum is having a shower. She usually has a shower at this time.
5 My relationship with my sister is getting better.
6 I don't believe everything my brother tells me.

5

Aim: to identify incorrect use of present tenses.

- Students now work individually to find six mistakes in a short paragraph.
- Remind them to read through the text once, underlining verbs which they think are incorrect.
- Encourage them to ask themselves the kind of questions that they were asked in exercises 3 and 4.
- Students should then work individually.
- Elicit answers.
- After students have completed this exercise, write this sentence on the board: *My mum is being a teacher and my dad is working as a waiter until he finds a better job.*
- Elicit from students why the *present continuous* is used in the underlined part of the sentence. (It is a temporary situation.)
- Elicit why 'is being a teacher' is incorrect. (The *present simple* is used for general truths: *My mum is a teacher…*)

Jenny
Thanks for all your comments! You all have really interesting families! Masha, you're doing a project on families too, so I thought I'd tell you about my family. There are five of us in my family – my mum and dad, me, my older brother, Alex and my younger sister, Lizzie. My mum's a newsreader on TV and my dad works in an office (I don't really know what he does!). I generally get on very well with Lizzie and Alex, but they're always playing tricks on me, and that's very annoying! I've also got two sets of grandparents, and they often come to visit us. In fact, Grandma Mollie and Grandpa Doug are staying with us at the moment, which is nice. I love my family!

ON THE BOARD

My mum is being a teacher and my dad is working as a waiter until he finds a better job.

Suggested homework

Assign Ex. 1, 2 and 3 – Workbook, p.6

V Vocabulary builder

1

Aim: to focus on adjectives used to describe people

- Either do this exercise as a class, or divide the class into small groups and encourage them to use a dictionary in order to find the meaning of any unknown words.
- Before students attempt this exercise, ask them to read through the sentences 1–11 and underline any other descriptive adjectives which might be useful as clues to help them do the exercise. Students should find the following adjectives: *successful, funny, upset, better.*
- Ask students to do the exercise.
- Elicit answers.

1 ambitious	5 generous	9 considerate
2 pessimistic	6 sensitive	10 modest
3 popular	7 optimistic	11 arrogant
4 amusing	8 selfish	

Additional task

- Write the headings *positive* and *negative* on the board.
- Ask students to look at the list of adjectives in the Student's Book and to tell you which they think are positive descriptions of someone's character and which are negative.

positive
ambitious / popular / amusing / generous / sensitive / optimistic / considerate / modest
negative
pessimistic / selfish / arrogant

- Brainstorm any other descriptive adjectives that they know and elicit which category they should fit into.
- Encourage individual students to come up and write their ideas on the board.

2

Aim: to practise forming negative adjectives by adding a prefix

- In this exercise students have to find the negative adjective. Remind students, however, that in exam-type word formation exercises, they will need to work out whether the word required should be positive or negative.
- Ask students to look at the adjectives in bold and brainstorm any opposites which they might know already and write them on the board.
- Students then work individually or with a partner to complete the sentences.
- Elicit answers.

1 unkind	5 dishonest
2 impolite	6 incapable
3 unattractive	7 illegal
4 unfair	8 irrelevant

Additional task

- Ask students, either individually or in pairs, to make a list of other adjectives they know which take the same prefixes.
- Get students to compare the lists they have come up with.

3

Aim: to introduce phrasal verbs with *up*

- Point out to students that phrasal verbs that share the same particle (*up, down, out,* etc) sometimes have meanings that have something in common. All the verbs here use *up* and they all have something to do with things appearing or being made to appear.
- Ask students to look at the phrasal verbs and ask: *Which phrasal verb might mean to have a sudden idea?* (*think up*)
- Students then work individually to complete the sentences.
- Elicit answers.
- Remind students that sometimes phrasal verbs can have more than one meaning.
- After students have completed this task, write on the board: *If you ________ with your friend, you become friends again.*
- Elicit which of the phrasal verbs from exercise 3 could fit this sentence. (*make up*)
- Encourage students to make a note of the different meanings of phrasal verbs in their notebooks under the particle (*up, down, out,* etc).

1 turns up	3 thinks up	5 brings up
2 comes up	4 makes up	

ON THE BOARD

If you ________________ with your friend, you become friends again.

4

Aim: to introduce students to metaphorical words used for describing people

- Ask students to look at the words in the box and to try to speculate about what kind of person they might be used to describe.
- Ask: *If I get angry easily, I might be described as what?* (*hot-tempered*)

- Explain that words connected to heat are often associated with anger and that words associated with cold are often used to describe a person who isn't very friendly or kind.
- Encourage students to underline other adjectives or phrases which appear in the sentences which might act as clues.
- Students then work individually or with a partner to complete the sentences.
- Elicit answers.

1 cold-hearted	4 cool
2 warm	5 icy
3 hot-tempered	

Suggested homework

Assign Ex. 1 and 2 – Workbook, p. 6–7

Listening

Warm up!

Aim: to introduce the topic and warm students up

- Ask students to think about their own families or other families they know. Ask them what problems can sometimes arise between family members. Make a list together on the board.
- If students are struggling for ideas, you might prompt them with: problems between brothers and sisters over clothes/games/etc; problems between children and parents over money/freedom/etc; problems between parents over money/work/etc.
- Ask students to listen out for any problems between family members as they do the listening tasks below.

1

Aim: to practise the skill of prediction

- Before students attempt this task, write on the board: *He was really annoyed because I didn't get back until midnight.*
- Ask them to read the first question in exercise 2 and tell you which of the three options could be matched with the sentence on the board (option A).
- Ask: *What might the teenager say to his friend if B was the correct answer?* (perhaps: *My dad came home and I was watching TV instead of doing my homework.*)
- Elicit any suggestions that the students may have and encourage them to offer similar suggestions for the last option.
- Do the same for the remaining questions.

ON THE BOARD

He was really annoyed because I didn't get back until midnight.

2

Aim: to listen for gist and practise an exam-type task

- Students now listen to five people talking in five different situations.
- Remind students that they will hear each extract twice and that they should listen to the whole of the extract before they decide on the answer.
- Play the listening text.
- Elicit answers, asking students to justify their answers by paraphrasing what they heard.

CD1, Track 2

1 B: *'He thinks I study as soon as I get home on Friday, but I normally go into his office and have a game of 'Net Killer' on the computer. He caught me and went mad.'*
2 C: *'... and she helps her clients to build whatever they want to build.'*
3 B: The speaker mentions speaking to his father and the fact that his uncle helped Josh (the brother) move into his new flat.
4 A: *'It's not expensive make-up, but that's not the point. It's really annoying when I'm going out and I can't find it ...'*
5 A: Mum says, *'We don't need to take presents,'* so it can't be her party. It can't be the speaker's brother's party because he has already had a party.

Soundbite

Aim: to practise listening for the sounds /i/ and /i:/

- Students now listen to hear the difference between the pronunciation of the sound /i/ in words such as *bit* and the sound /i:/ in words such as *beat.*
- Explain that they will hear someone say 10 words and that they should write down the number next to the word that they hear to reveal a ten-digit number.
- Play the listening text.
- Elicit the answer, checking pronunciation.
- Students now get the chance to play the game.
- Each student should write down a ten-digit number and, using the words from the Student's Book, say the corresponding words to their partner or to the whole class.
- Try this round the class with several students, making sure that they pronounce the words correctly.

CD1, Track 3

secret ten-digit number: 7640987420

Speaking

1

Aim: to practise giving personal details

- Remind students that the speaking sections of exams, such as the Cambridge First Certificate, often require candidates to give some personal details about themselves.
- Ask students to read what Julie says about her family and tell you if there is anything wrong with what Julie says. (No – this would be a very good way of starting an interview.)

Errors to watch out for

Remind students that they need to learn the English words for the schools they attend (see Student's Book page 103, exercise 5 for guidance) and also how to say which class they are in. For students at this level of English it is most likely that they will be in the second or third year at secondary school. Encourage students to learn phrases like *'I'm in the second year at (my local) secondary school.'*

2

Aim: to make students aware of common mistakes in spoken English

- Students now read two different ways of giving personal details, one of which is correct.
- Ask students to look at the first two options and tell you which they would say in an interview.
- Ask: *Why is 'My family consists of three members.' wrong?* (Although the sentence is grammatically correct, it is too formal to sound natural.)
- Divide the class into pairs and ask students to work together to choose the correct answer for the remaining two options.
- Elicit answers, asking for justification.

1 a	2 b	3 b

3

Aim: to practise giving personal details

- Before students do this exercise, ask them to study the **Speaking database** on page 165.
- Divide the class into pairs.
- Remind students to use the phrases to help them and to expand on the phrases to add some details of their own.
- Go round the class monitoring or helping where necessary. Check to make sure that students aren't making any of the mistakes from exercise 2.
- If you do this exercise as a whole-class activity, ask different students the questions and encourage them to expand on their answers.

Additional task

- Ask students to think of two more appropriate questions to ask and answer about family.

Use of English

1

Aim: to focus on stative verbs

- Before students do the exercises on this page, ask them to study pages 167–168 of the **Grammar database**, either in class or at home before the lesson starts.
- First, write these sentences on the board: *This cake is tasting really delicious!* and *I'm tasting the soup to see if it needs any more salt.*
- Elicit which sentence is correct/incorrect. (The first is incorrect because *taste* here should be used statively. The second is correct.)
- Students then work individually or with a partner to complete the exercise.
- Elicit answers.

1 think	4 owns
2 is seeing	5 sounds
3 doesn't look	6 are you thinking

ON THE BOARD

This cake is tasting really delicious!
I'm tasting the soup to see if it needs any more salt

Additional task

- Elicit the meaning of the verb in sentence 2 and ask why *seeing* is used in the continuous form here (Here it means *meeting.*).

2

Aim: to focus on lexico-grammatical word patterns

- First, write on the board: *If you care about/of the planet, join Greenpeace!*
- Elicit from students which is the correct preposition. (*about*)
- Ask students to look at the words in the box.
- Ask students to underline the prepositions in each of the sentences and to see if they can match each of the prepositions to one of the verbs.
- Do the first one together.
- Remind students to use the correct form of the verb.
- Students then work individually or with a partner to complete the exercise.
- Elicit answers.

1 blaming	3 accused	5 looks
2 deal	4 care	

ON THE BOARD

If you care about/of the planet, join Greenpeace!

3

Aim: to practise multiple-choice gap-filling

- Students now do a multiple-choice gap-fill, which is designed to practise some of what they have learned from exercises 1 and 2, as well as provide exam practice.
- Ask students to quickly read through the passage and tell you the main pieces of advice given about babysitting (stay calm, don't get depressed, be firm, don't shout). Elicit from students if any of them have ever looked after small children and if they agree with the advice given.
- Explain that at this stage it is not important to understand all of the words in the passage but draw students' attention to clues before and after the gaps that might help them find the answer. These include prepositions, articles, personal pronouns and determiners.
- Remind students that when they have completed the exercise, they should read it through again, inserting the missing word in the gap to check for sense.
- Students then work individually or with a partner to complete the exercise.
- Elicit answers.

1 D	3 A	5 D	7 B	9 A
2 B	4 C	6 A	8 D	10 B

Additional task

- To practise vocabulary, give students definitions of words that they might not know from the passage and ask them to tell you the word (eg *depressed, solution*).

Suggested homework

Assign Ex.1 and 2 – Workbook, p.7
Ex. 1 – Workbook, p.8

Writing

1

Aim: to focus on the purpose of informal letters/emails

- Before students do the exercises on this page, ask them to study page 154 of the **Writing database**, either in class or at home before the lesson starts.
- Ask students to read the writing task and to tell you who the letter should be written to (a female cousin).
- Elicit why the letter is informal.

> Because it is written to a member of the family / a cousin.

Additional task

- Encourage students to think about the kind of information that they might include in their letter to their cousin, especially one who lives abroad. (the weather, what the family did on a national holiday, any news about other members of the family, etc)
- Brainstorm ideas, writing any suggestions the students have on the board.
- Encourage students to make a paragraph plan before they start writing, with at least one piece of information that they would include in each paragraph.

2

Aim: to match formal and informal phrases

- Students now match formal and informal phrases.
- Students work individually or with a partner to complete the exercise.
- Elicit answers.

1 e	3 a	5 b	7 c
2 g	4 f	6 d	

Additional task

- If time allows, ask students to write a short letter based on the correctly ordered informal phrases. They should start and end the letter correctly and include at least three pieces of family news where they think appropriate.
- You may wish to set a time limit of seven or eight minutes for this.
- Ask students to exchange letters and invite one or two students to read them out to the rest of the class.

3

Aim: to provide a model answer for students to refer to

- Students now read the model answer to the question in exercise 1.
- Ask them to read the letter through once.
- Then ask them to read it again quickly and to underline all the pieces of family news that Martin has included in his letter.
- Encourage students to give their opinion on whether Martin has written a good letter and whether he has answered the question correctly.

> *Dear Tina,*
> *It was great to hear from you! Hope everything's okay. Have you started your exams yet? Good luck!*
> *Anyway, you asked me to tell you all the family news. Well, a lot's happened since you were here. The big news is that Uncle Tom got married! Can you believe it? His wife is lovely – she's a doctor and she's really beautiful. We all went to the wedding and had a wonderful time. Grandad danced! It was so much fun.*
> *Oh, and another thing! Dad's got a new job. Do you know the old shopping centre in town? They've built new shops there and Dad applied for a job as a manager and he got it! He's really excited. He starts next week.*
> *One last thing. Do you remember Fluffy, the cat? Well, we can't find her anywhere. We've got no idea where she's gone. It's a bit sad really. We all miss her. We're hoping she'll come back soon.*
> *We all miss you, too. Everybody sends their love. Can't wait to see you in the summer.*
> *All my love,*
> *Martin*

Additional task

- Divide the class into pairs.
- Ask students to look at the letter again and to work in pairs to replace the pieces of family news that they underlined with family news of their own.

4

Aim: to read for specific words and phrases

- First, ask students where in the letter they would normally expect to find words and phrases like these.
- Encourage them to visualise where the words and phrases should go.
- Remind them that these are words and phrases that they can learn and use in appropriate informal letters.
- Ask students to read the model answer in exercise 3 again and underline the informal words and phrases.
- Elicit answers.
- You may like to draw an outline of an informal letter on the board and invite individual students to write the words and phrases in the appropriate place.

> *Dear Tina,*
>
> *It was great to hear from you! Hope everything's okay. Have you started your exams yet? Good luck!*
>
> *Anyway, you asked me to tell you all the family news. Well, a lot's happened since you were here. The big news is that Uncle Tom got married! Can you believe it? His wife is lovely – she's a doctor and she's really beautiful. We all went to the wedding and had a wonderful time. Grandad danced! It was so much fun.*
>
> *Oh, and another thing! Dad's got a new job. Do you know the old shopping centre in town? They've built new shops there and Dad applied for a job as a manager and he got it! He's really excited. He starts next week.*
>
> *One last thing. Do you remember Fluffy, the cat? Well, we can't find her anywhere. We've got no idea where she's gone. It's a bit sad, really. We all miss her. We're hoping she'll come back soon.*
>
> *We all miss you, too. Everybody sends their love. Can't wait to see you in the summer.*
>
> *All my love,*
> *Martin*

5

Aim: to encourage students to think about the style of informal letters

- Remind students to look back at the model letter in exercise 3 to help them with the true or false questions.
- Elicit answers, asking students to justify by giving examples from the model letter.

> 1 F *'Good luck!', 'Can't wait to see you in the summer.'*
> 2 T *'It was great to hear from you!'*
> 3 T *'We've got no idea where she's gone.'*
> 4 T *'One last thing.', 'Oh, and another thing!'*
> 5 T *'okay', 'anyway', 'big', 'sad'.*

6

Aim: to prepare students for the writing task

- First, remind students of the importance of identifying who they are writing to.
- Ask them to look at the writing task and to tell you who they will be writing to.
- Ask: *Will you be writing to your pen friend or your brother?* (your brother)
- Ask: *Will you be writing about your family or your pen friend's family?* (pen friend's family)
- Ask: *Which country are you staying in?* (England)
- Elicit who the students will be writing to and why.

> Students are writing to their brother, Dean, to tell him about their pen friend's family, who they are staying with in England.

7

Aim: to encourage students to plan their writing

- This exercise is designed to encourage students to use their imagination and to make sure that they all have enough ideas before they start writing.
- Remind students that careful planning will improve their letters.
- Ask students to look at the questions and to make notes in their notebooks.
- Remind them that they should be answering the questions with one or two sentences.
- Go round the class monitoring or helping where necessary.
- At the end of the exercise, ask individual students to read out their ideas.
- Encourage students to make a note of any good ideas they hear from other students.
- If you have time, check that all students have completed the questions with appropriate information.

1	a
2	Students need to think of an appropriate surname for their pen friend's family. Common English surnames include: *Jones, Smith, Brown* and *Green.*
3	Students need to think of an English town. Easy towns/cities for students to remember (or ones that they might be familiar with) are: *London, Bath, Oxford, Cambridge* and *Manchester.*
4–8	students' own answers
9	Students should have a short introduction, 2/3 main paragraphs and a short ending to their letters.
10	*Love; Lots of love; All my love; Write to me soon; See you soon.*
11	first name only

- Ask students to turn to **Writing Planner 1** on page 155. Explain that each Writing Planner gives them a simple table to complete which helps them to put the right content in the right place in their piece of writing.
- Point out to students that each row of the table refers to a different part of their piece of writing and gives its purpose, together with useful expressions. Explain to students that they should complete the 'notes' column using their own ideas.
- Give students some time to complete the table. Invite a number of students to say what they have put in the 'notes' column for each part of the piece of writing. If possible, you may like to check the notes made by all students to ensure they have enough content to base their piece of writing on. Ask students to refer to the Writing Planner as they do their piece of writing.

8

Aim: to give students the opportunity to produce an informal letter

- This exercise can be done in class or set for homework.
- Remind students of the importance of using a conversational tone and of answering the question by including the information from their notes.

9

Aim: to encourage students to check their written work

- Draw students' attention to the checklist once they have finished writing and ask them to read each statement and to tick each one that is true for them.
- Ask them to make sure that they have ticked all of the boxes before handing their letter in to be marked.
- You might consider refusing to mark any letter that does not meet all the criteria in the checklist and asking the student to rewrite.

Additional task

In order to monitor whether students have checked their work carefully, you could ask them to underline in pencil on their letters places where they have 'used informal phrases', for example.

Alternatively, invite individual students to read parts of their letter to the rest of the class or get students to exchange letters with each other and to check each other's letters for mistakes before handing them in.

Look Back

Aim: to review the unit and to practise scanning for specific information

- Students now have the opportunity to go back through the unit to check what they have learned.
- Ask the whole class the questions from **Look Back**.
- Elicit answers from different students.
- Encourage students to scan the unit to find any information they can't remember.

1 an only child
2 present simple
3 sensitive
4 dishonest
5 They are not normally used in continuous tenses because they don't describe actions.

Suggested homework

Assign Ex. 1 and 2 – Workbook, p.9

Further material

- For further practice and consolidation, ask students to complete the Unit 1 tasks on the Student's CD-ROM.
- To test students' understanding of the material in Unit 1, you may like to administer the Unit 1 Test, which is in the Tests section of the Teacher's DVD-ROM. You may also like to construct your own test using the Test Generator material for Unit 1.

2

The Open Road

Target language

Grammar:	past simple and past continuous / *would, used to, be used to* / word patterns
Lexis:	topic vocabulary / confusable words / collocations (transport)
Reading skills:	scanning for specific information
Listening skills:	identifying location
Speaking skills:	comparing
Writing skills:	presenting an argument / essay
Pronunciation:	/æ/ and /e/

- The phrase *the open road* usually refers to roads in the countryside, where there is very little traffic, *eg Nothing quite beats the feeling you get from leaving the town behind and heading off on the open road.*
- Write the phrase *the open road* on the board.
- Ask students what they think the title refers to.
- Explain the meaning of the phrase *the open road.*
- Write the example sentence given above on the board.
- Elicit suggestions as to what the unit might be about.

ON THE BOARD

> *the open road*
> *Nothing quite beats the feeling you get from leaving the town behind and heading off on the open road.*

Start thinking!

Aim: to introduce the topic of transport through personal responses

- Ask students to work in pairs to talk about the questions in the Student's Book.
- Go round the class monitoring and helping where necessary.
- If you prefer, conduct a brief discussion involving the whole class by reading the questions and inviting different students to give their answers.
- Do not accept or reject answers at this stage.

Additional task

- First, write these phrases on the board: *public transport* and *private transport.*
- Elicit from the students which means of transport they would put into each category. You might need to offer a few suggestions, eg tram, train, motorbike, aeroplane, etc. (*Public transport* refers to means of transport that are used by the public and are often paid for by the government in some way, for example, buses, trams or the underground. *Private transport* refers to means of transport that are owned by individuals and includes cars, motorbikes and bicycles.)
- Ask students to write down as many means of transport as they can. You may wish to set a time limit of one or two minutes for this. Then ask them to tick those means of transport which are public and those which are private.

Reading CD1, Track 4

1

Aim: to scan for specific information

- Students are now going to read an extract from an encyclopaedia. Begin by asking them to predict which means of transport they might read about.
- Ask students to read the passage. This can be done individually or as a class activity with different students being asked to read different sections aloud to the rest of the class.
- Remind students that at this stage they do not need to understand all of the vocabulary as items will be covered in the **WORD BOX** section.
- Elicit answers from a few students to the questions in the **Start thinking!** section and ask them to justify their answers.

A horse can run at about 55 kilometres an hour.
Two American brothers, Wilbur and Orville Wright, invented the aeroplane.
Man first landed on the Moon in 1969.

Background information

- *A space shuttle is a vehicle which travels into space regularly and, although it sets off into space like a rocket, it returns to Earth like an aeroplane.*
- *A space tourist is a person who pays to go into space in order to enjoy the experience. Several high-profile multimillionaires, mostly from the USA, have already gone into space on such trips.*

Additional task

- In order to practise scanning for specific information from the passage, elicit the answers to the questions below.
- Remind students that they don't have to reread large parts of the passage but should look for clues or key words that might help them find the answer. The key words have been underlined in each sentence.

1. What did Richard Trevithick invent? (the first train)
2. When was the first bicycle with pedals invented? (around 1840)
3. Where was the first petrol-driven car invented? (Germany)
4. When was the wheel invented? (around 3500 BC)
5. What was the name of the Wright brothers' aircraft? (the Flyer)

2

Aim: to scan for specific information to complete sentences

- Read the first sentence together.
- Remind students that they can look at the extract but they don't need to read it in detail again.
- Elicit the answer and ask students to justify it by reading directly from the passage.
- Remind students of the importance of underlining where they found the answer in the passage.
- Ask students to work individually or with a partner to do the rest of the exercise.
- Elicit answers, asking for justification from the passage.

1. 3000: *'They probably first achieved this in northern countries before 3000 BC (before Christ) using skis.'*
2. 1804: *'In 1804, he took the first passengers, although they didn't have to buy a ticket.'*
3. 1840: *'… the bicycle didn't appear until around 1840 when a Scotsman, Kirkpatrick Macmillan, created the first one to have pedals.'*
4. 1980: *'It took around 140 years for Macmillan's design to develop into modern mountain bikes.'*

3

Aim: to practise an exam-type task

- Before students do this exercise, remind them of the best way to approach it so that they become familiar with exam technique.
- Remind them of the importance of looking for sentences from the passage which explain one of the four options A–D. They might also be able to work out from the passage which three options could not be the answer.
- Direct students' attention to the first question.
- Ask: *Could people travel fast before the wheel was invented?* (No – this eliminates option A.)
- Ask: *Did they invent the wheel or skis first?* (the wheel – this eliminates option B.)
- Ask: *Were the roads good when the wheel was invented?* (No – this means that option C must be the correct answer.)
- Explain that although people did use horses, this was because the roads were bad and carts couldn't travel as fast as horses could on them.
- Remind students of the importance of underlining where they found the answer within the passage, as this makes it much quicker and easier for them to be able to justify their answers.
- Ask students to work individually or with a partner to do the rest of the exercise.
- Elicit answers, asking for justification from the passage.

1. C: *'… but carts were very slow without roads.'*
2. B: *'During the first flight …'*
3. B: *'The railway developed gradually from carts on tracks.'*
4. B: *'Perhaps unexpectedly, the bicycle didn't appear until around 1840 …'*
5. A: *'… completely changed the way people thought about transport, and so did the aeroplane.'*

Additional task

- Have a class discussion about which means of transport students think has been the most important invention and why.

WORD BOX

4

Aim: to introduce new vocabulary

- Before students do this exercise, ask them to read the definitions.
- Remind them of the importance of looking back at the passage for clues if they are not sure of the meaning of any words.
- Ask students to work individually or with a partner to do the exercise.
- Elicit answers.
- Ask students if there were any other words in the passage which they didn't know the meaning of.

- Remind them to make a note of the words and to look them up in a dictionary before the start of the next lesson.
- Ask students if they enjoyed reading the extract and whether they learned anything from it or not and get them to justify their answers.

1 hydrofoil	4 tracks
2 vehicle	5 cart
3 hovercraft	6 pedal

Additional task

- Ask students to choose five means of transport and to write their own definitions for them.
- Students then swap their definitions with a partner and try to guess the means of transport that is being described.

Have your say!

Aim: to give students the opportunity to express their own opinions

- Put the students in pairs and get them to ask each other the questions. Ask them to make brief notes on their partner's answers. When they have finished, invite various students to tell the whole class what they discussed.
- Alternatively, you may like to do the activity as a whole class. Invite various students to give their opinions, encouraging them to agree or disagree with what other students have said. Encourage them to give reasons for their opinions.

Suggested homework

Assign Ex. 1 – Workbook, p.10–11
Ex. 1 – Workbook, p.11

G Grammar clinic

1

Aim: to review past tenses

- Before students do the exercises on this page, ask them to study pages 168–170 of the **Grammar database**, either in class or at home before the lesson starts.
- The first exercise refers back to the reading passage so that students can see the grammar in question being used in context.
- Read the sentences and ask students to tell you which tense is being used in each sentence.
- Ask students to match each sentence to its explanation.

1 d the past simple is used for a single, completed action
2 c the past continuous is used for an action in progress when another happened
3 a the past simple is used for repeated actions which don't happen now
4 b the past simple is used for past states

2

Aim: to practise identifying different uses of past tenses

- Ask students to look through the text again to find other examples of past tenses being used in these ways.
- Students can work individually or with a partner and should underline the examples they find.
- Elicit answers.

a single completed action: *'They probably first achieved this …'*
'The hot-air balloon made its first free flight in 1783.'
a repeated action in the past: *'Early humans dreamed of going faster and further than they could on foot.'*
an action in progress when another action happened: *'Two Frenchmen, the Montgolfier brothers, were working as papermakers when they had the idea for the balloon.' 'Unfortunately, they were travelling in the train when it began to fall off the tracks …'*
a past state (a feeling or situation, not an action): *'… carts were very slow without roads.' '… they were slow and not very popular.'*

3

Aim: to practise using past tenses

- Before students attempt this task, write this sentence on the board: *We drove along the road when one of the tyres burst.*
- Ask students to explain to you what is wrong with the sentence (One action is in progress when another action happened, so the first verb should be *were driving.*).
- Before students complete the sentences go through the first sentence together.
- Tell them to ignore the missing verb for the moment.
- Ask: *Is this a feeling or an action?* (an action)
- Ask: *Is it a single completed action or a repeated action in the past?* (a single, completed action)
- Ask: *What tense do we use for single, completed actions?* (*past simple*)
- Remind students to go through this process of asking themselves questions about the sentence before they fill in the gaps.
- Students may work individually or with a partner.
- Elicit answers.

1 flew	3 told	5 shouted
2 were flying	4 was telling	6 saw

ON THE BOARD

We drove along the road when one of the tyres burst.

4

Aim: to correct sentences using past tenses

- Before students correct the mistakes, go through the first one together.
- Ask: *Is this a feeling or an action?* (an action)
- Ask: *How many things are happening in the sentence?* (two – entering the station and noticing the train was late)
- Ask: *What tense do we use for an action in progress when another action happened? (past continuous)*
- Remind students to go through this process of asking themselves questions about the sentence before they correct it.
- Students may work individually or with a partner.
- Elicit answers, asking students to tell you which sentence is correct.

1 As we were entering the train station, I noticed the train was late.
2 I was sitting in a taxi when the accident happened so I saw the whole thing.
3 Mick rode his bike almost every day over the summer.
5 When you called, I was watching a programme about the history of transport.
Sentence 4 is correct.

5

Aim: to have controlled practice using past tenses

- Ask students to quickly read the text, ignoring the gaps for now. Ask them to say briefly what happened (The girl asked her dad to take the stabilisers off her bike. He pushed her and then let go and she rode the bike on her own.).
- Ask students to complete the text using the verbs given in the correct tense. Remind them that if they are not sure about a gap, they can go onto the next one and then come back to that gap later when there are fewer words left to choose from.
- Check answers orally.

1	learned	10	were riding
2	was	11	wanted
3	taught	12	got
4	was shining	13	started
5	took	14	told
6	had	15	was pushing
7	didn't	16	said
8	got	17	fell
9	saw	18	was

6

- Ask students if they remember learning to ride a bike. Ask them to say what happened, who helped them, how they learned and how they felt.
- Alternatively, you may like to put students into pairs and ask them to talk to each other about their experiences of learning to ride a bike. Ask them to report back to the whole class on their discussion.

Suggested homework

Assign Ex.1 and 2 – Workbook, p.12

V Vocabulary builder

1

Aim: to focus on vocabulary connected to public transport

- This exercise is probably best done as a whole class. If time allows, however, divide the class into small groups and encourage them to use a dictionary in order to find the meaning of any unknown words.
- First, ask students to read through the sentences 1–8 and underline any words which might act as clues.
- Elicit the clues and ask if there were any which they could do given the clues in the sentence.
- As an example of this you could direct students' attention to question 7. The word *taxis* suggests that the answer may be *taxi rank*. Even if students don't know what a *taxi rank* is, searching for clues can sometimes help them to make an educated guess.
- Elicit answers.

1 platform	4 underground	7 taxi rank
2 airline	5 fare	8 coach
3 terminal	6 cabin	

2

Aim: to practise using words which are easily confused

- Before students attempt this task, write on the board *journey* and *trip* and ask students to explain to you the difference and to give you an example sentence for each (A *journey* may be longer, and usually refers to just the period of travel. A *trip* may be shorter and usually refers to the period of travel, plus other activities such as sightseeing, etc.).
- Encourage students to learn collocations which will help them to remember how the words are used, such as school trip, business trip, a tiring journey.
- Ask them if they know words for any other types of journey (trek, voyage, crossing, excursion, etc).
- Elicit answers to numbers 1 and 2.
- Ask students to look at number 3 and elicit the answer. Don't negate the answer but encourage all students to either agree or disagree with the answer given and to justify whether *miss* or *lose* is used in this sentence.

- Ask students to look at number 4 and elicit the answer. Don't negate the answer but encourage all students to either agree or disagree with the answer given and to justify whether *on* or *in* is used in this sentence.

1 travel	2 trip	3 miss	4 on

ON THE BOARD

journey, trip

Errors to watch out for

- Students are often tempted to use *travel* as a noun in sentences such as, '*We went on a travel to the Peloponnese.*' Remind students that *travel* is only normally used as a verb and that in this case they should say, '*We travelled to the Peloponnese.*' or '*We went on a trip to the Peloponnese.*' *Travel* is only occasionally used as a noun, in phrases such as, '*Travel broadens the mind.*'
- *Excursion* is not a common word in English. Discourage students from using it instead of more natural collocations like *school trip.*

3

Aim: to practise collocations connected to transport

- Students now match the means of transport to the appropriate phrase.
- Ask students to work individually or with a partner to do the rest of the exercise.
- Elicit answers.

> get on / get off: bicycle, bus, horse, train, plane, motorbike, ferry, ship, trolleybus
> get in (*or* into) / get out of: car, helicopter, hot-air balloon, rowing boat, taxi

4

Aim: to match words to make compound nouns

- Explain to students that they need to match words from list A to words from list B to make compound nouns.
- Students may work individually or with a partner.
- Elicit answers.

> express train / radio taxi / double-decker bus / jet plane / sports car

5

Aim: to check students' understanding of the compound nouns from exercise 4

- Students now match one of the compound nouns from exercise 4 with a sentence to check their understanding.
- Students may work individually or with a partner.
- Elicit answers.

1 sports car	4 express train
2 double-decker bus	5 jet plane
3 radio taxi	

Suggested homework

Assign Ex.1 –Workbook, p.12
Ex.2 – Workbook, p.13

Listening

Warm up!

Aim: to introduce the topic and warm students up

- Ask students whether they would prefer to drive a train or a bus.
- Elicit answers, asking students to justify their opinions.

1

Aim: to focus on topic vocabulary

- Put students into pairs and ask them to brainstorm vocabulary connected to different means of transport.
- Ask them to make as long a list as they can. When they have finished, ask one pair to read out their list for 'bus'. Ask another pair to read out any words the first pair missed. Continue in this way until nobody has any more words or phrases connected to 'bus'.
- Do the same for the other means of transport. You may like to compile a master list on the board.

> (suggested answers)
> bus: bus stop, bus station, get on/off
> plane: take off, land, get on/off, runway, ticket, first class
> ship: sail, get on/off, sea, ticket, cabin
> train: train station, railway, first class, get on/off, platform

2

Aim: to listen to identify location

- Tell students that it's useful to listen for the location where a conversation is taking place. Elicit why that might be the case (because the location gives a context for the conversation and helps you to predict what the people are probably talking about).
- Ask students to listen to three short conversations and to identify where each conversation is taking place. Ask them to listen carefully to the vocabulary used and to decide which location they associate that vocabulary with.
- Play the listening text. Elicit answers, asking students to justify their opinions.

CD1, Track 5

1 a	2 b	3 c

3

Aim: to listen for specific information

- Ask students to quickly read the information provided. Ask them to think about what kind of information may be missing and what they should be listening for. Some students may be able to remember the answers from having listened once. Don't confirm the correct answers at this stage.
- Ask students to listen and complete the information with a word or short phrase from what they hear in each gap. Play the listening text.
- Elicit answers, asking students to justify their opinions.

CD1, Track 5

1 first class	4 cabin
2 10:45	5 over the bridge
3 about six hours	6 higher

Soundbite

Aim: to practise listening for the sounds /æ/ and /e/

- Students now listen to hear the difference between the pronunciation of the sound /æ/ in words such as *thank* and the sound /e/ in words such as *bed*.
- Explain that they will hear four words and should circle the two words which have the same vowel sound.
- Play the listening text.
- Elicit the answers, checking pronunciation.

CD1, Track 6

1 thank / cat	3 apple / ant
2 head / said	4 pet / send

Speaking

1

Aim: to introduce the idea of comparing

- Remind students that Part 2 of the FCE Speaking paper requires students to be able to talk about the similarities and differences between two photographs for one minute.
- Divide the class into pairs and ask them to make notes about the things that trains and buses have in common.
- Go round the class monitoring and helping where necessary.
- You might like to set a time limit of three or four minutes for this.
- Elicit ideas.

(suggested answers) They both carry passengers. / They both have a driver. / You get on and off a train and bus, rather than in (or into) and out of. / They both arrive and depart from stations (a bus station and a train station). / They can both cover long distances.

2

Aim: to practise comparing

- Repeat the procedure from exercise 1 about differences.

(suggested answers) Trains are faster than buses. / Buses can get stuck in traffic jams whereas trains cannot. / Trains often transport goods or materials while buses always carry passengers.

3

Aim: to practise expressing preference

- Ask students whether they prefer travelling by train or by bus.
- Elicit ideas, asking for justification.

4

Aim: to practise comparing photographs

- Before students do this exercise, ask them to study the **Speaking database** on page 165.
- Remind students that the questions they should answer will be printed above the pictures.
- Divide the class into pairs.
- Remind students to use the notes they made in exercises 1 and 2 and details of their own based on the photographs.
- Go round the class monitoring or helping where necessary.

Errors to watch out for

Students often start their description of a photo by saying, *'In this picture I can see …'*, which is not natural English. Encourage your students to use the more natural *'This is a picture of …'* or *'This picture shows …'*

Use of English

1

Aim: to focus on *would*, *used to* and *be used to*

- Before students do the exercises on this page, ask them to study page 170 of the **Grammar database**, either in class or at home before the lesson starts.
- First, write these sentences on the board: *My grandmother was used to read me bedtime stories when I was younger.* and *My grandmother would read me bedtime stories when I was younger.*
- Elicit which sentence is correct and which is incorrect (The first is incorrect because *be used to* means *to be familiar with something.* The second is correct.).

- Ask students to tell you the difference between *used to* and *would* in a sentence (*used to* can be used to talk about states in the past, but *would* can't).
- Ask students to tell you what follows *be used to* (a noun or *–ing* form).
- Students may work individually or with a partner.
- Elicit answers.

1 would	3 used to	5 get
2 am used to	4 used to	6 wasn't used to

ON THE BOARD

My grandmother was used to read me bedtime stories when I was younger.
My grandmother would read me bedtime stories when I was younger.

2

Aim: to practise *would, used to* and *be used to*

- Ask students to rewrite the sentences using the word in bold.
- Do the first one together.
- Students then work individually or with a partner.
- Elicit answers.

1. When he was a boy, my dad used to watch the steam trains go past.
2. Flying a helicopter is difficult at first, but you'll soon get used to it.
3. When she was four, my sister would ride her bike around the house.
4. My grandfather used to take me for rides in his old car when I was small.

Suggested homework

Assign Ex.1 and 2 – Workbook, p.13

3

Aim: to practise lexico-grammatical word patterns

- First, write on the board: *My mum always insists on / about walking with me to school.*
- Elicit from students which is the correct preposition (*on*).
- Remind them that the preposition which follows a gap often acts as a clue to the word in the gap.
- Ask students to underline the prepositions in each of the sentences and then see if they can match each of the prepositions to one of the verbs in the box.
- Do the first one together.
- Students may work individually or with a partner.
- Elicit answers.

ON THE BOARD

My mum always insists on / about walking with me to school.

1 insisted / insists	4 work
2 complain	5 reminds
3 take	

4

Aim: to practise gap-filling

- Students now do a gap-fill to practise some of what they have learned from exercises 2 and 3.
- Ask students to read through the passage and tell you what the gist of it is (the fact that more women are becoming pilots and what it's like to be one of them).
- Explain that at this stage it is not important to understand all of the words, but draw students' attention to clues before and after the gaps that might help them find the answer. These include prepositions, articles, personal pronouns and determiners.
- Remind students that when they have completed the exercise they should read it through again to check for sense.
- Remind students that they should write only one word in each gap, and that each word should be in capital letters.
- Students may work individually or with a partner.
- Elicit answers.

1 WOULD	5 WOULD	8 ME
2 AS	6 GOT	9 ABOUT
3 USED	7 TO	10 TAKE
4 ON		

Additional task

- To practise vocabulary, give students definitions of words or phrases that they might not know from the passage and ask them to tell you the word (eg *cabin crew, take into account, the majority* and *entering the field*).

Suggested homework

Assign Ex.1 and 2 – Workbook, p.14

Writing

1

Aim: to introduce the topic of essays

- Before students do the exercises on this page, ask them to study page 153 of the **Writing database**, either in class or at home before the lesson starts.
- Ask students to look at the questions and to make notes of their opinions, either individually or in pairs.
- Ask students to tell the rest of the class their opinions on the questions. Since they have already had time to think and have made notes, you should expect longer, more developed answers. Encourage them to expand on their answers.

1 Public transport usually includes buses, trolleybuses, trains, underground trains, trams, etc. Private transport usually includes cars, motorbikes, etc.
2 (suggested answers) it's cheaper / it's better for the environment / it runs on a schedule / you can relax and not worry about driving
3 (suggested answers) you cannot travel whenever you want / it might be dirty or uncomfortable / it might not take you to your destination

Additional task

- Encourage students to predict what they might be asked to write about in an essay based on the photograph (This might be connected to traffic problems in cities, how to get more people using public transport, what the advantages of public transport are, how we can help the environment, etc.).
- Brainstorm ideas, writing any suggestions the students have on the board.

2

Aim: to identify essay type

- Ask students to read the writing task and to tell you whether the essay should be formal or informal.
- Elicit why the essay is formal (Because it is an essay which is meant to be read by a teacher.).

1 formal
2 students' own answers

3

Aim: to introduce phrases that can be used in essays

- First, ask students if they know any phrases which could be used in an essay which they could use to connect their ideas.
- If they can't think of any, write these words in this order on the board: *to sum up, consequently, first of all, similarly, also, as well as this, firstly, it is my (strong) belief that, furthermore, since.*
- Elicit any ideas they have and write them on the board.
- Direct students' attention to the phrases in the Student's Book and ask them to complete the phrases using the words given.
- Elicit the answers orally. Ask students what other phrases they know, including any you have already written on the board, which are used for the same functions.

To begin with, …
In the first place, …
What is more, …
In addition to this, …
Because of this, …
This is due to …
On the one hand, …
On the other hand, …
I am convinced that …
I would argue that …

Additional task

- If time allows, ask students to write a mini-essay based on the correctly ordered formal phrases. They should include at least three reasons why they think people should or shouldn't be encouraged to use public transport where they think appropriate, each introduced by the correct phrase.
- You may wish to set a time limit of seven or eight minutes for this.
- Ask students to exchange essays and invite one or two students to read them out to the rest of the class.

4

Aim: to provide a model answer for students to refer to

- Students now read the model answer to the question in exercise 2.
- Ask them to read the essay through once and decide whether the writer agrees or disagrees with the statement (he/she agrees with the statement).
- Then ask them to read it again quickly and to underline all the discursive phrases that the writer has used.
- Encourage students to give their opinion on whether this is a good essay, whether it answers the question correctly and whether they agree or disagree with the writer's main arguments.

There is no doubt that traffic adds to pollution. Public transport offers a possible solution to the problem, since (because) many people can be transported in one vehicle. The government has a responsibility to encourage the public to use buses and the underground more. However, (But) there are a number of changes which need to be considered.
In the first place, (Firstly) public transport should be made free. The government should raise taxes to pay for the service. If it was free, most people would decide to leave their cars at home and travel by bus or train.
What is more, (In addition) the service must be clean and reliable. People need to know that they can get to work on time. They also need to know that their journey will be comfortable.
To sum up, (In conclusion) I would argue that a clean, reliable service which was free would encourage many people to use public transport. The government should take action on this to prevent environmental damage.
(answers to exercise 5 are in brackets)

5

Aim: to read for specific words and phrases

- Before students attempt this task, ask them where in the essay they would normally expect to find words and phrases like these.
- Encourage them to visualise where the words and phrases should go.
- Remind them that these are words and phrases that they can learn and use in appropriate essays.

- Ask students to read the model answer in exercise 4 again and replace some of the phrases that they underlined in exercise 4 with the phrases given here.
- Elicit answers.

6

Aim: to check students' understanding of text structure

- Ask students to read the model answer again and to choose which of the options, a or b, they think is correct.
- Students then work individually or with a partner to complete the exercise.
- Elicit answers.
- Remind students that exercise 6 is a paragraph plan that they can use when writing essays.
- Check that students have crossed out the incorrect option, so that they can clearly see the type of information that they should include in each paragraph.

1 a	2 b	3 b	4 a	5 a

7

Aim: to prepare students for the writing task

- First, remind students of the importance of identifying what they are writing about and who they are writing for.
- Ask them to look at the writing task and to tell you the subject that they will be writing about. Set a time limit of 10 seconds for this.
- Ask: *Will you be writing about the history of transport or about whether you think the invention of the car changed the world?* (whether you think the invention of the car changed the world)
- Then ask: *Will you be writing an essay or a formal letter?* (an essay)
- Then ask: *Should you express your personal opinion?* (yes)
- Elicit whether students agree or disagree with the statement that the invention of the car changed the world, asking them to provide justification for their answers.

8

Aim: to encourage students to plan their writing

- Remind students that careful planning will improve their essays.
- Ask students to look at the questions and to make notes in their notebooks.
- Remind them that they should be answering the questions with one or two sentences.
- Go round the class monitoring or helping where necessary.
- At the end of the exercise, ask individual students to read out their ideas.
- Encourage students to make a note of any good ideas they hear from other students.
- If you have time, check that all students have completed the questions with appropriate information.

1 students' own answers
2 whether I agree/disagree with the statement
3 some points in favour of my view
4 more points in favour of my view
5 a *To sum up, To conclude, In conclusion*
   b *I would argue that, I am convinced that, I believe, I'm of the opinion that*

- Ask students to turn to **Writing Planner 2** on page 155. Explain that each Writing Planner gives them a simple table to complete which helps them to put the right content in the right place in their piece of writing.
- Point out to students that each row of the table refers to a different part of their piece of writing and gives its purpose, together with useful expressions. Explain to students that they should complete the 'notes' column using their own ideas.
- Give students some time to complete the table. Invite a number of students to say what they have put in the 'notes' column for each part of the piece of writing. If possible, you may like to check the notes made by all students to ensure they have enough content to base their piece of writing on. Ask students to refer to the Writing Planner as they do their piece of writing.

9

Aim: to give students the opportunity to produce an essay

- This exercise can be done in class or set for homework.
- Remind students of the importance of using the correct phrases and of answering the question by including the information from their notes in exercise 8.

10

Aim: to encourage students to check their written work

- Draw students' attention to the checklist.
- When they have finished writing, ask them to read each statement and to tick each one that is true for them.
- Ask them to make sure that they have ticked all of the boxes before handing their essay in to be marked.
- You might consider refusing to mark any essay that does not meet all the criteria in the checklist and asking the student to rewrite.

Additional task

- In order to monitor whether students have checked their work carefully, you could ask them to underline in pencil places in their essays where they have 'used appropriate connecting phrases', for example.

Look Back

Aim: to review the unit and to practise scanning for specific information

- Students now have the opportunity to go back through the unit to check what they have learned.
- Ask the whole class the questions from **Look Back**.

- Elicit answers from different students.
- Encourage students to scan the unit to find any information they can't remember.

1 around 3500 BC
2 Two American brothers, Wilbur and Orville Wright.
3 past continuous
4 *Used to* can be used to talk about states in the past, but *would* can't.
5 *I would argue that…* (accept other correct answers)

Suggested homework

Assign Ex. 1 and 2 – Workbook, p.15

Webquest

- Ask students to complete the **Webquest** on page 198 of the Student's Book. You might ask students to work on this together in class if you have internet access, or you might assign it for homework.
- Explain to students that the answers to the questions are not in the Student's Book but that they need to find the answers online.
- Check the answers together and ask students to explain where they found the answers and how they found them (eg by typing terms into a search engine).

1 2004
2 Wright Flyer
3 Queensland
4 Mark Zuckerberg
5 the jet engine
6 John F. Kennedy International Airport
7 Neil Armstrong
8 The Tube
9 2011
10 1936

Further material

- For further practice and consolidation, ask students to complete the Unit 2 tasks on the Student's CD-ROM.
- To test students' understanding of the material in Unit 2, you may like to administer the Unit 2 Test, which is in the Tests section of the Teacher's DVD-ROM. You may also like to construct your own test using the Test Generator material for Unit 2.

Revision Units 1-2

1

1 C	3 D	5 A	7 C	9 A
2 A	4 B	6 D	8 B	10 A

2

1 is staying	5 fly
2 was doing	6 is having
3 eat	7 swam
4 am getting	8 is having

3

1 in	3 for	5 of	7 into
2 of	4 on	6 after	

4

1 illegal	5 unkind
2 unfair	6 irrelevant
3 dishonest	7 incapable
4 impolite	8 unattractive

5

1 divorced	5 rank
2 popular	6 coach
3 hydrofoil	7 selfish
4 pedals	

6

1 turn up	4 thought up
2 came up	5 making up
3 bring up	

7

1 am I seeing	4 tastes
2 don't believe	5 are you thinking
3 doesn't understand	

8

1 trip	5 on	8 up
2 do / did	6 rank	9 with
3 about	7 radio	10 bring
4 to		

3

Killing Time

Target language

Grammar: present perfect simple and present perfect continuous /articles / synonyms
Lexis: topic vocabulary / idioms (time) / phrasal verbs with *down* / metaphors (time)
Reading skills: recognising discourse markers
Listening skills: understanding attitude
Speaking skills: making suggestions
Writing skills: awareness of target reader / informal letter/email
Pronunciation: /ʌ/

- The phrase *killing time* means filling spare time, usually while waiting for something to happen, eg *We killed some time at the airport by watching the other planes take off and land.*
- Write the phrase *killing time* on the board.
- Ask students what they think the title refers to.
- Explain the meaning of the phrase *killing time.*
- Write the example sentence given above on the board.
- Explain that it is also very common to use the phrase *to have time to kill,* as in, *I had two hours to kill before my train left so I went shopping.*
- Elicit suggestions as to what the unit might be about.

ON THE BOARD

Killing time

We killed some time at the airport by watching the other planes take off and land.

Start thinking!

Aim: to introduce the topic of hobbies through personal responses

- Ask students to work in pairs to talk about the questions in the Student's Book.
- Go round the class monitoring and helping where necessary.
- If you prefer, conduct a brief discussion involving the whole class by reading the questions and inviting different students to give their answers.

> The first two questions depend on the students' own answers. Possible answers to the third question: stamps, comics, butterflies, coins

Reading CD1, Track 7

1

Aim: to read for gist

- Students are now going to read an article about hobbies in the past and in the present. Begin by asking students to guess what hobbies they might read about.
- Ask students to read the article. This can be done individually or as a class activity with different students being asked to read different sections aloud to the rest of the class.
- Remind students that at this stage they do not need to understand all of the vocabulary as items will be covered in the **WORD BOX** section.
- Elicit answers from a few students, asking them which hobby mentioned in the text sounds most interesting.

> stamp collecting, building models, playing computer games, running websites, communicating with friends around the world, fishing, gymnastics, sports, games

Background information

- *An 'arcade' is a place where young people go to play video games.*

Additional task

- In order to check your students' understanding of the gist of the passage, elicit the answers to the questions below.
- Remind students that they don't have to reread large parts of the passage but should look for clues or key words that might help them find the answer. The key words have been underlined in each sentence.

1 What appeared in the nineteenth century? (stamps)
2 Why are people not buying the same amount of stamps as before? (email)
3 What would people 50 years ago have thought was very strange? (computers)
4 Why is it easy now to start a new hobby? (There are websites on every hobby.)
5 What hobby did our grandparents enjoy that is still popular? (fishing)

2

Aim: to match discursive phrases with functions

- Ask students to quickly scan the text to find the phrases listed in a–d and to underline them.
- Remind them that the position of a phrase within a paragraph can often help them to understand the meaning or the function of the phrase.
- Ask them to tell you where in a paragraph they could expect to find the phrase *At first* (at the beginning of a paragraph).
- Go through the three remaining phrases in the same way, asking students to tell you where they might expect to find these phrases in a paragraph and indicating them to the students in the passage.
- Ask students to work individually or with a partner to do the rest of the exercise.
- Elicit answers.

1 d 2 b 3 c 4 a

3

Aim: to practise an exam-type task

- Before the students do this exercise, remind them of the best way to approach it so that they become familiar with exam technique.
- Ask them to read sentence A. Elicit which word or phrase might act as a clue to which gap the sentence fits (*as time has passed*).
- Remind students that they need to look for information before or after the gap.
- Remind them also of the importance of looking for discourse markers, such as relative and personal pronouns, defining and non-defining clauses and determiners.
- Elicit suggested answers but do not negate or confirm them at this stage.
- Encourage students to approach each of the sentences in the same way.
- Remind students of the importance of underlining the words which helped them find the answer within the passage, as this makes it much quicker and easier for them to be able to justify and check their answers.
- Finally, remind them that there is only one extra sentence which they do not need to use.
- Ask students to work individually or with a partner.
- Elicit answers, asking students to indicate the words or phrases which helped them choose the answer.

1 D *'... since ancient times.' 'However, most people in the past ...'*
2 F *'... people aren't buying stamps like they used to.' 'That in turn means that fewer children are becoming interested in the hobby.'*
3 C *'They proudly put these on display ...' 'Young people are still ... showing off these models.'*
4 E *'At first, they were seen as strange machines used by big businesses.' 'Gradually, however, the computer has become a part of almost every home ...'*
5 B *'Young people in the past had to rely on people they knew, or perhaps the local library, to learn about their hobby.' 'Today's teenagers ...'*
6 G *'Many young people fill their free time with activities that their parents and grandparents enjoyed.' 'For instance, people still go dancing, even if the rhythm of the music has changed.'*

Additional task

- Ask students to write a short paragraph of 50 words about hobbies which contains the extra sentence A.

WORD BOX

4

Aim: to introduce new vocabulary

- Before the students do this exercise, ask them to read the sentences.
- Remind them of the importance of deciding before they complete the sentences whether they need to look for a noun, adjective or verb in the article.
- Ask students to work individually or with a partner to do the exercise.
- Elicit answers.
- Ask students if there were any other words in the article which they didn't know the meaning of.
- Remind them to make a note of the words and to look them up in a dictionary before the start of the next lesson.
- Ask students if they enjoyed reading the article and whether they learned anything from it or not and get them to justify their answers.

1 valuable
2 afford
3 traditional
4 weird
5 rhythm
6 balance
7 video arcade

Additional task

- Read out definitions of five words from the **WORD BOX** and ask students to tell you the word that you have defined.

Have your say!

Aim: to give students the opportunity to express their own opinions

- Put the students in pairs and get them to ask each other the questions. Ask them to make brief notes on their partner's answers. When they have finished, invite various students to tell the whole class what they discussed.
- Alternatively, you may like to do the activity as a whole class. Invite various students to give their opinions, encouraging them to agree or disagree with what other students have said. Encourage them to give reasons for their opinions.

Suggested homework

Assign Ex.1 – Workbook, p.18–19

G Grammar clinic

1

Aim: to review *present perfect* tenses

- Before students do the exercises on this page, ask them to study pages 171–172 of the **Grammar database**, either in class or at home before the lesson starts.
- The first exercise refers back to the reading passage so that students can see the grammar in question being used in context.
- Read the sentences and ask which tense is being used in each sentence.
- Ask students to match each sentence to its explanation.

1 c	2 b	3 a

2

Aim: to practise identifying perfect tenses in context

- Before students attempt this task, write this sentence on the board: *I am living in Athens for two years.*
- Ask students to explain to you what is wrong with the sentence (The verb *live* should be in the *present perfect continuous* because it refers to a situation which has continued up to now.).
- Before students do the exercise, go through the first sentence together.
- Ask: *Is this a feeling or a situation?* (a situation)
- Ask: *Has the situation finished or is it continuing?* (continuing)
- Ask: *What tense do we use for a situation that continues up to now?* (*present perfect continuous*)
- Remind students to go through this process of asking themselves questions about the sentence before they choose true or false.
- Students then work individually or with a partner.
- Elicit answers, asking students to give reasons for their answers from the explanations a–c in exercise 1.

1 T	Present perfect continuous for actions continuing up to now
2 T	Present perfect rather than past simple, which would suggest he had died
3 F	Present perfect continuous for actions continuing up to now
4 T	A completed action when the time it occurred is not important.

ON THE BOARD

I am living in Athens for two years.

3

Aim: to correct sentences involving *present perfect* tenses

- Before students correct the mistakes, go through the first one together.
- Ask: *Is this a situation or an action?* (an action)
- Ask: *Is the time when the action took place mentioned?* (yes – last week)
- Ask: *What tense do we use for a single, completed action at a specific time in the past?* (*past simple*)
- Remind them also to look out for words and expressions which are often used with present perfect tenses (*This is the first time, just, yet, already, ever, never, for, since, so far, up to now*, etc).
- Remind students to go through this process of asking themselves questions about each sentence before they correct it.
- Ask students to work individually or with a partner.
- Elicit answers.

1 I saw Matt last week, when we were at the karate club.
2 I haven't played Monopoly for a long time.
4 This is the first time I have built a model plane.
Sentence 3 is correct.

4

Aim: to practise using *present perfect* tenses

- Before students complete the sentences, go through the first sentence together.
- Tell them to ignore the missing verb for the moment.
- Ask: *Is this a situation or a series of actions?* (a series of actions)
- Ask: *Did the series of actions finish a long time ago or recently?* (recently – the person is tired after the action so it can't have finished a long time before)
- Ask: *What tense do we use for an action over a period of time that has recently ended?* (*present perfect continuous*)
- Remind students to ask themselves these questions about the sentence before they fill in the gap.
- Ask students to work individually or with a partner.
- Elicit answers.

1 have been playing
2 has never met
3 Have you been following (note: we can use *follow* when we are referring to a series of programmes)
4 have been practising
5 have been waiting
6 has taken up

5

Aim: to have controlled practice using *present perfect* tenses

- Students now work individually to complete the passage.
- Encourage them to ask themselves the kind of questions that they were asked in exercises 3 and 4.
- Elicit answers.

1 have been planning	4 has read
2 have joined	5 have been thinking
3 have written	6 haven't made

Suggested homework

Assign Ex.1, 2 and 3 – Workbook, p.20

V Vocabulary builder

1

Aim: to focus on topic-based collocations

- Before students attempt this task, write this sentence on the board: *Emily has been doing horse-riding for three years.*
- Ask students to explain to you what is wrong with the sentence (The verb *go* is used with horse-riding rather than the verb *do*.).
- Ask students to look through the list of free-time activities.
- Write the words: *go, do* and *play* on the board and elicit from individual students which verbs precede each of the activities, writing the activity under the verbs as the students tell you them.
- Students then copy the information into their notebooks.

ON THE BOARD

Emily has been doing horse-riding for three years.
go
do
play

go	do	play
camping	ballet	basketball
horse-riding	karate	video games
swimming	judo	volleyball
skiing	gymnastics	the piano
fishing		
canoeing		

Errors to watch out for

Students may make the mistake of talking about going to *a camping*.
Remind students that they can say either, *'We go to a campsite every summer'*, or *'We go camping every summer'*.

2

Aim: to practise topic-based collocations

- Ask students to read the sentences and to decide if the word in bold is correct. If so, they should put a tick.
- If the word is incorrect, they should rewrite it correctly. Encourage them to refer to exercise 1 above to check the collocations used with different free-time activities.
- Go through the answers orally.

1 doing	3 ✓	5 do
2 ✓	4 playing	6 go

3

Aim: to develop awareness of idioms

- This exercise is probably best done as a whole class. If time allows, however, divide the class into small groups and encourage them to use a dictionary in order to find the meaning of the idioms given here.
- Before students attempt this exercise, ask them to read through the sentences and underline any words or phrases which might act as clues as to the meaning of the idiom.
- Students then work in small groups to match the two halves of the sentence.
- Elicit answers, asking for a definition of the idiom.
- Encourage students to make a note of idioms, their definitions and an example sentence in their notebooks.

1 c	3 f	5 b
2 e	4 a	6 d

take one's time = to do something slowly and carefully
be/start on time = (for people, trains, buses, etc) to arrive at a place at the right time / (for television programmes, concerts) to start at the right time
have time on one's hands = to have spare time
(just) in time = to manage to do something before it is too late
kill time = to fill spare time, usually when you have nothing better to do
make time for someone/something = to manage to find time to be with someone/do something

Additional task

- Brainstorm any other idioms that students might know connected to time (eg *one* (or *two*, etc) *at a time, about time, at the same time, from time to time, have (no) time for, time flies*, etc*)*.

4

Aim: to introduce phrasal verbs with *down*

- Point out to students that phrasal verbs that share the same particle (*up, down, out*, etc) sometimes have meanings that have something in common. All the verbs here use *down* and they all have negative meanings.
- Ask: *Which phrasal verb might mean to think you are better than someone? (look down on)*
- Elicit any ideas they have.
- Students then work individually to complete the sentences.
- Elicit answers.
- Remind students that sometimes phrasal verbs can have more than one meaning.
- After students have completed this task, write on the board: *If you ___________ something _________ on paper, you manage to write it down.*
- Elicit which of the phrasal verbs from exercise 4 could fit this sentence (*get down*).
- Encourage students to make a note of the different meanings of phrasal verbs in their notebooks.

1 turn down	4 puts (an animal) down
2 look down on	5 gets (you) down
3 come down with	

ON THE BOARD

If you ___________________ something __________ __________ on paper, you manage to write it down.

5

Aim: to introduce students to metaphorical words used for talking about time

- Ask students to look at the words in the box and tell you if they know any time phrases or expressions using these words.
- Ask: *If my time is valuable, what does that mean?* (I don't have much time to waste – I'm very busy.)
- Explain that words connected to time are often associated with money.
- Students then work individually or with a partner.
- Remind students that they may have to put the words into the correct form.
- Elicit answers.

1 save	3 spend
2 wasting	4 valuable

Suggested homework

Assign Ex. 1 and 2 – Workbook, p.21

Listening

Warm up!

Aim: to introduce the topic and warm students up

- Ask students to think about any hobbies they have or that people they know have. Ask them why people have hobbies and what they get out of them.
- You may like to get students to discuss hobbies briefly in pairs and then report back to the class on their discussion.

1

Aim: to focus on listening for attitude

- Students are now going to listen to two people talking about their hobbies.
- Ask students to read through the questions and the multiple choice options.
- Ask students to also listen for the hobby that each of the speakers is talking about.
- Play the listening text.
- Elicit answers, asking students to justify their answers by paraphrasing what they heard.

CD1, Track 8

1 b	*'… you have to practise constantly. I found that quite hard at first …'*
2 c	*'I find it entertains me when I haven't got anything better to do.'*

2

Aim: to listen for attitude and practise an exam-type task

- Before the students do this exercise, remind them of the best way to approach it so that they become familiar with exam technique.
- Remind them of the importance of listening for synonyms or similar words to any that appear in the sentences.
- Ask: *What words might someone use if they were talking about learning about other cultures?* (Words might include: *learn, understand, foreign countries, other/different people, way of life, traditions*, etc.)
- Ask students to read through the sentences B–E and to speculate about the vocabulary they might hear.
- Elicit their suggestions.
- Remind them to match each of the four speakers to one of the statements and that there is an extra statement.
- Play the listening text.
- Elicit answers, asking students to justify their answers by paraphrasing what they heard.
- Ask students if they can tell you the hobbies that each speaker was talking about.

CD1, Track 9

Speaker 1:
D karate: *'There's a lot of pressure on you to do all the moves perfectly.'*
Speaker 2:
B basketball: *'It's a sport that teaches you a lot about teamwork – you have to learn how to cooperate well with other people.'*
Speaker 3:
A watching TV: *'... and you learn about how people live in other countries ...'*
Speaker 4:
E drawing: *'... I can escape from my everyday problems that way.'*

Soundbite

Aim: to practise listening for the sound /ʌ/

- Students now listen for words which are spelled differently but which contain the same sound /ʌ/.
- Explain that they will hear four words and should circle the two words which have the same vowel sound.
- Play the listening text.
- Elicit the answers, checking pronunciation.

CD1, Track 10

1 come / luck	3 fun / fuss
2 run / won	4 truck / trust

Speaking

1

Aim: to develop language for making suggestions

- First, write this sentence on the board: *Mum suggested going to visit Grandma at Christmas.*
- Elicit students' suggestions for two other endings.
- Remind them that *suggest* can be followed by three things:
  suggest + noun (write on the board: *Mum suggested a visit to Grandma at Christmas.*)
  suggest + *that* clause (write on the board: *Mum suggested (that) we (should) visit Grandma at Christmas.*)
  suggest + *-ing* (as in the first sentence)
- Ask students to circle the correct words and phrases to complete the sentences.
- Elicit answers.

1 getting	3 Getting	5 buying
2 buy	4 might	6 getting

ON THE BOARD

Mum suggested going to visit Grandma at Christmas.
Mum suggested a visit to Grandma at Christmas.
Mum suggested (that) we (should) visit Grandma at Christmas.

Errors to watch out for

Students often use *suggest* with the full infinitive, eg *'He suggested me to go to the doctor.'* Remind them that *suggest* is never followed by the full infinitive.

2

Aim: to practise making suggestions and practise an exam-type task

- Before students do this exercise, ask them to study the **Speaking database** on page 165.
- Remind students that in the exam the questions they should answer will be printed above the photos.
- Remind students that they can use the structures in exercise 1 to make suggestions as well as other ways they know.
- Go round the class monitoring and helping where necessary. Check to make sure that students aren't making mistakes with *suggest.*
- You might want to set a time limit of three or four minutes for this.
- Elicit ideas.

Use of English

1

Aim: to focus on articles

- Before students do the exercises on this page, ask them to study pages 172–173 of the **Grammar database**, either in class or at home before the lesson starts.
- First, write this sentence on the board: *I used to play the guitar, but now I don't have much time because I have to study for the school.*
- Elicit what is wrong with the sentence (There shouldn't be an article before *school.*).
- Remind students that the definite article is used before musical instruments but not before places connected to education such as universities, schools or colleges.
- Elicit other objects, places or countries which take or don't take the definite article.
- Students then work individually or with a partner.
- Elicit answers.

1. In my free time, I listen to the music, go to the cinema and play the guitar.
2. The Head gave the Class 7 permission to organise an after-school club.
3. I go to the chess club at the weekend by the bus.
4. Jenny loves the swimming and she'd like to swim the English Channel.
5. We went to the USA and saw the Grand Canyon and the Mount Rushmore.
6. You need a hobby, like playing the flute or collecting the stamps.

ON THE BOARD

I used to play the guitar, but now I don't have much time because I have to study for the school.

2

Aim: to correct sentences where articles are missing

- Go through the first one together.
- Ask: *Do we need to put an article before: Oscar, time, hobbies, prison?* (no)
- Remind students that we only say that someone has gone to *the* prison or *the* hospital when they are just visiting.
- Ask: *Are there any other places where we need to insert 'a' or 'an'?* (yes – the phrase *a lot of time*)
- Remind students to go through this process of asking themselves questions about the sentence before they correct it.
- Ask students to work individually or with a partner to do the exercise.
- Elicit answers.

1. Oscar had a lot of time to start new hobbies when he was in prison.
2. I like comedies, whether they are on television or on the radio.
3. James has taken up a new hobby and spends the whole evening making models.
4. Hang-gliding is great fun, but you need hills or even a mountain nearby.
5. My hobby is drawing, so when I grow up I'd like to be an artist.

3

Aim: to develop awareness of transformations

- Remind students of the importance of learning what grammatical structures are possible for different verbs.
- Ask students to match the phrases which mean the same.
- Elicit answers.

1 c   2 a   3 d   4 b

Additional task

- Divide the class into pairs.
- Student A writes four short sentences using the verbs 1–4. Student B writes four sentences using the phrases a–d.
- Students then swap their sentences and rewrite their partner's sentences using the appropriate verb or phrase.
- Ask individual students to read their sentences out to the rest of the class.

4

Aim: to practise exam-type sentence transformations

- Students now do sentence transformations which are designed to practise what they have learned from exercise 3.
- Before they attempt the task, ask them to look at the word in bold in number 1.
- Based on what they have learned from exercise 3, ask them to tell you which words in the first sentence they might need to replace (*wanted to have*).
- Ask: *Which phrase from exercise 3 means, 'want to have'?* (*feel like doing*)
- Elicit the answer to number 1.
- Remind them that they will need to rewrite the first sentence using the word in bold so that the second sentence means exactly the same thing. They will need to use between two and five words, including the word given.
- Remind students that they should write the missing words in capital letters.
- Remind them that contractions such as *don't, doesn't, hasn't,* etc count as two words. The exception to this is *can't* which counts as one word (because it comes from *cannot*).
- Remind students that when they have completed the sentences they should read them through again to make sure they have followed the instructions properly.
- Students then work individually to complete the exercise.
- Elicit answers.

1. My parents asked me if I FELT LIKE HAVING ballet lessons.
2. The teachers DON'T/DO NOT APPROVE OF our playing football in the corridor.
3. I WISH I HADN'T/HAD NOT GIVEN up the trumpet at the age of 12.
4. I really CAN'T WAIT TO JOIN my local basketball team.
5. Dave IS LOOKING FORWARD TO TAKING part in the karaoke competition!
6. Why DO YOU OBJECT TO Sarah playing rugby?

Suggested homework

Assign Ex. 1 and 2 – Workbook, p.21
Assign Ex. 1 and 2 – Workbook, p.22

Writing

1

Aim: to introduce the topic of informal letters/emails

- Before students do the exercises on this page, ask them to study page 154 of the **Writing database**, either in class or at home before the lesson starts.
- Ask students to read the writing task and to tell you who the email should be written to (a friend called Craig).
- Elicit why the email is informal (because it is written to a friend).
- Encourage students to think about the kind of information that they **must** include in their email to Craig (make a suggestion for two possible concerts, check that Craig is arriving on June 19th, tell him that the Royal Orchestra is very good, tell him that you haven't got much money).

Additional task

- Check students' comprehension of the information they have been given by asking the following questions:

1 How much does it cost to see the Royal Orchestra? (€20)
2 What kind of music do the Wilson Brothers play? (country music)
3 How much are the cheapest tickets at *The Robbers'* concert? (€15)

2

Aim: to encourage students to think about the style of informal letters/emails

- Remind students that for exam purposes, an email simply means a letter sent electronically and that they should not use abbreviations such as 'CU', etc, in their emails.
- Remind students to look back at the writing task in exercise 1 to help them with the true or false questions.
- Elicit answers, asking students to justify their ideas based on their understanding of informal letters from Unit 1.

1 F	Some letters / emails are written to people you know and are informal.
2 T	This is a good way to start an informal letter / email.
3 T	Students will lose marks if they don't include all the points they should.
4 T	Students can expand on the information, as long as what they write is relevant

3

Aim: to provide a model answer for students to refer to

- Ask students to read the email through once.
- Encourage students to give their opinion on whether this is a good email, whether it answers the question correctly and whether Kelly has included all of the information she should have (Yes – this email would get a good mark in the exam.).

4

Aim: to read for specific information

- Before students attempt this task, ask them to read sentences 1–6 and tell you where in an informal email they would normally expect to find information like this.
- Encourage them to visualise where the information should be.
- Ask students to read the model answer in exercise 3 again and underline where the information appears.
- Elicit answers.
- Remind students that the order of this information provides a paragraph plan that they can learn and use in appropriate informal letters/emails.

From: *Kelly <kelly@dmail.com>*
To: *Craig <CriagSmith@friend.com>*
Subject: *Your visit!*

Dear Craig,

Hi! (1) Have your exams finished? I can't wait for you to arrive!

You said you want to go to a concert while you're here. (2) You're arriving on the 19th, aren't you? 'The Robbers' are playing up to the 18th, so we'll miss them. It's a shame because they're great!

So really you've got a choice of two concerts. (3) The first is the Royal Orchestra on the 20th or 21st. I've seen them and they were very good. Tickets are €20 each.

(4) The Wilson Brothers are playing after that. Have you heard of them? I don't know what they're like. Still, might be interesting. I don't have much money so we'd have to get the cheapest tickets. They're €25. (5) Decide which one you want to see and let me know. I'll get the tickets before you come.

(6) Got to go! Mum's calling me.

See you soon,
Kelly

5

Aim: to read for specific information to prepare students for the writing task

- First, remind students of the importance of identifying who they are writing to.
- Ask: *Will you be writing to a friend or a relation?* (a friend,Tom)
- Then ask: *Will you be writing about what you want to do when you visit him, or what he might want to do when he visits you?* (what he might want to do when he visits you)
- Then ask: *Do you need to include all of the information from your notes?* (yes)
- Elicit who the students will be writing to and why.
- Explain that the information from the leaflet given in exercise 1 on page 30 is the information for this writing task.

6

Aim: to encourage students to plan their writing

- This exercise is designed to encourage students to use their imagination and to make sure that all students have enough ideas before they start writing.
- Remind students that careful planning will improve their emails.
- Ask students to look at the questions and to make notes in their notebooks.
- Remind them that they should be answering the questions with one or two sentences.
- Go round the class monitoring or helping where necessary.
- At the end of the exercise, ask individual students to read out their ideas.
- Encourage students to make a note of any good ideas they hear from other students.
- If you have time, check that all students have completed the questions with appropriate information.

1	*Dear Tom,*
2	Students need to think of a question about Tom's news.
3	When he arrives and when he leaves.
4–5	students' own answers
6	It is birthday money.
7	Let me know which concert he wants to go to.
8	before 6th June
9	*Love; Lots of love; All my love; Write to me soon; See you soon.*

- Ask students to turn to **Writing Planner 3** on page 156. Explain that each Writing Planner gives them a simple table to complete which helps them to put the right content in the right place in their piece of writing.
- Point out to students that each row of the table refers to a different part of their piece of writing and gives its purpose, together with useful expressions. Explain to students that they should complete the 'notes' column using their own ideas.
- Give students some time to complete the table. Invite a number of students to say what they have put in the 'notes' column for each part of the piece of writing. If possible, you may like to check the notes made by all students to ensure they have enough content to base their piece of writing on. Ask students to refer to the Writing Planner as they do their piece of writing.

7

Aim: to give students the opportunity to produce an informal email

- This exercise can be done in class or set for homework.
- Remind students of the importance of using a conversational tone and of answering the question by including all the information from their notes.

8

Aim: to encourage students to check their written work

- Draw students' attention to the checklist.
- When they have finished writing, ask them to read each statement and to tick each one that is true for them.
- Ask them to make sure that they have ticked all of the boxes before handing their email in to be marked.
- You might consider refusing to mark any email that does not meet all the criteria in the checklist and asking the student to rewrite.

Look Back

Aim: to review the unit and to practise scanning for specific information

- Students now have the opportunity to go back through the unit to check what they have learned.
- Ask the whole class the questions from **Look Back**.
- Elicit answers from different students.
- Encourage students to scan the unit to find any information they can't remember.

1 in the nineteenth century
2 'He's been to India,' tells us that he has visited India and has now returned. 'He's gone to India,' suggests that he is on his way to India or is there and hasn't returned yet.
3 take your time
4 It makes you feel depressed.
5 (suggested answers) the Netherlands, the USA, the United Kingdom

Suggested homework

Assign Ex.1 – Workbook, p.22
Ex.2 and 3 – Workbook, p.23

Further material

- For further practice and consolidation, ask students to complete the Unit 3 tasks on the Student's CD-ROM.
- To test students' understanding of the material in Unit 3, you may like to administer the Unit 3 Test, which is in the Tests section of the Teacher's DVD-ROM. You may also like to construct your own test using the Test Generator material for Unit 3.

4

Work Wonders

Target language

Grammar:	past perfect simple and past perfect continuous / comparatives and superlatives
Lexis:	topic vocabulary / word formation (suffixes) / confusable words
Reading skills:	scanning for specific information
Listening skills:	listening for specific information
Speaking skills:	expressing uncertainty
Writing skills:	layout and text structure / report
Pronunciation:	silent letters (1)

- The phrase *to work wonders* means *to do somebody a lot of good,* eg *Regular exercise can work wonders for your general health.* Here it suggests that working can be an enjoyable and productive part of life.
- Write the phrase *to work wonders* on the board.
- Ask students what they think the title refers to.
- Explain the meaning of the phrase *to work wonders.*
- Write the example sentence given above on the board.
- Elicit suggestions as to what the unit might be about.

ON THE BOARD

to work wonders

Regular exercise can work wonders for your general health.

Start thinking!

Aim: to introduce the topic of occupations through personal responses

- Ask students to work in pairs to talk about the questions in the Student's Book.
- Go round the class monitoring and helping where necessary.
- If you prefer, conduct a class discussion.

Additional task

- Write these words on the board: *job* and *profession.*
- Elicit from the students which occupations they would put into each category. You might need to prompt them by offering a few suggestions, eg lawyer, secretary, taxi driver, doctor, etc. (*Job* usually refers to work which you do regularly to earn money. *Profession* refers to a type of job that you need a lot of training or education to do and includes lawyers, doctors and vets.)
- Ask students to write down as many occupations as they can.
- You may wish to set a time limit of one or two minutes for this.

Reading

1

Aim: to focus on the content of the text

- Students are going to read an article about different jobs. Before they read the text, ask them to look at the paragraph headings, which each refer to a different type of work.
- Ask students to comment on which type of work they would prefer to do, and to give reasons for their opinions.
- You might ask students to rank the types of work in order from 1 (the type of work they would prefer to do the most) to 5 (the type of work they would least prefer to do). Give them a few moments to rank the types of work, and then ask them to tell the class what ranking they have chosen and to say why.

Background information

- *'Voluntary work' is work that someone does, often for a charitable organisation, for which they don't get paid.*

2

Aim: to skim for gist to answer true or false questions

- Ask students to quickly read the whole text to get the general idea of what it's about. You might like to set a time limit, such as two minutes, for this.

- Ask students to read the statements given. Ask them to decide whether the statements are true or false from what they remember of the text. Ask them not to read the text again at this point.
- When they have finished, ask them to look at the text again to locate the parts of the text which give them the answers. Ask students to check their answers against the text.
- Go through the answers orally.

1 F	3 F	5 F
2 F	4 T	6 T

CD1, Track 11

3

Aim: to practise an exam-type task

- First, remind students of the best way to approach it so that they become familiar with exam technique.
- Remind them of the importance of looking for key words or phrases which are synonymous or similar in meaning to the words in the question.
- Remind them, too, of the importance of underlining where they found the answer within the passage, as this makes it much quicker and easier for them to be able to justify and check their answers.
- Finally, remind them that they can choose some of the paragraphs more than once and that some questions have more than one answer.
- Ask students to work individually or with a partner.
- Elicit answers, asking for justification from the passage.

1 and 2 B / E (in any order)
3 C
4 and 5 A / D (in any order)
6 C
7 and 8 A / C (in any order)
9 and 10 A / D (in any order)

Additional task

- Ask students to write a short paragraph of 50 words explaining why they would be suitable for one of the kinds of work in the text. Ask them to write about their personality and their qualities and why those make them suitable for that kind of work.

WORD BOX

4

Aim: to introduce new vocabulary

- Before students do this exercise, ask them to read the sentences.
- Remind them of the importance of deciding before they complete the sentences whether they need to look for a noun, adjective or verb in the passage.
- Ask students to work individually or with a partner to do the exercise.
- Elicit answers.
- Ask students if there were any other words in the passage which they didn't know the meaning of.
- Remind them to make a note of the words and to look them up in a dictionary before the start of the next lesson.
- Ask students if they enjoyed reading the article and whether they learned anything from it or not and get them to justify their answers.

1 salary	5 applicant
2 application form	6 voluntary work
3 expenses	7 staff
4 in writing	

Additional task

- Ask students to choose five words from the **WORD BOX** and to jumble up the letters to create an anagram.
- Students then swap their anagrams with a partner who must try to find the word.

Have your say!

Aim: to give students the opportunity to express their own opinions

- Put the students in pairs and get them to ask each other the questions. Ask them to make brief notes on their partner's answers. When they have finished, invite various students to tell the whole class what they discussed.
- Alternatively, you may like to do the activity as a whole class. Invite various students to give their opinions, encouraging them to agree or disagree with what other students have said. Encourage them to give reasons for their opinions.

Suggested homework

Assign Ex.1 – Workbook, p.24–25
Ex.1 – Workbook, p.24

G Grammar clinic

1

Aim: to review *past perfect* tenses

- Before students do the exercises on this page, ask them to study pages 174–175 of the **Grammar database**, either in class or at home before the lesson starts.
- The first exercise refers back to the reading passage so that students can see the grammar in question being used in context.
- Read the sentences and ask students to tell you which tense is being used in each sentence.
- Ask students to decide if the statements are true or false.

1 T, T
2 T, F (It's possible that the action was completed before the main time in the past, but we can't say for sure, and the context makes it unlikely.)

Additional task

- Ask students to write two sentences of their own using the *past perfect simple* and two using the *past perfect continuous.*

2

Aim: to practise using *past perfect* tenses

- First, write this sentence on the board: *By the time we got to the bus station, the bus left.*
- Ask students to explain to you what is wrong with the sentence (The *past perfect*, rather than the *past simple*, is used to talk about actions and states before the main time in the past we are interested in.).
- Before students circle the correct answer, go through the first sentence together.
- Ask: *Are there any phrases in the sentence which might act as a clue?* (yes – *by the time* is used with perfect tenses)
- Ask: *Which action in the past occurred first?* (Claire working for 20 years)
- Ask: *What tense do we use for actions that occurred for a long time in the past up to the time in the past that we are interested in?* (*past perfect continuous*)
- Remind students to go through this process of asking themselves questions about the sentence before they fill in the gaps.
- Ask students to work individually or with a partner to do the rest of the exercise.
- Elicit answers.

ON THE BOARD

By the time we got to the bus station, the bus left.

1 had been working	4 had finished
2 had called	5 decided
3 had worked	

3

Aim: to correct sentences using *past perfect* tenses

- Before students correct the mistakes, go through the first one together.
- Ask: *Are there any phrases in the sentence which might act as a clue?* (yes – *all morning* is often used with *present* and *past perfect continuous*)
- Ask: *Did the action happen in the present or in the past?* (in the past)
- Remind students to look out for words and expressions which are often used with past perfect tenses such as *before, after, when, already, as soon as, It was the first time, all morning/day/week/*etc, *just, for, since,* etc.
- Remind students to go through this process of asking themselves questions about the sentence before they correct it.
- Ask students to work individually or with a partner to do the exercise.
- Elicit answers.

2 Because he had never worked from home, my brother didn't know what to expect.
3 Somebody else got the job before I had had a chance to send in my application form.
4 Dad had been driving all day so he was really tired when he got home from work.
Sentence 1 is correct.

4

Aim: to practise using *past perfect* tenses

- Before students complete the sentences, go through the first sentence together.
- Tell them to ignore the missing verb for the moment.
- Ask: *Are there any phrases in the sentence which might act as a clue?* (yes – *it was the first time* is used with *past perfect simple*)
- Remind students to go through this process of asking themselves questions about the sentence before they fill in the gap.
- Ask students to work individually or with a partner to do the rest of the exercise.
- Elicit answers.

1 had worked	4 had been having
2 had already written	5 had worked
3 had been waiting	6 had been trying

Suggested homework

Assign Ex. 1, 2 and 3 – Workbook, p.26

V Vocabulary builder

1

Aim: to focus on occupations

- This exercise is probably best done as a whole class. If time allows however, divide the class into small groups and encourage them to use a dictionary in order to find the meaning of any unknown occupations before they begin the exercise.
- Before students attempt to match the occupation to the definition, ask them to read through the sentences 1–10 and underline any key words. These key words might be useful as clues to help them do the exercise.
- Go through the first sentence as an example.
- Elicit the key words *physical work* and *repairing roads.*
- Ask: *Which job is difficult, physical and might involve repairing roads?* (labourer)
- Ask students to complete the exercise.
- Elicit answers.

1 labourer	6 miner
2 architect	7 plumber
3 accountant	8 civil engineer
4 journalist	9 electrician
5 civil servant	10 sales rep

Additional task

- Students play a game of 'This morning I have been …' round the class.
- Tell students to choose one of the jobs from exercise 1 in the Student's Book or think of another job they know. They must explain to the class what they have been doing as part of their job so that the rest of the class can work out which job they do.

2

Aim: to develop topic vocabulary knowledge

- This exercise is probably best done in pairs. If time allows however, encourage each pair to use a dictionary in order to find the meaning of any unknown words or phrases before they begin the exercise.
- Encourage students to make a note of any new expressions or phrases that they learn in their notebooks.
- Elicit answers.

1 work	3 more	5 stop
2 lose	4 better	

Additional task

- After students have done this exercise, ask them to close their books and then ask individual students to give you the definitions for each of the phrases given here.

3

Aim: to practise forming nouns by adding a suffix

- Before students attempt this task, draw a three-column table on the board with the following headings: *verb, noun* and *adjective.*
- Ask students to look at the words and brainstorm any forms of the words which they might know already and write them on the board in the appropriate column.
- Encourage students to copy the table into their notebooks. Remind them that these tables will help them when doing word formation exercises which they have to do in Part 3 of the FCE Use of English paper.
- Remind students that if a word is spelled incorrectly, they will lose marks.
- Students then work individually or with a partner to make the nouns using the suffixes that they are given.
- Elicit answers and encourage individual students to come up and write the words on the board, checking that the words are spelled correctly.

1 activity	6 employment
2 enjoyment	7 attraction
3 kindness	8 payment
4 majority	9 promotion
5 politeness	10 laziness

ON THE BOARD

verb / noun / adjective

4

Aim: to practise using derivatives formed in exercise 3

- Explain to students that the words missing from the sentences in exercise 4 are all words they have just formed in exercise 3.
- Explain that each word appears once and only once in the sentences.
- You might like to get students to do this task in pairs. Ask them to decide together which word is missing from each sentence. Then ask different pairs to compare their answers and discuss any disagreements until they settle on the correct answers.
- Alternatively, get students to complete the task individually and then go through the answers orally.

1 activities	6 laziness
2 employment	7 kindness
3 majority	8 promotion
4 politeness	9 attractions
5 enjoyment	10 payment

Suggested homework

Assign Ex. 1 and 2 – Workbook, p.27

Listening

Warm up!

Aim: to introduce the topic and warm students up

- Ask students if they know what a 'careers officer' is (someone who visits schools and advises students on their future career options). Ask if they have anything like that in their country.
- If students do have careers officers, ask what kind of advice they normally give and how useful they are.
- If students don't have careers officers, ask if they think it would be a good idea to have careers officers in schools to advise students on future careers.

1

Aim: to introduce the listening task

- Students are now going to listen to an extract from an interview with two careers officers.
- Ask students to read through the sentences and predict the information that they might hear.
- Remind them that they will need to listen for numbers and figures.
- Play the listening text.
- Elicit answers, asking students to justify their answers by paraphrasing what they heard.

CD1, Track 12

1 17: '… *over the 17 years I've been doing the job it hasn't changed much.'*
2 50: *'My area includes around 50 schools and I visit each one about once a year.'*
3 5,000: *'My area is similar, with around 5,000 pupils aged 17 to 18.'*
4 10: '… *we can only speak to each person for about 10 minutes …'*

Background information

- *A 'careers officer' is a person who gives advice to young people on whichever career they are interested in pursuing. Normally, careers officers will visit schools in their local area and interview students who are on the point of making a decision about which subjects to study at school.*

Additional task

- In order to check your students' understanding, ask them if they can tell you the answers to the following questions:

1 What is the name of the radio show that Craig and Susan appear on? ('World of Work')
2 What is Craig's surname? (Philips)
3 How often does Craig visit each of the schools? (about once a year)
4 How old are the pupils that Susan sees? (17 or 18 years old)

2

Aim: to listen for specific information and practise an exam-type task

- Before students listen to the complete interview, ask them to read through the questions and try to think about the information that they will need to listen for.
- Remind students that they will hear the interview twice. The first time they listen they should circle an answer and the second time they hear the interview they should check their answers.
- Play the listening text.
- Elicit answers, asking students to justify their answers by paraphrasing what they heard.

CD1, Track 13

1 B *'… over the 17 years I've been doing the job it hasn't changed much.'*
2 A *'… we do get a lot of people who want to follow a career as a doctor or a lawyer. Unfortunately, only about 10% of them will actually make it.'*
3 B *'I really wasn't certain what advice would be best, so in the end I suggested he join the air force.'*
4 A *'Try to have a clear idea of what you want, but be prepared to change.'*
5 C *'You can't really want to do a job unless you know something about it first.'*

Soundbite

Aim: to raise student awareness of silent letters

- Ask students to look at the list of words in the Student's Book and underline any letters they think are not pronounced.
- Play the listening text.
- Elicit the answers, encouraging students to pronounce the words correctly.

CD1, Track 14

listen, plumber, lamb, climber, comb, tomb, pneumonia, knight

Speaking

1

Aim: to practise expressing uncertainty

- Ask students to look at the phrases in italics which can be used to express uncertainty or speculate.
- Elicit answers, encouraging students to give you an example sentence using the expressions.

1 I'm not sure / I'm not certain
2 but I suppose / but I imagine
3 might / could

2

Aim: to give students practice in exam-type tasks

- Before students do this exercise, ask them to study the **Speaking database** on page 165.
- Ask students to choose at least four of the questions from the list and to discuss their ideas with their partner.
- Remind them to use the phrases from exercise 1 when expressing uncertainty.
- Go round the class monitoring and helping, where necessary.

- Ask students to report back to the whole class on the ideas they have discussed.

Use of English

1

Aim: to focus on comparatives and superlatives

- First, ask students to study pages 175–176 of the **Grammar database**, either in class or at home before the lesson starts.
- Write these sentences on the board: *Our new teacher is much more funny than the last one.* and *Our new teacher is much more interesting than the last one.*
- Elicit which sentence is correct and which is incorrect (The first one is incorrect because *funny* is a two-syllable adjective and two-syllable adjectives ending in *-y* usually form the comparative by adding *-ier* rather than *more.*).
- Ask students to tell you why the second sentence is correct (*Interesting* is a four-syllable adjective so it takes *more* in the comparative form.).
- Remind students that with some two-syllable adjectives, there is a choice: *clever – cleverer – cleverest* or *clever – more clever – the most clever.* We usually use the forms with *more* and *the most.*
- Students then work individually or with a partner.
- Elicit answers.

1 easier	3 the most confident
2 more challenging	4 better

ON THE BOARD

Our new teacher is much more funny than the last one.
Our new teacher is much more interesting than the last one.

2

Aim: to practise sentence transformations

- First, ask students to look at the word in bold in number 1.
- Ask which words in the first sentence they might need to replace (such as *boring*).
- Ask: *Do we need to replace 'boring' with a comparative or superlative adjective?* (superlative)
- Ask: *Do we need to use least or most?* (*least*)
- Elicit the answer to number 1.
- Remind them that they will need to rewrite the first sentence using the word in bold so that the second sentence means exactly the same thing. They shouldn't change the word given and they will need to use between two and five words.
- Remind them that contractions such as: *don't, doesn't, hasn't,* etc count as two words. The exception to this is *can't* which counts as one word (because it comes from *cannot*).
- Remind students that when they have completed the sentences they should read them through again to make sure they have followed the instructions properly.
- Students then work individually.
- Elicit answers.

1 This is the least interesting book about being an actor I have ever read.
2 The job wasn't as difficult as I had expected.
3 Kim finished her work more quickly than everyone else in the office.
4 I am less satisfied than I was in my old job.

3

Aim: to practise an exam-type task

- Before the students do this exercise, remind them of the best way to approach it so that they become familiar with exam technique.
- Remind them of the importance of reading through the passage once before they start to get an idea of the gist of it.
- Direct students' attention to the first sentence.
- Explain the importance of reading whole sentences rather than just single lines, as there may be additional information given on the following line or lines which affect how the word should be changed.
- Remind students that some words have more than one meaning and that might affect which word is required.
- Remind students, too, that they will need to think about not only whether the word should be a verb, noun, adjective or adverb but whether the word is plural or singular or positive or negative.
- Emphasise that spelling is extremely important and that words which are spelled incorrectly will be marked as wrong.
- Remind them that the first word is given as an example.
- Once they have finished the exercise remind them to read the passage again to check for sense.
- Remind students that they should write only one word in each gap, and that each word should be in capital letters.
- Finally, remind students that they should always fill in an answer, even if they are not sure it is correct.
- Ask students to work individually or with a partner to do the rest of the exercise.
- Elicit answers.

1 LABOURER	6 PRETTIEST
2 EMPLOYMENT	7 ACTIVITIES
3 MAJORITY	8 ATTRACTIONS
4 BETTER	9 EXPENSES
5 EASIER	10 ENJOYMENT

Suggested homework

Assign Ex. 1 and 2 – Workbook, p.27
Ex. 1, 2 and 3 – Workbook, p.28

Writing

1

Aim: to introduce the topic of reports

- Before students do the exercises on this page, ask them to study page 151 of the **Writing database**, either in class or at home before the lesson starts.
- Ask students to read the writing task and to tell you who has asked them to write the report.
- Ask students what the report is about.
- Elicit why the report should be formal (because it is going to be read by a teacher at school).

> The report is for their teacher and the report is about a job that a member of their family does and which they spent a day observing.

Additional task

- Encourage students to think about the kind of information that should be included in this report and to make a paragraph plan. In pairs, get them to make notes on what each part of the report might contain.

2

Aim: to encourage students to think about the style of reports

- Remind students to look back at the writing task in exercise 1 to help them with the true or false questions.
- Ask students to work individually or with a partner to do the exercise.
- Elicit answers.

> 1 T
> 2 F: It is usually a good idea to give your opinion or make a suggestion in the last paragraph.
> 3 F: Reports are formal pieces of writing.
> 4 T: A short heading should tell the reader exactly what the paragraph is about.
> 5 T
> 6 F

3

Aim: to provide a model for students to refer to

- Explain to students that the four extracts all come from the same report and have been put in random order.
- Ask students, working individually or in pairs, to reassemble the report by putting the parts in the correct order.
- Give students some time to complete the task and then check the answers.

> 1 C 2 B 3 D 4 A

Additional task

- You might ask students to work together in pairs to come up with alternative headings for each of the two main paragraphs.

4

Aim: to focus on the content of the writing model

- Ask students to read the model again. Tell them that they should read the parts of the model in the correct order.
- Ask students to complete the sentences with a word or short phrase from the model.
- Give students some time to complete the task and then elicit answers.

> 1 learn about
> 2 accountant
> 3 the office / Rachel's office
> 4 meetings
> 5 financial problems
> 6 vet

5

Aim: to prepare students for the writing task

- Before students begin these exercises, remind them of the importance of identifying who they are writing to.
- Ask: *Who will you be writing your report for?* (a teacher)
- Then ask: *What will you be writing about?* (about the main features of a particular career and why it would/wouldn't be suitable for you)

6

Aim: to focus students' attention on the information they need

- Before going through this task in class, you may like to ask students to find information about their chosen career for homework. This might involve searching for information online. There are a number of careers websites that provide that kind of information, and students should be able to easily locate a suitable one through a search engine. If students know someone, such as a member of their family, who does a particular job they wish to write about, they could speak to them to collect information.
- Alternatively, you could do the task in class, with students working either individually or in pairs, using their imagination or what they already know to complete the task.
- Invite different students to read their answers to the questions to the rest of the class. Ask them to comment on the information they have found.

> students' own answers, based on information they have found

7

Aim: to encourage students to further plan their writing

- This exercise is designed to encourage students to use their imagination and to make sure that they all have enough ideas before they start writing.

- Remind students that careful planning will improve their reports.
- Ask students to look at the questions and to make notes in their notebooks.
- Remind them that they should be answering the questions with one or two sentences.
- Go round the class monitoring or helping where necessary.
- At the end of the exercise, ask individual students to read out their ideas.
- Encourage students to make a note of any good ideas they hear from other students.
- If you have time, check that all students have completed the questions with appropriate information.

> ***To:*** *Mr/Mrs/Ms* [name of teacher]
> ***From:*** [their first and second names]
> ***Subject:*** *Being a / Working as a* [chosen occupation]
> 2–8 students' own answers

- Ask students to turn to **Writing Planner 4** on page 156. Explain that each Writing Planner gives them a simple table to complete which helps them to put the right content in the right place in their piece of writing.
- Point out to students that each row of the table refers to a different part of their piece of writing and gives its purpose, together with useful expressions. Explain to students that they should complete the 'notes' column using their own ideas.
- Give students some time to complete the table. Invite a number of students to say what they have put in the 'notes' column for each part of the piece of writing. If possible, you may like to check the notes made by all students to ensure they have enough content to base their piece of writing on. Ask students to refer to the Writing Planner as they do their piece of writing.

8

Aim: to give students the opportunity to produce a report

- This exercise can be done in class or set for homework.
- Remind students of the importance of using headings and formal language and of answering the question by including the information from their notes in exercises 6 and 7.

9

Aim: to encourage students to check their written work

- Draw students' attention to the checklist.
- When they have finished writing, ask them to read each statement and to tick each one that is true for them.
- Ask them to make sure that they have ticked all of the boxes before handing their report in to be marked.
- You might consider refusing to mark any report that does not meet all the criteria in the checklist and asking the student to rewrite.

Additional task

- In order to monitor whether students have checked their work carefully, you could ask them to underline in pencil places in their reports where they have 'used formal phrases', for example.
- Alternatively, invite individual students to read parts of their report to the rest of the class or get students to exchange reports with each other and to check each other's reports for mistakes before handing them in.

Look Back

Aim: to review the unit and to practise scanning for specific information

- Students now have the opportunity to go back through the unit to check what they have learned.
- Ask the whole class the questions from **Look Back**.
- Elicit answers from different students.
- Encourage students to scan the unit to find any information they can't remember.

> 1 an application form
> 2 the government
> 3 laziness
> 4 careers officer
> 5 climber

Suggested homework

Assign Ex. 1, 2 and 3 – Workbook, p.29

Webquest

- Ask students to complete the **Webquest** on page 198 of the Student's Book. You might ask students to work on this together in class if you have internet access, or you might assign it for homework.
- Explain to students that the answers to the questions are not in the Student's Book but that they need to find the answers online.
- Check the answers together and ask students to explain where they found the answers and how they found them (eg by typing terms into a search engine).

> 1 postcards
> 2 teddy/stuffed/toy/etc bears
> 3 numismatist
> 4 oologist
> 5 flags
> 6 the Chancellor of the Exchequer
> 7 (income) tax
> 8 hair
> 9 National Insurance
> 10 wholesale

Further material

- For further practice and consolidation, ask students to complete the Unit 4 tasks on the Student's CD-ROM.
- To test students' understanding of the material in Unit 4, you may like to administer the Unit 4 Test, which is in the Tests section of the Teacher's DVD-ROM. You may also like to construct your own test using the Test Generator material for Unit 4.

Revision Units 3-4

1

1 B	3 B	5 D	7 A	9 D
2 A	4 C	6 B	8 C	10 B

2

1 have known
2 had left
3 has been cooking
4 have seen
5 have been learning
6 had been working
7 has visited
8 have finished / finish

3

1 went	4 playing	6 doing
2 does	5 going	7 been
3 Going		

4

1 Take	3 in
2 hands	4 make / find

5

1 B	2 A	3 A	4 A

6

1 the	3 –	5 –	7 –
2 the	4 a	6 –	

7

(2 marks for each correct answer)

1 employment	6 working
2 laziness	7 enjoyment
3 politeness	8 activity
4 kindness	9 attraction
5 promotion	10 unhappiness

5

The Global Village

Target language

Grammar:	the passive / countable and uncountable nouns / homonyms
Lexis:	topic vocabulary / phrasal verbs with *on* / idioms (the media)
Reading skills:	scanning for specific information
Listening skills:	listening for gist
Speaking skills:	talking about experiences
Writing skills:	using descriptive language / story
Pronunciation:	/ɜː/

- The phrase *the global village* refers to the modern world where all countries depend on each other and seem to be closer together because of modern communication and transport systems, eg *Life in the global village means it's as easy to find out what's happening on the other side of the world as at the end of your street.*
- Write the phrase *the global village* on the board.
- Ask students what they think the title refers to.
- Explain the meaning of the phrase *the global village.*
- Write the example sentence given above on the board.
- Elicit suggestions as to what the unit might be about.

ON THE BOARD

> ***the global village***
>
> ***Life in the global village means it's as easy to find out what's happening on the other side of the world as at the end of your street.***

Start thinking!

Aim: to introduce the topic of the media through personal responses

- Ask students to work in pairs to talk about the questions in the Student's Book.
- Go round the class monitoring and helping where necessary.
- If you prefer, conduct a brief discussion involving the whole class by reading the questions and inviting different students to give their answers.

Background information

- *'The media' generally includes radio, television, newspapers, the internet and magazines.*

Reading CD1, Track 15

1

Aim: to scan for specific information

- Students are now going to read a magazine article. Begin by asking them to predict which types of media they might read about.
- Ask students to read the passage. This can be done individually or as a class activity with different students being asked to read different sections aloud to the rest of the class.
- Remind students that at this stage they do not need to understand all of the vocabulary as items will be covered in the **WORD BOX** section.
- Elicit answers from a few students as to what is surprising about the history of television.

> It is surprising that such an important invention as television was thought of by a thirteen-year-old boy.

Background information

- *Telecommunications is the technology of sending information by telephone, radio, television, email, etc.*

Additional task

- In order to check your students' ability to scan for specific information, elicit the answers to the following questions:

- Remind students that they don't have to reread large parts of the passage again but should look for clues or key words that might help them find the answer. The key words have been underlined in each sentence.

> 1 What was <u>invented in 1837</u>? (the telegraph)
> 2 What invention allowed people <u>to send messages through the air</u>? (the radio)
> 3 Who was <u>Justin Tolman</u>? (Philo T. Farnsworth's teacher)
> 4 What was Farnsworth's <u>first job after university</u>? (repairing radios)

2

Aim: to scan for specific information

- Ask students to quickly scan the text to find the years listed in 1–6 and to underline them.
- Ask students to work individually or with a partner to complete the exercise.
- Elicit answers.

1 d	3 f	5 a
2 b	4 c	6 e

3

Aim: to practise an exam-type task

- Before the students do this exercise, remind them of the best way to approach it so that they become familiar with exam technique.
- Ask them to read sentence A. Elicit which word or phrase might act as a clue to which gap the sentence fits (*as it still is*).
- Remind students that they need to look for information before or after the gap.
- Remind them also of the importance of looking for discourse markers such as relative and personal pronouns, defining and non-defining clauses and determiners.
- Elicit suggested answers but do not negate or confirm them at this stage.
- Encourage students to approach each of the sentences in the same way.
- Remind students of the importance of underlining the words which helped them find the answer within the passage, as this makes it much quicker and easier for them to be able to justify and check their answers.
- Finally, remind them that there is only one extra sentence which they do not need to use.
- Ask students to work individually or with a partner.
- Elicit answers, asking students to indicate the words or phrases which helped them choose the answer.

> 1 C *'For the first time, people's voices could be sent over long distances.' 'However, wires were needed to connect people who wanted to communicate.'*
> 2 F *'Although images were sent, they were very basic.' 'In order to develop, television needed to be electronic …'*
> 3 G *'… his brain played with the idea of television.' 'Gradually, an idea formed in his mind.'*
> 4 E *'He drew diagrams on the blackboard explaining how it would work.' 'Over the next few weeks, they developed the ideas together …'*
> 5 B *'… he was looking out for the chance to raise money to develop his world-changing invention.' 'It finally came when he got a job with two rich investors …'*
> 6 A *'Television became a part of everyday life, as it still is.' 'Billions of us every day around the world stay up to date with the news headlines.'*

Additional task

- Ask students to write a short paragraph of 50 words about TV which contains the extra sentence D.

WORD BOX

4

Aim: to introduce new vocabulary

- Before the students do this exercise, ask them to read the definitions.
- Remind them of the importance of deciding before they complete the definitions whether they need to look for a noun, adjective or verb in the article.
- Ask students to work individually or with a partner to do the exercise.
- Elicit answers.
- Ask students if there were any other words in the article which they didn't know the meaning of.
- Remind them to make a note of the words and to look them up in a dictionary before the start of the next lesson.
- Ask students if they enjoyed reading the article and whether they learned anything from it or not and get them to justify their answers.

> 1 turn over
> 2 global
> 3 telecommunications
> 4 images
> 5 broadcast (irregular: broadcast – broadcast – broadcast)
> 6 up to date
> 7 headlines

Additional task

- Ask students to choose five words or phrases from the **WORD BOX** and to write their own sentences with the word missing.

- Students then swap their sentences with a partner and try to fill in the missing word.

Have your say!

Aim: to give students the opportunity to express their own opinions

- Put the students in pairs and get them to ask each other the questions. Ask them to make brief notes on their partner's answers. When they have finished, invite various students to tell the whole class what they discussed.
- Alternatively, you may like to do the activity as a whole class. Invite various students to give their opinions, encouraging them to agree or disagree with what other students have said. Encourage them to give reasons for their opinions.

Suggested homework

Assign Ex. 1 – Workbook, p.32–33
Ex. 1- Workbook, p.33

G Grammar clinic

1

Aim: to review the passive

- Before students do the exercises on this page, ask them to study pages 176–177 of the **Grammar database**, either in class or at home before the lesson starts.
- The first exercise refers back to the reading passage so that students can see the grammar in question being used in context.
- Read the sentences and phrases and ask students to tell you from the list a–d when the passive is used.
- Ask students to work individually or with a partner to underline all the examples of the passive that they can find in the article.
- Elicit answers.

Students should have ticked options a, b and c.
Other examples of the passive in the article are:
'The telegraph, which was invented …'
'… meant that messages could be sent …'
'… wires were needed …'
'Although images were sent …'
'He was fascinated …'
'Magnets could be used …'
'… until they were convinced …'
'… Philo's family was forced to move to find work'
'… TV pictures were being broadcast into homes …'

Additional task

- Ask students to write three sentences of their own about television or the media using the passive.

2

Aim: to practise rewriting sentences in the passive

- Go through the first sentence together with the students.
- Explain that the first sentence is in the *past simple*. To make it passive, we put the object first, then the verb *to be* in the right tense (here, *past simple*), then the past participle of *suggest*.
- Ask: *What is the object of the sentence?* (the idea of the internet)
- Ask: *What is the subject of the sentence?* (*someone*)
- Ask: *What verb do we need to use after the object?* (the verb *to be*)
- Ask: *And what follows the verb to be?* (the past participle of the verb *suggest*)
- Elicit the answer to number 1, reminding students that we don't need to say *by someone* at the end of the sentence.
- Remind students to go through this process of asking themselves questions about the sentence before they rewrite it.
- Students then work individually or with a partner to do the exercise.
- Elicit answers.

1 The idea of the internet was first suggested in the 1960s in America.
2 Our newspaper is delivered to the house every morning.
3 I was told that the BBC is planning a new channel.
4 The internet is said to be a great way to receive international news.
5 I was given a great book about working in the media by Jill.

3

Aim: to practise identifying passive and active sentences

- Before students attempt this task, write these sentences on the board: *Kevin's cousin is teaching him English.* and *Kevin ________________ English by his cousin.*
- Ask students to complete the second sentence so that it means the same as the first.
- Ask: *Which verb do we need to use?* (*teach*)
- Ask: *Is the action happening now or in the past?* (now – *present continuous*)
- Explain that to make the sentence passive, we put the object first (in this case, *Kevin*), then the verb *to be* in the right tense (here, *present continuous*), then the past participle of *teach*.
- Complete the sentence on the board *(Kevin is being taught English by his cousin.)*.
- Remind students that we do not need to say who did the action when it's unimportant or obvious. When we do want to say who did it, we normally use *by*.
- Ask students to work individually or with a partner to do the exercise.
- Elicit answers.

1 b	2 a	3 b	4 b

ON THE BOARD

Kevin's cousin is teaching him English.
Kevin ________________ English by his cousin.

4

Aim: to further practise the passive

- Students now work individually to rewrite a passage about communication.
- Encourage them to ask the kind of questions that they were asked in exercises 2 and 3 in order to establish how to change the sentences.
- Remind students that they need to use the passive voice.
- Students should then work individually to rewrite the passage.
- Elicit answers.

The first modern email was sent in 1971. The first text message was sent in 1992. The world has been changed by both of these forms of communication. People have been brought together and the world has been made smaller. Today, over 300 billion email messages are sent per day! And over 1 billion text messages are sent per week – in just the UK!

Suggested homework

Assign Ex.1 and 2 – Workbook, p.34

V Vocabulary builder

1

Aim: to focus on types of television programme

- This exercise is probably best done as a whole class. If time allows, however, divide the class into small groups and encourage them to use a dictionary in order to find the meaning of any unknown words.
- First, ask students to read through sentences 1–6 and underline any key words. These key words might be useful as clues to help them do the exercise.
- Go through the first sentence as an example.
- Elicit the key words: *funny, lasts for half an hour* and *same characters.*
- Ask: *Which programme is funny, half an hour long and has the same characters in it?* (*sitcom*)
- Remind students that a soap opera is also usually half an hour long and has the same characters in it but is not usually funny. Many soap operas last for an hour.
- Ask students to do the exercise.
- Elicit answers.

1 sitcom	4 soap opera
2 documentary	5 game show
3 chat show	6 reality show

students' own answers

- Students are then asked if they can name one of each type and what they prefer to watch.

2

Aim: to further develop topic vocabulary

- This exercise is probably best done individually or in pairs. You could also work through the exercise as a whole class.
- Encourage students to make a note of any new vocabulary that they learn in their notebooks.
- Elicit answers.

1 f	3 d	5 c
2 a	4 e	6 b

3

Aim: to introduce phrasal verbs with *on*

- Point out to students that phrasal verbs that share the same particle (*up, down, out,* etc) sometimes have meanings that have something in common. All the verbs here use *on* and they all have something to do with *starting* or *continuing.*
- Ask students to look at the phrasal verbs and ask: *Which phrasal verb might mean to start something like a radio or television working?* (*turn on*) and *Which phrasal verb might mean to connect to the internet?* (*log on*)
- Elicit any ideas they have.
- Students then work individually to choose the correct phrasal verb in each sentence.
- Elicit answers.
- Students now match the phrasal verbs to the definitions.
- Remind them to put each phrasal verb in the infinitive.
- Elicit answers.
- Remind students that sometimes phrasal verbs can have more than one meaning.

1 turn on	3 growing on	5 get on
2 carry on	4 log on	6 put on

have a good relationship: get on with
broadcast on TV: put on
start something working: turn on
connect to the internet: log on
continue: carry on
become more attractive to you after some time: grow on
Other phrasal verbs which mean *continue* are *go on* or *keep on.*

4

Aim: to speculate on the meaning of idioms

- This exercise is best done in pairs.
- Before students attempt this exercise, ask them to read through the idioms and underline any words which might act as clues as to the meaning of the idiom.

- Students then work in pairs to speculate on the meanings of the idioms.
- Elicit suggestions.
- If time allows, encourage each pair to use a dictionary to find the meaning of the idioms given here.
- Write the example sentences on the board and encourage students to make a note of idioms, their definitions and an example sentence in their notebooks.

be front-page news = be the most important item of news
a couch potato = a person who enjoys sitting in front of the TV for long periods of time
be on the spot = be in the exact place where something is happening
hit the headlines = become famous by being reported in the news (*headlines* are the titles above reports in newspapers)
be on the air = be broadcast at a particular time

ON THE BOARD

The princess' new baby was front-page news all over the world.
If you want to get fit, you'd better stop being such a couch potato!
An ambulance was on the spot within 10 minutes of the accident happening.
Zlatan Ibrahimovic's decision to leave Milan has hit the headlines.
The new radio show is on the air at 6.30 tonight.

Suggested homework

Assign Ex. 1 and 2 – Workbook, p.35

Listening

Warm up!

Aim: to introduce the topic and warm students up

- Ask students to quickly name as many different kinds of TV programme as they can.
- Ask them to name examples of the different types which are popular in their country. Ask them to name any shows of the same type that they know in English.

1

Aim: to practise listening for gist

- First, ask students to give you definitions of the television programmes listed in a–e.
- Elicit the type of language that they might expect to hear someone use in a documentary.
- Ask: *Would you expect a documentary to contain formal or informal language?* (formal language)
- Elicit their suggestions for each of the programmes.
- Remind students that they should also be listening for the tone and style of the extract. Explain that a sitcom is likely to contain a dialogue, whereas a documentary might be a formal monologue.
- Play the listening text.
- Elicit answers, asking students to justify their answers by paraphrasing what they heard.

CD1, Track 16

Extract 1 c: *'Well, let's go play Super Money!'*
Extract 2 d: *'My next guest has been called a genius …'*
Extract 3 e: the whole recording
Extract 4 b: the whole recording and the audience laughter
Extract 5 a: *'Tonight on* Global Focus, *we investigate the government's claims that the unemployment figures have fallen every month for the last three years.'*

2

Aim: to listen for gist

- Students now hear the extracts again in a different order.
- Remind students that they will hear each extract twice and that they should listen to the whole of the extract before they decide on the answer.
- Play the listening text.
- Elicit answers, asking students to justify their answers by paraphrasing what they heard.

CD1, Track 17

1 B	*'You see, Brad isn't really your cousin at all. I know you'll find this hard to believe, but … he's your brother. Brad is my son.'*
2 A	*'… we investigate the government's claims that the unemployment figures have fallen every month for the last three years.'*
3 B	*'Sorry, dear. I forgot my passport. It's in the cupboard I think.'*
4 C	*'Currently starring in the hit show 'Girls and Guns'…'*
5 B	*'Now, Amy, your two thousand euros is safe – that's yours to take back home with you to Manchester whatever happens.'*

Soundbite

Aim: to practise listening for the sound /ɜː/

- Students now listen to recognise the vowel sound /ɜː/ which appears in words such as *word* and *bird.*
- Explain that they will hear someone say four words and that they should circle two words which have the same vowel sound in them.
- Play the listening text.
- Elicit the answers, making sure that students pronounce the words correctly.

CD1, Track 18

1 word / bird	4 learn / burn
2 heard / murder	5 sir / occur
3 fur / first	

Speaking

1

Aim: to prepare for the speaking task

- Remind students that in Part 1 of the Speaking exam they are asked questions about themselves and their own experience.
- Ask students to look at the questions in exercise 1.
- Ask students to make brief notes in answer to each of the questions about themselves.

2

Aim: to practise an exam-type task

- Before students do this exercise, ask them to study the **Speaking database** on page 165.
- Point out the useful phrases that follow the exercise. Encourage students to use these phrases when they do the task.
- Ask students to interview each other in pairs, asking the questions given and making a note of their partner's answers.
- Remind students that they should give reasons, explanations, examples, etc.
- Go round the class monitoring the task.
- Ask each pair to report back to the whole class on what they discussed.
- You might prefer to do the task as a whole class. Ask the questions and invite different students to talk about their opinions and experiences.

Use of English

1

Aim: to focus on countable and uncountable nouns

- First, ask students to study pages 177–178 of the **Grammar database**, either in class or at home before the lesson starts.
- Write these sentences on the board: *Sarah is tall with really long hairs.* and *There were lots of hair in the sink, so I had to clean it.*
- Elicit what is wrong with each of the sentences (*Hair* can be both countable and uncountable. In the first sentence it should be uncountable and in the second sentence countable.).
- Remind students that some nouns can be countable with one meaning and uncountable with another (*coffee, a coffee, chicken, a chicken*).This often happens when we talk about a material or substance and a thing made out of it.
- Students then work individually or with a partner to complete the exercise.
- Elicit answers.
- Point out that most uncountable nouns are singular and take a singular verb: *Her advice was helpful.* However, there are also some plural uncountable nouns *(jeans, scissors, clothes, trousers)* which take a plural verb: *These jeans are a bit short.*
- With the nouns that can be both countable and uncountable, ask students to explain what the difference in meaning is.

countable
sheep – (plural=sheep)
fact
journey

uncountable

advice	information
equipment	jeans
furniture	money
news	trousers
luggage	rice
clothes	

both
wood (the material / a collection of trees)
chicken (the material or food / an individual animal)
paper (the material / a newspaper)
hair (the growth on the head / one individual hair)
chocolate (the material or food / one from a box of chocolates)
interest (the feeling / a hobby)
bone (the material / an individual bone)

ON THE BOARD

Sarah is tall with really long hairs.
There were lots of hair in the sink, so I had to clean it.

2

Aim: to further practise countable and uncountable nouns

- Before students correct the mistakes, go through the first one together.
- Ask: *Is this sentence correct?* (no)
- Ask: *Which noun in the sentence is uncountable?* (*equipment*)
- Remind students to go through this process of asking themselves questions about the sentence before they correct it.
- Ask students to work individually or with a partner.
- Elicit answers.

1 Any television studio has a lot of valuable equipment in it.
2 The programme was interrupted to bring the viewers important news.
3 Most people who read the news on TV wear a suit, rather than jeans.
4 I used to write for a paper and give advice to readers with problems.
Sentence 5 is correct.

3

Aim: to raise awareness of homonyms

- Point out to students that the same word can have more than one meaning. When they do some exercises, such as word formation, it is important that they realise which meaning is relevant.
- Ask students to read the verbs given and to match each to two different meanings.
- Elicit answers.

1 argue	5 realise	9 order
2 run	6 run	10 feel
3 suggest	7 suggest	11 order
4 feel	8 argue	12 realise

4

Aim: to practise an exam-type task

- Before the students do this exercise, remind them of the best way to approach it so that they become familiar with exam technique.
- Remind them of the importance of reading through the passage once before they start to get an idea of the gist of it.
- Direct students' attention to the first sentence.
- Explain the importance of reading whole sentences rather than just single lines, as there may be additional information given on the following line or lines which affect how the word should be changed.
- Remind students that some words have more than one meaning and that might affect which word is required.
- Remind students, too, that they will need to think about not only whether the word should be a verb, noun, adjective or adverb but whether the word is plural or singular or positive or negative.
- Emphasise that spelling is extremely important and that words which are spelled incorrectly will be marked as wrong.
- Remind them that the first word is given as an example.
- Once they have finished the exercise remind them to read the passage again to check for sense.
- Remind students that they should write only one word in each gap, and that each word should be in capital letters.
- Finally, remind students that they should always fill in an answer, even if they are not sure it is correct.
- Ask students to work individually or with a partner to do the rest of the exercise.
- Elicit answers.

1 PRESENTER	6 COMEDY
2 VARIETY	7 PRODUCERS
3 CONTESTANTS	8 VIEWERS
4 POPULARITY	9 REALITY
5 BROADCAST	10 EARLIER

Suggested homework

Assign Ex.1 and 2 – Workbook, p.35
Ex. 1 and 2 – Workbook, p.36

Writing

1

Aim: to focus on descriptive language

- This exercise is probably best done as a whole class. If time allows however, divide the class into small groups and encourage them to use a dictionary in order to find the meaning of any unknown adjectives.
- Before students attempt this exercise, remind them that descriptive language is important in a story as it can help to bring the characters and the narrative to life.
- Draw a three-column table and write the headings: '*very good*', '*very bad*' and *feelings* at the top of each column.
- Invite individual students to come up and write the adjectives under the correct heading.
- Encourage students to think of other adjectives and to add them to the list on the board.
- Check that students have copied the table into their notebooks.

ON THE BOARD

'very good' *'very bad'* *feelings*

'very good' (suggested answers)
wonderful (wonderfully), fantastic (fantastically)
terrific (terrifically), brilliant (brilliantly)
great (greatly), excellent (excellently)
cool (coolly), awesome (awesomely)
perfect (perfectly)
amazing (amazingly)
(answers to exercise 2 are in brackets)

'very bad' (suggested answers)
terrible (terribly), nasty (nastily)
dreadful (dreadfully), appalling (appallingly)
awful (awfully), terrifying (terrifyingly)
horrible (horribly)
(answers to exercise 2 are in brackets)

feelings (suggested answers)
excited (excitedly), anxious (anxiously)
depressed, enthusiastic (enthusiastically)
nervous (nervously)
(answers to exercise 2 are in brackets)

2

Aim: to identify adjectives which become adverbs by adding *-ly*

- Ask students to look through the list of adjectives on the board.
- Elicit which adjectives can be made into adverbs by adding *-ly*.
- Elicit how the other adjectives form adverbs.
- Invite individual students to come up and write the adverb next to the adjective, making sure that students spell the adverb correctly.

3

Aim: to introduce the topic of a story and focus on the reader

- First, ask students to study page 152 of the **Writing database**, either in class or at home before the lesson starts.
- Ask students to read the writing task and to tell you who is going to read the story.

> The story will be read initially by the people judging the competition who work at the radio station. However, the people who are the real audience for the story are the listeners of the radio station.

Additional task

- Encourage students to think about the type of details that they could include in this story (why I was on the news, why it was a surprise, the response of my family and friends, whether I enjoyed /disliked the experience, if anything happened to me after I had appeared on the news, etc).

4

Aim: to provide a model answer for students to refer to and to focus on useful phrases used in stories

- Ask students to read the model story through once. Ask them who they think is going to read this story.
- Then ask them to read it again quickly and to underline all the descriptive adjectives and adverbs that the writer has included.
- Encourage students to give their opinion on whether this is a good story, whether it answers the question correctly and whether the writer has used appropriate descriptive language (Yes – this story would be given a high mark in the exam.).

Additional task

- In order to check students' understanding of story writing, ask them to paraphrase the sequence of events in the story.

> ***IT WASN'T ME!***
>
> *I had never imagined I would see myself on the news. It was awful! The newsreader was talking about a robbery and there, on the screen, was a picture of me.*
>
> *'Mum! I'm on television!' I shouted, and she ran into the living room.*
>
> *'That's great!' she said and then suddenly stopped. She looked at me, and then back at the screen.*
>
> *'I didn't do it. I'm innocent!' I said quickly. 'What should I do?'*
>
> *My mum suggested that we go to the police station. I wasn't sure. I didn't want to go to prison for a crime I hadn't committed! Mum said that I had to convince them that they wanted the wrong person.*
>
> *We got to the police station and I went inside nervously. I explained who I was and they asked me lots of questions. I answered them honestly. Eventually, they believed I was innocent. It was a wonderful feeling when I finally walked out of the police station!*
>
> *The next night, they said on the news that the police had caught the person who committed the robbery. He looked a little like me. My nightmare was finally over.*

5

Aim: to encourage students to think about the style of a story

- Remind students to look back at the model story in exercise 4.
- Elicit answers.

> 1 T The writer begins the story with, *'I had never imagined I would see myself on the news.'*
> 2 T *'It was awful!'; 'She looked at me, and then back at the screen.'; 'I answered them honestly.'*
> 3 T *'"That's great!" she said …'; '"I didn't do it. I'm innocent!" I said quickly.'*
> 4 T *'"Mum! I'm on television!" I shouted.'*
> 5 F

6

Aim: to encourage students to plan their writing

- This exercise is designed to encourage students to use their imagination and to make sure that all students have enough ideas before they start writing.
- Ask students to look at the questions and to make notes in their notebooks.
- Remind them that they should be answering the questions with one or two sentences.
- Go round the class monitoring or helping where necessary.
- At the end of the exercise, ask individual students to read out their ideas.
- Encourage students to make a note of any good ideas they hear from other students.

- If you have time, check that all students have completed the questions with appropriate information.

1	at the beginning of the story
2–9	students' own answers

- Ask students to turn to **Writing Planner 5** on page 157. Explain that each Writing Planner gives them a simple table to complete which helps them to put the right content in the right place in their piece of writing.
- Point out to students that each row of the table refers to a different part of their piece of writing and gives its purpose, together with useful expressions. Explain to students that they should complete the 'notes' column using their own ideas.
- Give students some time to complete the table. Invite a number of students to say what they have put in the 'notes' column for each part of the piece of writing. If possible, you may like to check the notes made by all students to ensure they have enough content to base their piece of writing on. Ask students to refer to the Writing Planner as they do their piece of writing.

7

Aim: to give students the opportunity to produce a story

- This exercise can be done in class or set for homework.
- Remind students of the importance of using descriptive language and of creating drama using direct speech.

8

Aim: to encourage students to check their written work

- Draw students' attention to the checklist.
- When they have finished writing, ask them to read each statement and to tick each one that is true for them.
- Ask them to make sure that they have ticked all of the boxes before handing their story in to be marked.
- You might consider refusing to mark any story that does not meet all the criteria in the checklist and asking the student to rewrite.

Additional task

- In order to monitor whether students have checked their work carefully, you could ask them to underline in pencil places in their story where they have 'used descriptive language', for example.
- Alternatively, invite individual students to read parts of their story to the rest of the class or get students to exchange stories with each other and to check each other's stories for mistakes before handing them in.

Look Back

Aim: to review the unit and to practise scanning for specific information

- Students now have the opportunity to go back through the unit to check what they have learned.
- Ask the whole class the questions from **Look Back**.
- Elicit answers from different students.
- Encourage students to scan the unit to find any information they can't remember.

1 13
2 the headline
3 the verb 'to be'
4 a person who enjoys sitting in front of the TV for long periods of time
5 facts
6 'quarrel' or 'row' and 'make a point'

Suggested homework

Assign Ex. 1, 2 and 3 – Workbook, p.37

Further material

- For further practice and consolidation, ask students to complete the Unit 5 tasks on the Student's CD-ROM.
- To test students' understanding of the material in Unit 5, you may like to administer the Unit 5 Test and Term Test 1, which are in the Tests section of the Teacher's DVD-ROM. You may also like to construct your own test using the Test Generator material for Unit 5.

6

Come Rain or Shine

Target language

Grammar: the future (1): *will, going to,* present simple and present continuous / question tags / connectors
Lexis: topic vocabulary / collocations (weather) / confusable words
Reading skills: understanding main concepts
Listening skills: listening for specific information
Speaking skills: speculating
Writing skills: selecting appropriate style / article
Pronunciation: weak forms (1)

- The phrase *come rain or shine* means that something will definitely happen no matter what the weather may be, eg *West Ham United are going to win the Cup on Saturday, come rain or shine.*
- Write the phrase *come rain or shine* on the board.
- Ask students what they think the title refers to.
- Explain the meaning of the phrase *come rain or shine.*
- Write the example sentence given above on the board.
- Elicit suggestions as to what the unit might be about.

ON THE BOARD

come rain or shine

West Ham United are going to win the Cup on Saturday, come rain or shine.

Start thinking!

Aim: to introduce the topic of the weather through personal responses

- Ask students to work in pairs to make notes about the weather in each season.
- Go round the class monitoring and helping where necessary.
- If you prefer, divide the class into small groups and give each group a different part of the world (Antarctica, Africa, Europe, Russia, Australia, etc) to make notes about.
- If time allows, conduct a discussion involving the whole class by inviting different groups to talk about the notes they made.

Additional task

- Ask students to speculate about what the climate might be like in the following countries: China, England, Canada.

Reading CD1, Track 19

1

Aim: to read for gist

- Students are now going to read an extract from a book. Begin by asking them to look at the title of the extract and predict what the extract might be about.
- Elicit ideas.
- Ask students to read the extract. This can be done individually or as a class activity with different students being asked to read different sections aloud to the rest of the class.
- Remind students that at this stage they do not need to understand all of the vocabulary as items will be covered in the **WORD BOX** section.
- Elicit answers from a few students as to whether they would like to try forecasting the weather and ask them to justify their answers.

Background information

- *'Do-It-Yourself' (or DIY) usually refers to the hobby of making or repairing things for your home instead of getting someone else to do them for you. Here it refers to trying to forecast the weather yourself without relying on official weather forecasts.*
- *'A weather station' is a place where instruments record information about the weather.*
- *'Cloud cover' refers to the amount and density of cloud covering a particular area.*
- *A 'wind meter' is an instrument used to measure the speed of the wind.*
- *'Static' is the unpleasant noise that you hear on a radio when it isn't tuned to any particular station.*

2

Aim: to read to understand main concepts

- Read the first sentence together.
- Remind students that they can look at the extract but they don't need to read it in detail again.
- Elicit the answer and ask students to justify it by reading directly from the extract.
- Remind students of the importance of underlining where they found the answer in the extract.
- Ask students to work individually or with a partner.
- Elicit answers, asking for justification from the extract.

1 Agrees
'Many cultures have traditional ideas about how to forecast the weather … not very accurate.'
2 Disagrees
The whole of paragraph 2 explains where meteorologists get their data from.
3 Agrees
'You need to know about the climate in the area where you live.'
4 Agrees
'Soon, you'll be able to plan your day better.'

3

Aim: to give students practice in an exam-type task

- First, remind students of the best way to approach it so that they become familiar with exam technique.
- Remind them of the importance of looking for sentences from the passage which explain one of the four options A–D. It is also possible that they might be able to work out from the passage which three options could not be the answer.
- Direct students' attention to the second question.
- Ask: *Where does the writer mention collecting information about the weather very high in the atmosphere?* (*Weather balloons tell us what is happening at high altitude.*) and tell students that this eliminates option A.
- Ask: *Where does the writer mention the amount of cloud over an area?* (*Satellites give us images of cloud cover…*) and tell students that this eliminates option C.
- Ask: *Where does the writer mention the way the wind is blowing?* (*and wind direction*) and tell students that this eliminates option D.
- Remind students of the importance of underlining where they found the answer within the passage, as this makes it much quicker and easier for them to be able to justify their answers in class and check their work in the exam.
- Ask students to work individually or with a partner to do the rest of the exercise.
- Elicit answers, asking for justification from the passage.

1 B: *'Many cultures have traditional ideas about how to forecast the weather …'*
2 B: This isn't mentioned in the passage.
3 B: *'You need to know about the climate in the area where you live.'*
4 C: *'Start to keep records of the temperature …'*
5 C: *'Is your barometer rising and do the clouds seem to be getting higher?'*
6 A: *'With a little practice, your forecasts will become more accurate.'*

Additional task

- Have a class discussion about any extremes of weather that the students can remember and what problems were caused.

WORD BOX

4

Aim: to introduce new vocabulary

- Before the students do this exercise, ask them to read the definitions.
- Remind them of the importance of looking back at the passage for clues if they are not sure of the meaning of any words.
- Ask students to work individually or with a partner to do the exercise.
- Elicit answers.
- Ask students if there were any other words in the passage which they didn't know the meaning of.
- Remind them to make a note of the words and to look them up in a dictionary before the start of the next lesson.
- Ask students if they enjoyed reading the extract and whether they learned anything from it or not and get them to justify their answers.

1 e	3 f	5 h	7 a
2 d	4 b	6 g	8 c

Additional task

- Ask students to choose five words from the **WORD BOX** and to write their own sentences with the word missing.
- Students then swap their sentences with a partner and try to fill in the missing word.

Have your say!

Aim: to give students the opportunity to express their own opinions

- Put the students in pairs and get them to ask each other the questions. Ask them to make brief notes on their partner's answers. When they have finished, invite various students to tell the whole class what they discussed.

- Alternatively, you may like to do the activity as a whole class. Invite various students to give their opinions, encouraging them to agree or disagree with what other students have said. Encourage them to give reasons for their opinions.

Suggested homework

Assign Ex. 1 – Workbook, p.38–39
Ex.1 – Workbook, p.38

G Grammar clinic

1

Aim: to review the future

- First, ask students to study pages 178–179 of the **Grammar database**, either in class or at home before the lesson starts.
- The first exercise refers back to the reading passage so that students can see the grammar in question being used in context.
- Read the list of ways that we can talk about the future.
- Ask students to work individually or with a partner to underline all the examples of the future that they can find in the extract.
- Elicit answers.

be going to
'Or have you heard that when cows lie down it's going to rain?'
'...a sunny Christmas Day means we're going to have a warm Easter.'
'...when you are trying to understand what the weather is going to do next.'
'...that probably means that the weather is going to get worse.'
'It could mean that it's going to rain.'
'...a few minutes spent outside will tell you whether it's going to rain or not.'
could / might
'They could affect the wind.'
'That could affect rainfall.'
'It could mean that it's going to rain.'
'You might even beat the experts!'
will
'...that the weather tomorrow will be more or less the same as today.'
'...your forecasts will become more accurate.'
'...a few minutes spent outside will tell you...'
present continuous
'Are you playing football tomorrow?'
'Are you going skiing next week?'

Additional task

- Ask students to write four sentences of their own which use each of the four ways of referring to the future.

2

Aim: to practise identifying different uses of future tenses

- Ask students to look at the first sentence.
- Ask: *Which way of referring to the future is being used here?* (*be going to*)
- Ask: *Do we arrange the weather or do we predict the weather?* (we predict or forecast the weather)
- Remind students that when we make predictions based on evidence we can see now, such as a hurricane or rain clouds, we often use *be going to.*
- Ask students to work individually or with a partner.
- Elicit answers, asking for students to justify their answers with grammatical rules. Refer to the **Grammar database** if there is any confusion.

1 b 2 a 3 b 4 a

Errors to watch out for

Students often use *will* to talk about the future in clauses after *when, until, if* and *what*, particularly in sentences like *'I'm going to call my friend when I will finish my homework'*. Remind students that they should use the present simple.

3

Aim: to practise choosing the correct future forms

- Students now work individually to choose the correct phrases to complete the email.
- Encourage students to ask the kind of question they were asked in exercise 2 in order to establish which way of referring to the future is appropriate and why.
- Give the students some time to complete the task and then elicit the answers.

1 I'm meeting
2 Are you still going
3 we'll have
4 will be
5 I'll
6 I'm going to
7 Are
8 I'll text
9 I

4

Aim: to correct sentences using future tenses

- Before students correct the mistakes, go through the first one together.
- Ask: *Which way of referring to the future is being used here? (present continuous)*
- Ask: *Do we arrange the weather or do we predict the weather?* (we predict or forecast the weather)
- Remind students that when we make predictions based on evidence we can see now we often use *be going to* but often we can talk about predictions using *will* with no difference in meaning.
- Write these sentences on the board: *I think it will rain this afternoon.* and *I think it's going to rain this afternoon.* And explain that there is no difference in meaning between them.
- Remind students to go through this process of asking themselves questions about the sentence before they correct it.

- Ask students to work individually or with a partner to do the exercise.
- Elicit answers.

1 The forecast says it's going to rain later today.
2 I'm meeting Ben at the café at six.
3 We are going to have a storm!
5 It'll start raining in a minute, I bet! / It's going to start raining in a minute, I bet!
6 I think that in 100 years' time we will be able to control the weather.
Sentence 4 is correct.

ON THE BOARD

I think it will rain this afternoon.
I think it's going to rain this afternoon.

Suggested homework

Assign Ex. 1, 2 and 3 – Workbook, p.40

V Vocabulary builder

1

Aim: to focus on vocabulary connected to the weather

- This exercise is probably best done as a whole class. If time allows however, divide the class into small groups and encourage them to use a dictionary in order to find the meaning of any unknown words.
- First, ask students to read through the sentences 1–7 and underline any words which might act as clues.
- Elicit the clues and ask if there were any which they could do given the clues in the sentence.
- As an example of this you could direct students' attention to question 7. The words *hot weather* suggest that the answer may be *heatwave.* Even if students don't know the word *heatwave,* searching for clues can sometimes help them to make an educated guess.
- Elicit answers.
- Ask: *Which three words can we add '-y' to to make adjectives?*
- Elicit the answers.
- Ask students to work in pairs to brainstorm other adjectives ending in *-y* which describe the weather.
- Elicit their ideas.

1 hail	5 mist (misty)
2 shower (showery)	6 hurricane
3 blizzard	7 heatwave
4 frost (frosty)	

(suggested answers)
rainy, sunny, windy, cloudy, chilly, breezy, foggy, snowy

2

Aim: to match words to make words and phrases connected to the weather

- Ask students to look at the pictures and to complete the words and phrases using the words in the box.
- Encourage students to make a note of any new vocabulary that they learn in their notebooks.
- Elicit answers.

snowflake / raindrop / hailstone / a flash of lightning / a gust of wind / a puddle of water

3

Aim: to practise collocations

- Before students attempt this task, write this sentence on the board: *Tom came home from school ________ wet because it had been ________ with rain.*
- Explain that two of the options a–c in number 1 complete the sentence *(dripping / pouring).*
- Elicit the phrases *dripping wet* and *pouring with rain* and ask students to speculate on what they mean.
- Encourage students to make a note of any new vocabulary that they learn in their notebooks.
- Elicit answers.

1 c 2 a 3 b 4 c 5 a

ON THE BOARD

Tom came home from school ________ wet because it had been ________ with rain.

4

Aim: to practise using words which are easily confused

- Before students attempt this task, write on the board: *look, see* and *watch.* Ask students to explain to you the difference between the words and to give you an example sentence for each of them (*Look* means to move your eyes toward something so you can see it. *See* means to notice something with your eyes. *Watch* means to look at someone or something for a period of time and is most commonly used with sporting activities and television.).
- Encourage students to learn collocations which will help them to remember how the words are used, such as *look at something or someone, watch television* or *see the sights.*
- Remind students to put the words in the correct form and ask them to do the task.
- Elicit answers to numbers 1, 2 and 3.
- Ask students to look at numbers 4 and 5 and elicit the answers. Don't negate the answers but encourage all students to either agree or disagree with the answers given and to justify whether *nervous* or *upset* is used in each sentence.
- Remind them that if you are *nervous,* you feel worried or anxious about something and if you are *upset*, you feel sad or angry about something.
- Ask students to look at numbers 6, 7 and 8 and elicit the answers. Don't negate the answers but encourage all students to either agree or disagree with the answers given and to justify whether *have, spend* or *pass* is used in each sentence.

- Remind them that people *have a good time* when they enjoy themselves, they *spend time doing something* and you do something to *pass the time* or make it go quicker.
- Encourage students to learn these definitions by heart.

ON THE BOARD

look / see / watch

1 watching	4 upset	7 have
2 looking	5 nervous	8 pass
3 seen	6 spend	

Errors to watch out for

Students will often say things like *'I will pass your house later to see you.'* Remind students that this doesn't sound natural in English and that they should learn to use the more natural, *'I will come round to your house later to see you'*.

Suggested homework

Assign Ex. 1 and 2 – Workbook, p.41

Listening

Warm up!

Aim: to introduce the topic and warm students up

- Ask students what they already know about rainbows. Ask if anyone knows what causes a rainbow.
- Do not at this stage confirm the accuracy of students' suggestions, but encourage them to agree or disagree with each other.

1

Aim: to introduce the listening task and listen for specific information

- Students now listen to an extract from an interview about rainbows.
- Ask them to read through the questions and try to predict the kind of information that they will need to listen for.
- Play the listening text.
- Elicit answers, asking students to justify their answers by paraphrasing what they heard.

CD1, Track 20

1 'Tell Me Why': *'"Tell Me Why", the programme that answers questions that you have about science.'*
2 what a rainbow is: *'It's from Nicola in Derby and she says, "Dear Tell Me Why, what is a rainbow?"'*
3 at the Science Museum: *'I've got with me in the studio Dr Kate Williams of the Science Museum.'*

2

Aim: to listen for specific information

- Students now listen to the whole of the interview.
- First, remind students of the best way to approach it so that they become familiar with exam technique.
- Remind them to listen for key words or phrases which could fit the gaps.
- Ask: *What kind of information should you be listening for to complete number 1?* (a noun)
- Encourage students to do the same for numbers 2–7 in pairs or as a whole class.
- Elicit their suggestions.
- Remind them that they will hear the whole interview twice. The first time they listen they should take notes and the second time they listen they should check their answers.
- Encourage students to complete all of the gaps. If they are not certain of an answer, they should make an educated guess.
- Finally, remind students that they only need to write a word or a short phrase.
- Play the listening text.
- Elicit answers, asking students to justify their answers by paraphrasing what they heard.

CD1, Track 21

1 radio waves: *'... the energy from the sun is actually made up of radio waves, microwaves and light of lots of different colours.'*
2 dust: *'When it reaches the Earth, dust in the atmosphere bends the light.'*
3 raindrop (on a leaf): *'Next time you're out in the rain, look closely at a raindrop on a leaf.'*
4 frozen: *'In winter, at high altitudes, the raindrops are frozen ...'*
5 spraying water: *'For example, you can often create your own rainbow. If you've got a garden hose, try spraying water into the air.'*
6 piece of card: *'And you'll need a bowl, a small mirror and a piece of card.'*
7 lightning: *'Alison wants to know what causes lightning.'*

Soundbite

Aim: to practise weak forms

- Explain to students that some words sound different when they are in a sentence. Some common words, such as *and, can* and *for* have 'weak forms' that we use when the word is not stressed. They may have to listen carefully to hear these words.
- Ask students to read the sentences given.
- Play the listening text and ask students to listen carefully.
- Ask student volunteers to repeat the sentences, doing their best to use the weak forms of the words.
- Play the listening text again if necessary.

CD1, Track 22

Speaking

1

Aim: to practise speculating

- Tell students that some exams, such as the Cambridge FCE, ask them to talk about photographs.
- Explain that it might be possible that they are asked to talk about something in a photograph which is not clear to them or which they are not familiar with.
- Remind them that there are phrases and expressions which they can learn to show that they are not clear what something is.
- Ask students to look at the images in the Student's Book.
- Ask students to look at the expressions and talk with their partner about what they think the images might be.
- Go round the class monitoring and helping where necessary.
- You might want to set a time limit of three or four minutes for this.
- Elicit ideas.

> These visual puzzles are designed to encourage students to think laterally.
> 1 a giraffe walking past a window
> 2 a bear climbing a tree
> 3 a man wearing a big hat riding a bicycle
> 4 a witch standing behind a wall

2

Aim: to practise speculating about a photograph

- Before students do this exercise, ask them to study the **Speaking database** on page 165.
- Divide the class into pairs.
- Explain to students that they should take it in turns to ask and answer the questions given. Point out to them that they are not expected to know the answers to the questions and that it might be difficult to tell from the photograph. Tell them that they have to speculate, using the phrases they have practised in exercise 1.
- Go round the class monitoring or helping where necessary. Check to make sure students aren't making mistakes with speculation.

Use of English

1

Aim: to focus on question tags

- Before students do the exercises on this page, ask them to study page 180 of the **Grammar database**, either in class or at home before the lesson starts.
- Before students attempt this task, write these sentences on the board: *The weather forecast said it's going to snow, isn't it?* and *The weather forecaster said it's going to snow, didn't she?*
- Elicit which sentence is correct and which is incorrect (The first is incorrect because when the sentence doesn't have an auxiliary verb, we use the verb *do* – the question tag should be *didn't it?* The second is correct.).
- Students then work individually or with a partner to complete the exercise.
- Elicit answers.

1 doesn't it	4 shouldn't they
2 hasn't there	5 have you
3 did they	

ON THE BOARD

The weather forecast said it's going to snow, isn't it?
The weather forecaster said it's going to snow, didn't she?

2

Aim: to practise using connectors

- Ask students to read the sentences, completing the gaps using the words given.
- Elicit answers.
- Point out that *since* has two meanings (Here it means *because*, not *from that time.*).
- Point out that *in spite* is followed by *of* and *despite* isn't.

1 although	4 in spite
2 since	5 so
3 despite	6 However

3

Aim: to practise an exam-type task

- Students now do a multiple choice gap-filling which is designed to practise what they have learned from exercises 1 and 2.
- Ask students to read through the passage, ignoring the gaps, and tell you what *seasonal affective disorder* is (a medical condition which causes its sufferers to be depressed during the winter months).
- Explain that at this stage it is not important to understand all of the words but draw students' attention to clues before and after the gaps that might help them find the answer. These include prepositions, articles, personal pronouns and determiners.
- Remind students that when they have completed the exercise they should read the text through again, inserting the missing word in the gap to check for sense.
- Students then work individually or with a partner to complete the exercise.
- Elicit answers.

1 C	3 D	5 B	7 A	9 C
2 A	4 C	6 D	8 D	10 B

Additional task

- To practise vocabulary, give students definitions of words that they might not know from the passage and ask them to tell you the word.

- Words which they might not know but could guess from the context are: *mood, depressed, medical, condition* and *cure.*

Suggested homework

Assign Ex. 1 and 2 – Workbook, p.41
Ex. 1 – Workbook, p.42

Writing

1

Aim: to introduce the topic of an article and focus on the reader

- First, ask students to study page 153 of the **Writing database**, either in class or at home before the lesson starts.
- Ask students to read the writing task and to tell you who is going to read the article.
- Ask students what the article should be about (the local climate and how it affects people's way of life).
- Elicit why the report shouldn't be too formal (because it is going to be read by young students).

> students from around the world who read the international students' magazine in question

Additional task

- Encourage students to think about the kind of information that they could include in their article (Things to include might be: what the weather is like throughout the year – mild winters and long, hot summers which go from May to October, people spend a lot of time outside in the summer, many people don't work during August, state schools are closed for a three-month summer holiday, people go swimming a lot, sleep in the afternoons when it's at its hottest, etc.).
- Brainstorm ideas, writing any suggestions the students have on the board.

2

Aim: to encourage students to think about the style of an article

- Ask students to work in pairs to answer the questions.
- Elicit answers, asking for justification based on what they have learned about articles from the **Writing database**.

> 1 a The article will be read by students who are about the same age as the writer.
> 2 b An article for students should be fairly informal and 'chatty' in order to maintain the readers' interest.
> 3 b An article like this should be entertaining and interesting to read.
> 4 a A conversational style will make the article more appealing to teenagers.
> 5 a The same is true of all articles in magazines or newspapers.

3

Aim: to provide a model answer for students to refer to

- Students now read the model answer once.
- Then ask them to read it again quickly and to underline all the phrases that the writer has used which are conversational.
- Encourage students to give their opinion on whether this is a good article, whether it answers the question correctly and whether the writer has used a conversational style (Yes – this article would be given a good mark in the exam, in spite of the few mistakes the student has made.).

> <u>*Is your idea of fun lying on the beach, or is skiing more your style? In my area we are doing both!*</u>
> *I live on the east coast of Greece and we have a Mediterranean climate. We do have cold days, but the sun is never far away.*
> *The summers are warm and dry. Temperatures can reach at 40° Celsius, although it's not usually so hot. The days are sunny and bright and most people spend their time swimming or sitting in cafés.*
> *Autumn can be wet and windy. We have great storms, with lots of thunder and lightnings, and people usually visit friends or stay at home.*
> *The winters are mild and sunny. It might snow in February or March, but it doesn't last long. Everybody loves to go for the lunch in villages in the mountains and play in the snow.*
> *Spring finally arrives and the days get warmer again. Some people like going for picnics in a countryside.*
> *My area has a wonderful climate, which is why we get such many tourists. Everybody enjoys themselves, whatever season it is.*

4

Aim: to practise coming up with titles

- Remind students that articles should have a title, as they do in magazines and newspapers.
- Have a class discussion about which of the titles would be most suitable for the model article in exercise 3, asking for students to justify their suggestions with examples from the article.

> 1 is too formal and 2 is irrelevant. The best title is 3, *Fun All Year Round*

5

Aim: to correct mistakes in a model article

- Ask students to read the model article in exercise 3 again.
- Explain that the writer has made one mistake in each paragraph.
- Students then work individually or with a partner to underline the mistakes.
- Elicit answers, asking students to read you the corrected paragraphs.

Is your idea of fun lying on the beach, or is skiing more your style? In my area we do both! I live on the east coast of Greece and we have a Mediterranean climate. We do have cold days, but the sun is never far away.
The summers are warm and dry. Temperatures can reach at 40° Celsius, although it's not usually so hot. The days are sunny and bright and most people spend their time swimming or sitting in cafés.
Autumn can be wet and windy. We have great storms, with lots of thunder and lightning, and people usually visit friends or stay at home.
The winters are mild and sunny. It might snow in February or March, but it doesn't last long. Everybody loves to go for the lunch in villages in the mountains and play in the snow.
Spring finally arrives and the days get warmer again. Some people like going for picnics in the countryside.
My area has a wonderful climate, which is why we get so many tourists.
Everybody enjoys themselves, whatever season it is.

6

Aim: to prepare students for the writing task

- Before students begin these exercises remind them of the importance of identifying what they are writing about and who they are writing for.
- Ask them to look at the writing task and to tell you the subject that they will be writing about.
- Ask: *Will you be writing about the weather in your country or the problems that the weather causes?* (the problems that the weather causes)
- Then ask: *Will you be writing an article or an informal letter?* (an article)
- Then ask: *Should you give your article a title?* (yes)
- Elicit who is going to be reading the article.

Again, students from around the world who read the international students' magazine in question.

7

Aim: to encourage students to plan their writing

- This exercise is designed to encourage students to use their imagination and to think 'around' the subject.
- Ask students to look at the questions and to make notes in their notebooks.
- Remind them that they should be answering the questions with one or two sentences.
- Go round the class monitoring or helping where necessary.
- At the end of the exercise, ask individual students to read out their ideas.
- Encourage students to make a note of any good ideas they hear from other students.
- If you have time, check that all students have completed the questions with appropriate information.

1–5 students' own answers
6 informal, because an article for students should be fairly informal and 'chatty' in order to maintain the readers' interest

- Ask students to turn to **Writing Planner 6** on page 157. Explain that each Writing Planner gives them a simple table to complete which helps them to put the right content in the right place in their piece of writing.
- Point out to students that each row of the table refers to a different part of their piece of writing and gives its purpose, together with useful expressions. Explain to students that they should complete the 'notes' column using their own ideas.
- Give students some time to complete the table. Invite a number of students to say what they have put in the 'notes' column for each part of the piece of writing. If possible, you may like to check the notes made by all students to ensure they have enough content to base their piece of writing on. Ask students to refer to the Writing Planner as they do their piece of writing.

8

Aim: to give students the opportunity to produce an article

- This exercise can be done in class or set for homework.
- Remind students of the importance of starting their article with a question, of using a conversational style and of answering the question by including the information from their notes in exercise 7.

9

Aim: to encourage students to check their written work

- Draw students' attention to the checklist.
- When they have finished writing, ask them to read each statement and to tick each one that is true for them.
- Ask them to make sure that they have ticked all of the boxes before handing their article in to be marked.
- You might consider refusing to mark any article that does not meet all the criteria in the checklist and asking the student to rewrite.

Additional task

- In order to monitor whether students have checked their work carefully, you could ask them to underline in pencil places in their articles where they have 'used an informal style', for example.
- Alternatively, invite individual students to read parts of their article to the rest of the class or get students to exchange articles with each other and to check each other's articles for mistakes before handing them in.

Look Back

Aim: to review the unit and to practise scanning for specific information

- Students now have the opportunity to go back through the unit to check what they have learned.

- Ask the whole class the questions from **Look Back**.
- Elicit answers from different students.
- Encourage students to scan the unit to find any information they can't remember.

1 sounds seem clearer than usual and there is a kind of ring around the Sun or Moon
2 a barometer measures pressure in the atmosphere / atmospheric pressure
3 present continuous
4 a heavy snowstorm
5 check whether something is true

Suggested homework

Assign Ex. 1 and 2 – Workbook, p.43

Webquest

- Ask students to complete the **Webquest** on page 199 of the Student's Book. You might ask students to work on this together in class if you have internet access, or you might assign it for homework.
- Explain to students that the answers to the questions are not in the Student's Book but that they need to find the answers online.
- Check the answers together and ask students to explain where they found the answers and how they found them (eg by typing terms into a search engine).

1 Merry Christmas
2 48°C (in Athens, Greece, on 10th July 1977)
3 USA / America
4 red, orange, yellow, green, blue, indigo and violet
5 a soap opera
6 wind speed
7 *Nineteen Eighty-Four* by George Orwell (1903–1950), an English writer
8 typhoons
9 World Wide Web
10 It snowed (in London and other parts of the UK).

Further material

- For further practice and consolidation, ask students to complete the Unit 6 tasks on the Student's CD-ROM.
- To test students' understanding of the material in Unit 6, you may like to administer the Unit 6 Test, which is in the Tests section of the Teacher's DVD-ROM. You may also like to construct your own test using the Test Generator material for Unit 6.

Revision Units 5-6

1

1 B	3 D	5 B	7 A	9 D
2 C	4 C	6 A	8 A	10 B

2

1 reality
2 argument
3 information
4 entertainment, entertainer
5 knowledge
6 decision
7 relationship
8 advice, adviser (also spelled 'advisor')

3

1 isn't she
2 wasn't it
3 isn't there
4 hasn't he
5 will you
6 shall we
7 doesn't she

4

1 upset
2 pass
3 seen
4 nervous
5 spends

5

(2 marks for each correct answer)

1 The church near our house was damaged by a storm.
2 While the new road was being built, it was very noisy here.
3 TV news is thought to be very shocking.
4 My books have been taken out of my bag!
5 The match will probably be won by South Africa.
6 Everyone has been told about the changes to the timetable.
7 We were each given €100 to spend at the fair.

6

1 get on
2 put on
3 grows on
4 turn on / put on
5 carry on / go on
6 pick on

7

1 global
2 hail
3 chat show
4 forecast
5 presenter
6 meteorologist
7 amateur
8 heatwave
9 realise
10 blizzard

7

A Matter of Taste

Target language

Grammar:	reported speech / indirect questions / prepositions
Lexis:	topic vocabulary / phrasal verbs with *out* / collocations (cooking)
Reading skills:	grammatical referencing
Listening skills:	identifying roles
Speaking skills:	agreeing and disagreeing
Writing skills:	using prompts / formal letter/email
Pronunciation:	/ k /, / g / and / ŋ /

- The phrase *a matter of taste* means that our preferences for most things, from food to furniture, are a matter of personal preference, eg *I wouldn't like to have that painting on my wall, but I suppose it's just a matter of taste.* Here it refers to our preferences for certain foods.
- Write the phrase *a matter of taste* on the board.
- Ask students what they think the title refers to.
- Explain the meaning of the phrase *a matter of taste.*
- Write the example sentence given above on the board.
- Elicit suggestions as to what the unit might be about.

ON THE BOARD

> a matter of taste
> *I wouldn't like to have that painting on my wall, but I suppose it's just a matter of taste.*

Start thinking!

Aim: to introduce the topic of food and drink through personal responses

- Ask students to work in pairs to talk about the questions in the Student's Book.
- Go round the class monitoring and helping where necessary.
- If you prefer, conduct a brief discussion involving the whole class by reading the questions and inviting different students to give their answers.

Reading CD1, Track 23

1

Aim: to read for gist

- Students are now going to read a magazine article. Begin by asking them to look at the title of the article and predict what it might be about.
- Elicit ideas.
- Ask students to read the article. This can be done individually or as a class activity with different students being asked to read different sections aloud to the rest of the class.
- Remind students that at this stage they do not need to understand all of the vocabulary as items will be covered in the **WORD BOX** section.
- Elicit answers from a few students as to whether their answers to the questions in the **Start thinking!** section were correct.

1 Peru ('It all started in Peru.')
2 The Belgians, although it has not been proved. ('...the Belgians claim that they invented fried potatoes, although nobody really knows for sure.')
3 1853 ('Everybody agrees that a Native-American chef, George Crum, made the first crisps in 1853.')

Background information

- *The title 'Chips with everything!' refers to the fact that if you have chips with everything, it means that you have no imagination when it comes to cooking.*

Additional task

- In order to check your students' ability to scan for specific information from the article, elicit the answers to the questions below.
- Remind students that they don't have to reread large parts of the article but should look for clues or key words that might help them find the answer. The key words have been underlined in each sentence in case students need help.

1. When did Peruvians start growing potatoes? (over 2,000 years ago)
2. Which other vegetables were introduced into Europe in the 16th century? (tomatoes and sweet potatoes)
3. Who wrote about chips in 1859? (Charles Dickens)
4. Which people eat over 20 million tons of chips a year? (the Americans)
5. What was the name of the man who made the first crisps? (George Crum)

2

Aim: to practise grammatical referencing

- Ask students to quickly scan the text to find the words listed in numbers 1–4 and to underline them.
- Remind them that the position of a word within a sentence can often help them to understand the meaning or the function of the word.
- Ask them to tell you what the sentence *They weren't like the ones we know today* (before the second gap) is talking about (potatoes).
- Ask students what *They* and *the ones* in this sentence refer to (*They* refers to the potatoes the people in Peru had and *the ones* refers to the potatoes we have today.).
- Go through the rest of the words in the same way, asking students to tell you what the words refer to.
- Remind students that these grammatical markers can often help them to identify the missing sentence.

1 potatoes
2 other vegetables
3 the customer
4 your friends

3

Aim: to recognise grammatical references and practise an exam type task

- Before the students do this exercise, remind them of the best way to approach it so that they become familiar with exam technique.
- Ask them to read sentence A. Elicit which word or phrase might act as a clue to which paragraph the sentence fits (*He*).
- Remind students that they need to look for information before or after the gap where a man (*He*) mentions frying *chips of potato* in one of his books.
- Remind them of the importance of looking for grammatical markers (eg relative and personal pronouns, defining and non-defining clauses and determiners).
- Elicit the answer but do not negate or acknowledge it at this stage.
- Encourage students to approach each of the sentences in the same way.
- Remind students of the importance of underlining the words which helped them find the answer within the passage, as this makes it much quicker and easier for them to be able to justify their answers in class and check their work in the exam.
- Finally, remind them that there is one extra sentence which they do not need to use.
- Ask students to work individually or with a partner to do the exercise.
- Elicit answers, asking students to indicate the words or phrases which helped them choose the answer.

1 G *'They are everywhere, eaten by everyone with practically every meal.' 'We seem to love potatoes however they are cooked.'*
2 D *'They weren't like the ones we know today.' 'The original potatoes ...'*
3 F *'People generally didn't like the potato.' 'They were given to slaves and prisoners because they were so cheap.'*
4 C *'He planted them in the royal gardens,...' 'Ordinary people stole them and planted them in their own gardens.'*
5 A *'The first mention of "chips" in England is by the writer Charles Dickens in 1859.' 'He mentions "chips of potato" fried ...'*
6 B *'When they arrived, he said they weren't thin enough.' 'He kept sending them back to be sliced again.'*

Additional task

- Conduct a class survey on other popular food and why certain types of food (such as chips) are especially well-liked.
- Ask students to justify their answers.

WORD BOX

Aim: to introduce new vocabulary

- First, ask students to read the sentences.
- Remind them of the importance of deciding before they complete the sentences whether they need to look for a noun, adjective or verb in the article.
- Ask students to work individually or with a partner to do the exercise.
- Elicit answers.
- Ask students if there were any other words in the article which they didn't know the meaning of.
- Remind them to make a note of the words and to look them up in a dictionary before the start of the next lesson.
- Ask students if they enjoyed reading the article and whether they learned anything from it or not and get them to justify their answers.

1 fried	5 slice
2 flavour	6 jacket potato
3 chips, French fries	7 bitter
4 crisps, chips	

Additional task

- Ask students to choose five words or phrases from the **WORD BOX** and to write a short paragraph using those words.

Have your say!

Aim: to give students the opportunity to express their own opinions

- Put the students in pairs and get them to ask each other the questions. Ask them to make brief notes on their partner's answers. When they have finished, invite various students to tell the whole class what they discussed.
- Alternatively, you may like to do the activity as a whole class. Invite various students to give their opinions, encouraging them to agree or disagree with what other students have said. Encourage them to give reasons for their opinions.

Suggested homework

Assign Ex. 1 – Workbook, p.46–47
Ex. 1 – Workbook, p.47

G Grammar clinic

1

Aim: to review reported speech

- Before students do the exercises on this page, ask them to study pages 181–182 of the **Grammar database**, either in class or at home before the lesson starts.
- The first exercise refers back to the reading passage so that students can see the grammar in question being used in context.
- Read the sentence and ask students to tell you which tense is being used (*past simple*).
- Ask students to tell you exactly what the person said.
- Encourage students to justify their answer by telling you that we usually have to change the tense if the reporting verb is in the past.

b: Past simple in reported speech is present simple in direct speech.

2

- Write this sentence on the board: *'The sausages are burnt!' my mum said.*
- Ask a volunteer to come up to the board and rewrite the sentence using reported speech (*My mum said the sausages were burnt.*).
- Ask students to explain what kind of changes have to be made in reported speech.
- Write this sentence on the board: *My cousin asked me what had I bought from the record shop.*
- Ask students to tell you whether the sentence is correct or incorrect (*My cousin asked me what I had bought from the record shop.*).
- Remind students that with *wh-* questions (*what, who,* etc), we repeat the question word and change the tense and the word order.
- Ask students to work individually or with a partner.
- Elicit answers, asking for grammatical justification.

1 b 2 b 3 a 4 b

ON THE BOARD

'The sausages are burnt!' my mum said.
My cousin asked me what had I bought from the record shop.

3

Aim: to practise changing direct speech to reported speech

- Before students attempt this task, write these sentences on the board: *'I saw John here last night,' Phil said.* and *Phil said he had seen John here last night.*
- Ask students to explain to you what is wrong with the second sentence (words which refer to time and place also need changing).
- Elicit the correct answer (*Phil said that he had seen John there the night before/the previous night.*).
- Before students do the exercise, go through the first sentence together.
- Ask: *What tense is being used?* (*past simple*)
- Ask: *What does past simple become in reported speech?* (*past perfect simple*)
- Ask: *Are there any other references to time or place which need changing?* (yes – *last night* becomes *the night before* or *the previous night*)
- Remind students to repeat this process with every question.
- Students then work individually or with a partner to do the exercise.
- Elicit answers.

1. George said that they had eaten in a great restaurant the night before / the previous night.
2. Mr Brown said that he would have chicken and another glass of the wine.
3. Tom's father told him not to put his knife in his mouth.
4. My friend asked me if I was having chips.
5. She asked her husband what he had cooked for dinner.

ON THE BOARD

'I saw John here last night,' Phil said.
Phil said he had seen John here last night.

4

Aim: to match reporting verbs to the correct meaning

- Remind students of the importance of identifying which verb is the reporting verb.
- Ask students to work individually or with a partner to do the exercise.
- Elicit answers.

1 b	2 d	3 e	4 c	5 a

5

Aim: to practise using reporting verbs

- Before students complete the sentences go through the first sentence together.
- Tell them to ignore the missing verb for the moment.
- Ask: *What tense is being used? (present simple)*
- Ask: *What does* present simple *become in reported speech? (past simple)*
- Ask: *Are there any other references to time or place which need changing?* (no)
- Ask: *Which reporting word from the box fits the context of the sentence best? (claimed)*
- Remind students to repeat this process with every question.
- Ask students to work individually or with a partner.
- Elicit answers.

1 The owner claimed that they served the best food in town.
2 She admitted eating the cake in the fridge.
3 Sally refused to cook her husband's dinner while he watched TV.
4 Oliver denied drinking all of the orange juice.
5 Ron suggested all of us meet / we all meet outside Burger Bar at nine.

Suggested homework

Assign Ex. 1, 2 and 3 – Workbook, p.48

V Vocabulary builder

1

Aim: to focus on cooking vocabulary

- This exercise is probably best done as a whole class. If time allows however, divide the class into small groups and encourage them to use a dictionary in order to find the meaning of any unknown ways of cooking, before they begin the exercise.
- Ask students to work individually or with a partner to do the exercise.
- Elicit answers.
- Point out to students: *bake* = cook in the oven in dry heat (cake, bread, etc)/*roast* = cook in the oven in oil (meat, vegetables, etc).

1 d	2 b	3 e	4 c	5 a

Additional task

- Draw a five-column table on the board.
- Write the headings: *fry, boil, bake, grill, roast* at the top of each column.
- At the side of the table write the following words: *sausages, bread rolls, a chocolate cake, an egg, potatoes, chips, a chicken, a lamb chop, bacon, pasta, moussaka, pizza*
- Invite individual students to come up and write the word on the board under the appropriate heading(s).
- Remind students that some of the words can fit under more than one heading.
- Elicit any other foods that the students can think of.

Sausages, an egg, chips, chicken, a lamb chop and bacon could all be fried. An egg, potatoes and pasta could all be boiled. Bread rolls, a chocolate cake, potatoes, moussaka and pizza could all be baked. Sausages, chicken, a lamb chop, bacon and a pizza could all be grilled. Sausages, potatoes, a chicken and a lamb chop could all be roasted.

2

Aim: to further develop cooking vocabulary

- Ask students to read through the passage and tell you what the gist of it is (what cookery books are).
- Ask them to read again, this time using the words given to complete the passage.
- Remind students to reread the passage when they have completed it to check for sense.
- Ask students to work individually or with a partner to do the exercise.
- Elicit answers.
- Encourage students to make a note of any new words or phrases that they learn in their notebooks.

1 chefs	5 raw	8 cooker
2 recipes	6 dairy	9 meal
3 dishes	7 saucepans	10 snack
4 ingredients		

Errors to watch out for

Students often make mistakes with the words *cooker* and *chef*, saying things like *'My uncle is a great cooker.'* Remind them that a *cooker* is a machine which cooks food. A *cook* is a person who cooks for a living (or who cooks at home for pleasure) but who isn't usually professionally qualified. Compare, for example: *'John works as a cook in the pub down the road'* and *'My mum is a really great cook.'* A *chef* is a person with a formal qualification in cooking. *'Sally has started training to be a chef.'*

3

Aim: to develop vocabulary for describing different tastes

- This exercise is probably best done as a whole class.
- Ask students to think about the flavour and smell of the foods and to choose the best adjective to describe them.
- Elicit answers.
- Ask students to name other kinds of food that might be described in the same way.

1 bitter	3 salty	5 spicy
2 sour	4 sweet	

4

Aim: to introduce phrasal verbs with *out*

- Point out to students that phrasal verbs that share the same particle *(up, down, out,* etc*)* sometimes have meanings that have something in common. All the verbs here use *out* and they all have something to do with things *stopping* or *disappearing*.
- Students then work individually to complete the sentences.
- Elicit answers.
- Encourage students to make a note of the different meanings of phrasal verbs in their notebooks.

1 f	3 g	5 e	7 d
2 b	4 a	6 c	

5

Aim: to match collocations connected to cooking

- Ask students to look at the words and to try and match them to make phrases.
- Students then work individually or in pairs to make phrases.
- Elicit answers.

1 d	2 c	3 b	4 e	5 a

Additional task

- Ask students to write example sentences for the phrases in their notebooks but to delete the phrase.
- Students then swap their sentences with a partner who must fill in the missing collocation.

6

Aim: to practise using cooking collocations

- Ask students to look at each picture. They all show items of cooking equipment mentioned in exercise 5.
- Ask students to match each picture to a phrase from exercise 5.
- Give students some time to do the task and then elicit answers.

1 baking tray	4 serving spoon
2 mixing bowl	5 carving knife
3 frying pan	

Suggested homework

Assign Ex. 1 – Workbook, p.48
Ex. 2 – Workbook, p.49

Listening

Warm up!

Aim: to introduce the topic and warm students up

- Ask students if they like eating out. Ask them to comment on their favourite places to eat out and who they normally eat out with.
- Ask if anybody has ever had any problems in a restaurant. Ask if they / their parents complained and what happened after that.

1

Aim: to introduce the listening task and to identify speakers

- Ask students to read through the sentences.
- Ask students to predict what they might hear each of the four speakers talk about.
- Ask: *What kind of things might the owner of a restaurant talk about?* (the expenses of running a business, meeting customers, why they started up the restaurant, etc)
- Ask: *What kind of things might a waiter talk about?* (serving food, taking orders, getting tips, etc)
- Ask the same question for a customer, a chef, a student and a restaurant manager.
- Elicit answers, asking students to justify their answers by paraphrasing what they heard.

CD1, Track 24

1 C	2 C	3 A	4 B

2

Aim: to practise listening for specific information

- Ask students to read the questions. Explain that there is one question about each of the four extracts.
- Ask students to guess the answers from what they remember from the first listening. At this stage, do not confirm whether students' guesses are right or wrong.
- Play the listening text.
- Elicit answers, asking students to justify their answers by paraphrasing what they heard.

CD1, Track 24

1 A	*'And what about the menu for this month?'* *'Well, I'd like to include …'*
2 B	*'Yes. Now that you know what it's like, you'll know what you're talking about when customers ask about it.'*
3 A	*'Okay, I'll give it a go.'*
4 C	*'Could you recommend something to go with the lamb?'* *'Well, it's quite spicy, so you might want to consider something simple like a selection of seasonal vegetables and mashed potatoes.'*

Soundbite

Aim: to practise listening for the sounds /k/, /g/ and /ŋ/

- Students now listen for words which have similar endings and end with either /k/, /g/ and /ŋ/.
- Explain that they will hear someone say four words which all end differently.
- Play the beginning of the listening text.
- Ask individual students to repeat the words that they have heard, paying particular attention to the endings.
- Students will now hear four sets of three words with a different ending.
- Remind them that they must decide in which order they heard the words and write the letters a to c next to the appropriate word.
- Play the rest of the listening text.
- Elicit the answers, checking pronunciation.

CD1, Track 25

1 thing c	think b	thick a
2 sang c	sank a	sag b
3 sick b	sink c	sing a
4 bring a	brick c	brink b

Speaking

1

Aim: to present useful phrases for agreeing and disagreeing

- First, write this sentence on the board: *I am agreeing with you about that.*
- Ask students to tell you what is wrong with the sentence (*agree* is a stative verb and isn't normally used in the continuous form).
- Elicit other ways of agreeing or disagreeing with someone that the students know and write these on the board.
- Students then work individually or in pairs to make phrases.
- Elicit answers.

1 d	2 e	3 a	4 c	5 b

ON THE BOARD

I am agreeing with you about that.

Errors to watch out for

Students often make the mistake of saying *'I am agree (or agreeing) with you.'* and *'You have right.'* Remind students that they should learn the phrases from exercise 1 by heart and use these correctly.

2

Aim: to practise agreeing and disagreeing through an exam-type task

- Before students do this exercise, ask them to study the **Speaking database** on page 165.
- Divide the class into pairs.
- Remind students that they should use the prompts numbered 1–5 from exercise 1.
- Encourage them to use other ways of agreeing and disagreeing that they know to talk about the pictures.
- Remind them that they should try to allow time at the end to select two choices which they will suggest to their families.
- Go round the class monitoring and helping where necessary.
- Get each pair to report back to the group.

Use of English

1

Aim: to focus on indirect questions

- Before students do the exercises on this page, ask them to study pages 182–183 of the **Grammar database**, either in class or at home before the lesson starts.
- Ask your students if they know what a fortune cookie is (a kind of biscuit you get at the end of a Chinese meal with a piece of paper inside that makes a prediction).
- Ask students to read the direct questions and the indirect questions.
- Direct your students' attention to the two true or false statements.
- Elicit answers, asking for grammatical justification.

a F	We don't use question word order in the second part of the sentence.
b F	Some indirect questions need a question mark at the end and some don't.

2

Aim: to practise asking indirect questions

- Before students attempt this task, write this sentence on the board: *I wonder could you tell me who invented the fortune cookie?*

- Elicit what is wrong with the sentence (When the direct question is a *yes/no* question, we use *if* or *whether* and don't need question word order in the indirect question. Also, sentences which start with *I wonder* don't need a question mark.).
- Elicit the correct answer (*I wonder if/whether you could tell me who invented the fortune cookie.*).
- Then, write this sentence on the board: *Could you tell me what is the price of this jacket.*
- Ask students to tell you what is wrong with the sentence.
- Elicit that we use an introductory phrase (*Could you tell me ...*) followed by the normal word order (*... what the price of this jacket is?*). Also, sentences which start with '*Could you tell me ...*' need a question mark.
- Remind students that they need to start with the words given.
- Students then work individually or with a partner to complete the exercise.
- Elicit answers.

1 I wonder if you could tell me if/whether you like Chinese food.
2 Could you tell me if/whether you have ever been to China?
3 Do you know the capital of China? / what the capital of China is?
4 I would like to know how much a fortune cookie costs.
5 Could you tell me where the nearest Chinese restaurant is?

ON THE BOARD

I wonder could you tell me who invented the fortune cookie?
Could you tell me what is the price of this jacket.

3

Aim: to practise using prepositions

- Before students attempt this task, remind them that phrases which come before or follow a gap often act as clues.
- Ask students to look at the prepositions in the box.
- Do the first one together.
- Students then work individually or with a partner to complete the exercise.
- Elicit answers.
- Remind students to make a note in their notebooks of any prepositional phrases that they have learned in this exercise.

1 back	4 on	7 at / during
2 on	5 about	8 to
3 At	6 in	

4

Aim: to answer direct and indirect questions

- Students now read a passage which contains the answers to the direct and indirect questions in exercise 1.
- Ask students to read through the passage and tell you what the gist of it is (what fortune cookies are and where they come from).
- Ask individual students the indirect questions from exercise 1.
- Elicit answers, asking students to paraphrase what they have read in the passage.

A fortune cookie is a small biscuit which is traditionally served at the end of a meal in a Chinese restaurant.
Fortune cookies have a piece of paper inside them, which has your fortune written on it.
The fortune cookie was invented in China in the 13th century.

5

Aim: to practise an exam-type task

- Students now do a gap-fill which is designed to practise what they have learned from exercises 2 and 3.
- Explain that at this stage it is not important to understand all of the words, but draw students' attention to clues before and after the gaps (eg prepositions, articles, personal pronouns and determiners).
- Remind students that when they have completed the exercise they should read it through again to check for sense.
- Remind students that they should write only one word in each gap, and that each word should be in capital letters.
- Students then work individually or with a partner to complete the exercise.
- Elicit answers.

1 ABOUT	6 BACK
2 IF/WHETHER	7 ON
3 AT	8 TO
4 ON	9 ON
5 IN	10 AT / DURING

Suggested homework

Assign Ex. 1 and 2 – Workbook, p.49
Ex. 1 and 2 – Workbook, p.50

Writing

1

Aim: to introduce the topic of formal letters/emails and develop awareness of style

- First, ask students to study page 150 of the **Writing database**, either in class or at home before the lesson starts.
- Ask students to read the writing task and to tell you who the email should be written to (a chef who works at a local restaurant).

- Ask students what the purpose of the email is (to give the chef more information about an interview).
- Elicit why the email is formal.

> because you are writing to someone that you don't know

Additional task

- Encourage students to think about the kind of information that they **must** include in their email (tell Denise the questions she will be asked in the interview; suggest the morning of either the 12th or 13th March; ask her if she can bring examples of easy food for children to prepare; ask her if we can take some photographs of her, etc).
- Remind them that they need to look at their notes and include all the information in their email.
- Encourage students to make a paragraph plan before they start writing an email, with at least one piece of information that they would include in each paragraph.

2

Aim: to provide a model answer for students to refer to

- Remind students that for exam purposes, an email simply means a letter sent electronically and that they should not use abbreviations such as 'CU', etc, in their emails.
- Students now read the model answer to the question in exercise 1.
- Ask them to read the email through once.
- Encourage students to give their opinion on whether this is a good email, whether it answers the question correctly and whether the writer has included all of the information she should have (Yes – this email would be given a high mark in the exam.).

3

Aim: to read to identify indirect questions

- Before students attempt this task, ask them to read questions 1–4.
- Ask students to read the model answer in exercise 2 again and underline where Maria has mentioned those points.
- Elicit answers.
- Ask students which of the sentences are indirect questions.
- Elicit answer (1, 2, 3).
- Remind students that in formal letters/emails it is more polite to use indirect questions and that they should try to avoid asking direct questions where possible.

> ***From:*** *Maria*
> ***To:*** *Denise Jordan*
>
> ***Subject:*** *Your interview*
> *Dear Mrs Jordan,*
>
> *I work for my school magazine, 'Talking in Class'. Our editor has asked me to give you more information about the interview you have agreed to do.*
> *We are very interested in your new series. Would you mind if we asked you a few questions about it?*
> *(1) We would also like to ask you about your experiences working in a hotel.*
> *(2) I wonder if you would be available on either the twelfth or the thirteenth of March. The interview would take place at about ten o'clock in the morning, because of the school timetable.*
> *Your new series is about learning to cook easy dishes.*
> *(3) I wonder if you could bring some examples to show us what you mean.*
> *(4) Would you mind if we took photographs during the interview?*
>
> *Please contact me if you need more information.*
>
> *Yours sincerely,*
> *Maria Zerva*

> Indirect questions: 1, 2, 3

4

Aim: to prepare students for the writing task

- Before students begin these exercises, remind them of the importance of identifying who they are writing to.
- Ask them to look at the writing task and to tell you who they will be writing to.
- Ask: *Will you be writing to a person you know or don't know?* (a person I don't know)
- Ask: *Will you be writing to give more information or to ask for more information?* (to give more information)
- Then ask: *Do you need to include all of the information from your notes?* (yes)

5

Aim: to encourage students to plan their writing

- This exercise is designed to encourage students to use their imagination and to make sure that all students have enough ideas before they start writing.
- Remind students that careful planning will improve their emails.
- Ask students to look at the questions and to make notes in their notebooks.
- Remind them that they should be answering the questions with one or two sentences.
- Go round the class monitoring or helping where necessary.
- At the end of the exercise, ask individual students to read out their ideas.
- If you have time, check that all students have completed the questions with appropriate information.

1	c
2–3	students' own answers
4	(suggested answers) *Would an interview at your restaurant be convenient for you? / I wonder if an interview at your restaurant would be possible.*
5	(suggested answers) *Would you mind preparing some recipes for students? / I wonder if you could prepare some recipes for students.*
6	(suggested answers) *Could you let me know if/whether we could take photographs? / Would you mind if we took photographs?*
7	b
8	c

- Ask students to turn to **Writing Planner 7** on page 158. Explain that each Writing Planner gives them a simple table to complete which helps them to put the right content in the right place in their piece of writing.
- Point out to students that each row of the table refers to a different part of their piece of writing and gives its purpose, together with useful expressions. Explain to students that they should complete the 'notes' column using their own ideas.
- Give students some time to complete the table. Invite a number of students to say what they have put in the 'notes' column for each part of the piece of writing. If possible, you may like to check the notes made by all students to ensure they have enough content to base their piece of writing on. Ask students to refer to the Writing Planner as they do their piece of writing.

6

Aim: to give students the opportunity to produce a formal email

- This exercise can be done in class or set for homework.
- Remind students of the importance of using indirect questions and of answering the question by including all the information from their notes.
- Ask students to write their email to Peter Murphy.

7

Aim: to encourage students to check their written work

- Draw students' attention to the checklist.
- When they have finished writing, ask them to read each statement and to tick each one that is true for them.
- Ask them to make sure that they have ticked all of the boxes before handing their email in to be marked.
- You might consider refusing to mark any email that does not meet all the criteria in the checklist and asking the student to rewrite.

Additional task

- In order to monitor whether students have checked their work carefully, you could ask them to underline in pencil places in their emails where they have 'used indirect questions', for example.
- Alternatively, invite individual students to read parts of their email to the rest of the class or get students to exchange emails with each other and to check each other's emails for mistakes before handing them in.

Look Back

Aim: to review the unit and to practise scanning for specific information

- Students now have the opportunity to go back through the unit to check what they have learned.
- Ask the whole class the questions from **Look Back**.
- Elicit answers from different students.
- Encourage students to scan the unit to find any information they can't remember.

1 in 1853	3 sour	5 in 1849
2 chips	4 no	

Suggested homework

Assign Ex. 1 – Workbook, p.50
Ex. 2 and 3 – Workbook, p.51

Further material

- For further practice and consolidation, ask students to complete the Unit 7 tasks on the Student's CD-ROM.
- To test students' understanding of the material in Unit 7, you may like to administer the Unit 7 Test, which is in the Tests section of the Teacher's DVD-ROM. You may also like to construct your own test using the Test Generator material for Unit 7.

8

Out and About

Target language

Grammar: full infinitives (with *to*) and *-ing* forms after verbs / *prefer, would rather, had better*
Lexis: topic vocabulary / word formation (irregular forms) / metaphors (life)
Reading skills: text type and function
Listening skills: listening for specific information
Speaking skills: giving examples
Writing skills: expressing opinion, review
Pronunciation: /s/ and /z/

- The phrase *out and about* means out of the house, travelling around, eg *My grandma's quite old so she doesn't get out and about much these days.*
- Write the phrase *out and about* on the board.
- Ask students what they think the title refers to.
- Explain the meaning of the phrase *out and about.*
- Write the example sentence given above on the board.
- Elicit suggestions as to what the unit might be about.

ON THE BOARD

out and about

My grandma's quite old so she doesn't get out and about much these days.

Start thinking!

Aim: to introduce the topic of travel and tourism through personal responses

- Ask students to work in pairs to talk about the questions in the Student's Book.
- Go round the class monitoring and helping where necessary.
- If you prefer, conduct a brief discussion involving the whole class by reading the questions and inviting different students to give their answers.

Reading CD1, Track 26

1

Aim: to read to understand gist

- Students are now going to read a magazine article. Begin by asking them to look at the title of the article and predict what it might be about.
- Elicit ideas.
- Ask students to read the article. This can be done individually or as a class activity with different students being asked to read different sections aloud to the rest of the class.
- Remind students that at this stage they do not need to understand all of the vocabulary as items will be covered in the **WORD BOX** section.
- Elicit answers from a few students as to which holiday sounds most interesting and why.

Background information

- *'Wish you were here' is a typical greeting which holidaymakers write on postcards which they send while on holiday.*
- *Farm holidays are quite popular in Britain with young families. The family has its own accommodation and the freedom to explore the farm and take part in any farming duties that they are interested in. They are especially suitable for children and adults who like the countryside.*

Additional task

- In order to check your students' ability to scan for specific information, elicit the answers to the questions below.
- Remind students that they don't have to reread large parts of the passage but should look for clues or key words that might help them find the answer. The key words have been underlined in each sentence.

1 Who went on holiday for 10 days? (Amy Barker)
2 Who thought their holiday would be great for young children? (Hanna Bridgeman)
3 Who went on an adventure holiday? (Rebecca Key)
4 Who had been to their destination before? (Ryan Fletcher)
5 Who had to travel for only an hour to get to their destination? (Simon Watson)

2

Aim: to encourage students to think about text type and function

- Ask students to read the questions 1–3 and answer them without looking back at the passage.
- Elicit answers, asking for justification.

1 a   2 b   3 b

3

Aim: to give students practice in an exam-type task

- Before the students do this exercise, remind them of the best way to approach it so that they become familiar with exam technique.
- Remind them of the importance of looking for key words or phrases which are synonymous or similar in meaning to the words in the question.
- Remind them, too, of the importance of underlining where they found the answer within the passage, as this makes it much quicker and easier for them to be able to justify their answers in class and check their work in the exam.
- Finally, remind them that they can choose some of the teenagers' reports more than once and that some questions have more than one answer.
- Ask students to work individually or with a partner.
- Elicit answers, asking for justification from the passage.

1 E: *'... I thought, "That's great for my sister ... but what about me?"'*
2 A: *'We were exhausted when we arrived because the flight takes about 24 hours ...'*
3 B: *'... so we went out every night, which was great.'*
4 and 5 (in any order)
B: *'I'd had enough of the beach, really, after two weeks.'*
D: *'There wasn't much to do and I was glad to get home.'*
6 and 7 (in any order)
B: *'... but I met a couple of local people my age ...'*
C: *'I soon made friends and we had a lot of fun.'*
8 and 9 (in any order)
B: *'We go abroad every year ...'*
D: *'Usually, it's Italy or Spain.'*

Additional task

- Ask students to write a short paragraph of 50 words in a similar style about their last holiday.

WORD BOX

Aim: to introduce new vocabulary

- Before the students do this exercise, ask them to read the sentences.
- Remind them of the importance of deciding before they complete the sentences whether they need to look for a noun, adjective, verb or adverb in the passage.
- Ask students to work individually or with a partner to do the exercise.
- Elicit answers.
- Ask students if there were any other words in the passage which they didn't know the meaning of.
- Remind them to make a note of the words and to look them up in a dictionary before the start of the next lesson.
- Ask students if they enjoyed reading the teenagers' reports and whether they learned anything from them or not and get them to justify their answers.

1 self-catering	6 stopover
2 brochure	7 Adventure holiday
3 resort	8 abroad
4 jet lag	9 souvenir
5 destination	

Additional task

- Ask students to choose five words or phrases from the **WORD BOX** and to jumble up the letters to create an anagram.
- Students then swap their anagrams with a partner who must try to find the word.

Have your say!

Aim: to give students the opportunity to express their own opinions

- Put the students in pairs and get them to ask each other the questions. Ask them to make brief notes on their partner's answers. When they have finished, invite various students to tell the whole class what they discussed.
- Alternatively, you may like to do the activity as a whole class. Invite various students to give their opinions, encouraging them to agree or disagree with what other students have said. Encourage them to give reasons for their opinions.

Suggested homework

Assign Ex.1 – Workbook, p.52–53
Ex. 1 – Workbook, p.53

G Grammar clinic

1

Aim: to focus on full infinitives and *-ing* forms

- First, ask students to study page 183–184 of the **Grammar database**, either in class or at home before the lesson starts.
- The first exercise refers back to the reading passage so that students can see the grammar in question being used in context.
- Ask students to read the sentences and look back at the article and underline the verbs which are followed by the full infinitive or the *-ing* form.

'… suggested going …'
'… decided to try …'
'… want to do …'
'… prefer staying …'
'… planning to go …'
'… expected to help …'
'… enjoyed swimming …'
'… seemed to enjoy …'
'… like looking …'
'… looking forward to going …'

2

Aim: to practise using full infinitives and *-ing* forms

- Go through the first sentence together.
- Tell them to ignore the missing verb for the moment.
- Ask what the gist of the sentence is (We don't have enough money for a holiday this year.).
- Ask: *Do we say 'afford to do something' or 'afford doing something'?* (*afford to do*)
- Ask students to work individually or with a partner.
- Elicit answers.
- Remind students to make a note of the verbs which are followed by the full infinitive and those followed by *-ing* and learn them by heart.

1 to go	4 swimming	6 to be
2 to find	5 to meet	7 booking
3 to visit		

Errors to watch out for

Students often make the mistake of thinking that the verb *suggest* is followed by the full infinitive. Draw students' attention to item 7 in exercise 2, emphasising what structures are possible after *suggest*: a noun; an *-ing* form (possibly with a possessive pronoun); a *that* clause (possibly with *should*).

3

Aim: to practise using full infinitives and *-ing* forms

- Go through the first one together.
- Tell them to ignore the missing words for the moment.
- Ask: *Which verb is followed by another verb?* (*imagine*, followed by *see*)
- Ask: *Do we say 'imagine to do something'* or *'imagine doing something'?* (*imagine doing something*)
- Remind students to go through this process of asking themselves questions about the sentence before they complete the notes.
- Remind them, too, that there might be more than one verb in a sentence which they will need to change.
- Students then work individually or with a partner.
- Elicit answers. Draw students' attention to item 6 in particular, where three verbs appear in a row; *refuse* followed by the full infinitive and *consider* followed by the *-ing* form.

1 Imagine seeing the sun as it goes down behind the Pyramids!
2 A trip around the world involves making a lot of arrangements.
3 When I was there last year, the local people seemed to be very friendly and offered to help us.
4 We decided to avoid staying in places where lots of tourists go.
5 Tina promised to bring me back a souvenir from South Africa.
6 My grandmother refuses to consider going on foreign holidays.

4

Aim: to practise verbs which change their meaning when followed by the full infinitive or *-ing* form

- Elicit from students which verbs they know which change their meaning depending on whether they are followed by the infinitive or the *–ing* form (*remember*, *forget*, *stop*, *try*, *go on*, *regret*, *like*).
- Write these sentences on the board: *John worked for the company for 20 years and went on to become the manager.* and *I told my brother to turn down his music but he went on playing it really loudly.*
- Ask students to tell you the difference in meaning between the two sentences (In the first sentence *go on* means *to progress* or *develop* whereas in the second sentence, *go on* means *to continue* or *carry on.*).
- Remind students to go through this process of asking themselves questions about the meaning of the verb before they circle the correct answer.
- Students then work individually or with a partner.
- Elicit answers.

1 seeing	3 asking	5 to open
2 to get	4 to pick	

ON THE BOARD

John worked for the company for 20 years and went on to become the manager.

I told my brother to turn down his music but he went on playing it really loudly.

5

Aim: to identify incorrect use of full infinitives and *-ing* forms

- Students now work individually to find mistakes in a text message.
- Remind them to read through the text once, underlining those verbs which they think are incorrect.
- Encourage them to ask the kind of questions that they were asked in exercises 2, 3 and 4 in order to establish which form is appropriate and why.

- Students should then work individually to correct the verbs that they think are incorrect. These sentences should be rewritten correctly in their notebooks.
- Elicit answers.
- Remind students that when a preposition is followed by a verb, the verb is always in the *-ing* form.

> Hi from New York! Got here last night and planning to stay for about two days. The shops are fantastic! I've managed to find some great clothes! We hope to go up the Statue of Liberty tomorrow. Sharon's refused to come, but I've agreed to go with Mum and Dad. Not sure if I'll enjoy climbing all those stairs or not! I promise to get you an I♥NY T-shirt – if I can afford to buy it!

Suggested homework

Assign Ex. 1, 2 and 3 – Workbook, p.54

V Vocabulary builder

1

Aim: to focus on vocabulary connected to travel and tourism

- This exercise is probably best done as a whole class. If time allows however, divide the class into small groups and encourage them to use a dictionary in order to find the meaning of any unknown words.
- First, ask students to read through the definitions 1–9 and underline any words which might act as clues.
- Elicit the clues and ask if there were any which they could do given the clues in the definition.
- As an example of this you could direct students' attention to item 4. The word *checked* suggests that the answer may be *check in*. Even if students don't know the answer, searching for clues can sometimes help them to make an educated guess.
- Elicit answers.

1 pack	6 holiday rep
2 travel agent	7 route
3 departure lounge	8 customs
4 check in	9 sightseeing
5 package holiday	

Additional task

- Ask students if any of them have ever flown. Discuss what happens at an airport. Encourage students to use appropriate vocabulary for describing the process. You might like to use leaflets in English showing the layout of a nearby airport.

2

Aim: to practise using vocabulary connected to travel and tourism

- This exercise is probably best done in pairs.
- Ask students to read through the passage and tell you what the gist of it is (the problems that someone had when they went on holiday).
- Students then complete the passage with the correct form of the words from exercise 1.
- Remind students to reread the passage when they have completed it to check for sense.
- Ask students to work with a partner to do the exercise.
- Elicit answers.

1 checked in	5 holiday rep
2 departure lounge	6 customs
3 to pack	7 route
4 travel agent	8 package holiday

3

Aim: to practise irregular forms

- Before students attempt this task, remind them that there are verbs, adjectives and nouns which are irregular and some which don't take regular suffixes or prefixes.
- Go through the first one together.
- Ask students to read the first sentence and tell you whether they need to complete it with a noun, adjective, verb or adverb (a noun).
- Elicit the noun from the adjective *deep* (*depth*).
- Emphasise that spelling is extremely important and that words which are spelled incorrectly will be marked as wrong.
- Ask students to work individually or with a partner to do the rest of the exercise.
- Elicit answers. Get students to spell out the words.

1 depth	3 variety	5 heights
2 explanation	4 choice	6 beliefs

4

Aim: to introduce students to metaphorical words and phrases used for talking about life

- Ask students to look at the words in the box and tell you if they know any phrases or expressions connected with life that can be made from these words.
- Explain that words connected to *life* are often associated with *travel* and *journeys*. We think of life as a journey, so we often use the language of journeys to describe life.
- Remind students that they may have to change the form of a word to complete the sentences.
- Students then work individually or with a partner to complete the sentences.
- Elicit answers.

1 pace	4 going through
2 arrived	5 step
3 direction	6 progress

Suggested homework

Assign Ex. 1 and 2 – Workbook, p.54–55

Listening

Warm up!

Aim: to introduce the topic and warm students up

- Ask students if they have ever been on holiday. Ask them to say where they have been and whether they enjoyed it or not.
- Ask students if they have ever had any problems on holiday (with, for example, the food, the accommodation, etc). Ask them to talk about what happened and how they felt.

1

Aim: to listen for specific information and introduce the listening task

- Students are now going to listen to a woman being asked questions about a recent holiday.
- Before students listen, ask them to read the list of problems and to predict the vocabulary and the information that they might hear.
- Remind them that they will need to listen for four problems and that they should write the numbers 1–4 next to the problems they hear being talked about.
- Play the listening text.
- Elicit answers, asking students to justify their answers by paraphrasing what they heard.

CD1, Track 27

1 problems with the food: *'And then there were nights in local restaurants. I'm afraid we found those rather disappointing.'*
2 problems with the journey: *'... coming back was a bit of a nightmare. The first thing was that our plane was cancelled.'*
3 problems with pollution: *'The thing we didn't like was the atmosphere.'*
4 problems with the weather: *'... I don't think it stopped raining the whole time we were there ... it made life very difficult.'*

2

Aim: to practise listening for specific information and to practise an exam-type task

- Tell students that they are going to listen to the interview again.
- Before the students do this exercise, remind them of the best way to approach it so that they become familiar with exam technique.
- Remind them of the importance of listening for key words or phrases which could fit the gaps.
- Encourage students to complete all of the gaps. If they are not certain of an answer, they should make an educated guess.
- Finally, remind students that they only need to write a short phrase.
- Play the listening text.
- Walk around the class monitoring the students.
- Play the listening text again if necessary.

CD1, Track 27

1 ten days
2 places to visit
3 museums and art galleries
4 public transport
5 traditional dancing
6 was cancelled

Soundbite

Aim: to practise listening for the sounds /s/ and /z/

- Write the phrase *summer holidays* on the board. Underline the letter 's' in each word. Ask students if these two letters are pronounced the same (No – the first is like 's' in *see* and the second is like 'z' in *zebra.*).
- Ask students to look at the words given and to decide which of the two sounds each letter 's' represents.
- Explain to students that they will now hear someone say a sentence containing each word and they should tick whether the word contains a /s/ sound or a /z/ sound.
- Play the listening text.
- Elicit the answers, making sure that students pronounce the words correctly.

ON THE BOARD

summer holidays

CD1, Track 28

like 's' in see	like 'z' in zebra
stress, interested, increase	says, advise, doesn't, peas

Speaking

1

Aim: to practise giving examples

- Ask students to quickly read the text, ignoring the gaps for now. Ask them to say what the text is about (examples of problems you might have on holiday).
- Explain that each gap is part of a way of introducing an example. Students should put the words from the box in the correct gaps to complete the useful phrases.
- Ask students, individually or in pairs, to complete the task. Then elicit the answers.

1 One	3 Another	5 such
2 For	4 instance	6 like

2

Aim: to practise an exam-type task

- Before students do this exercise, ask them to study the **Speaking database** on page 165.
- Explain to students that they are going to work in pairs to discuss the question given. Ask them to read the question and the prompts.
- Remind students to use the phrases from exercise 1 to introduce examples.
- Ask the students to do the task and go round the class monitoring and helping where necessary. If you notice any mistakes that you would like to focus on, make a brief note as you monitor.
- Ask pairs to report back to the class on what they have discussed. Encourage students to give examples using the phrases they know.
- If you have noted any mistakes you would like to focus on, do this now as a whole class. Do not mention which pairs made these mistakes, but focus on them as things you would like the whole class to get right.

Use of English

1

Aim: to focus on *prefer, would rather* and *had better*

- Before students do the exercises on this page, ask them to study page 184 of the **Grammar database**, either in class or at home before the lesson starts.
- First, write these sentences on the board: *I'd rather go to the beach than swim in the hotel pool.* and *You'd better take some suntan lotion with you if you're going to the beach.*
- Ask students if these sentences are correct (yes).
- Underline *I'd* in the first sentence and *You'd* in the second. Ask students which words have been contracted (In the first sentence *would* is contracted and in the second sentence *had* is contracted.).
- Remind students that *had better* is used for saying what someone should do.
- Remind students that we don't say *would better* (See **Errors to watch out for**).
- Students then work individually or with a partner.
- Elicit answers.

1. I'd prefer to travel by ferry to France when we go on holiday this summer.
2. We had better call the hotel to see if they still have any rooms.
3. I prefer seeing the sights to lying on the beach all day. / I'd prefer to see the sights rather than lie on the beach all day.
4. Vietnam was great but I didn't like eating some of the local dishes.
5. I would/I'd rather not stay in a hotel where there are lots of other tourists.

ON THE BOARD

I'd rather go to the beach than swim in the hotel pool.
You'd better take some suntan lotion with you if you're going to the beach.

Errors to watch out for

Students often make the mistake of using *would better*. Remind students to try not to confuse *would better* with *had better* when saying what someone should do.

2

Aim: to practise using *prefer*, *would rather* and *had better*

- Before students attempt this task, ask them to look at the word in bold in item 1.
- Based on what they have learned from exercise 1, ask them to tell you which words in the first sentence they might need to replace (… *I'd prefer to go* …).
- Ask: *What follows 'would rather'?* (*would rather* + bare infinitive … *than* + bare infinitive …)
- Elicit the answer to item 1.
- Remind them that they will need to rewrite the first sentence using the word in bold so that the second sentence means exactly the same thing. They shouldn't change the word given and they will need to use between two and five words.
- Students then work individually or with a partner to rewrite the sentences.
- Elicit answers.

1. This year, I would rather go to Spain than go to France.
2. Mum says she would rather not visit countries she has been to before.
3. 'You had better take some time off work to relax,' my doctor said.
4. Sometimes, I prefer staying at home to travelling.

3

Aim: to practise changes in parts of speech

- Remind students what the phrase *parts of speech* means (types of word, such as noun, verb, adjective, etc).
- Explain to students that one of the things they may have to do with a sentence transformation exercise is to change the part of speech.
- Look at the first row together. Ask: *What is the noun from 'agree'?*
- Elicit the answer and the negative form (*agreement/disagreement*).
- Ask students to work individually or with a partner to do the rest of the exercise.
- Elicit answers, asking individual students to spell out the words.

verb	noun	adjective
(dis)agree	disagreement	…
(dis)appear	disappearance	…
apply	application applicant	…
damage	damage	…
describe	description	…
…	difficulty	difficult
discuss	discussion	…
interest	interest	(un)interesting (un)interested
…	(ir)responsibility	(ir)responsible
visit	visit visitor	…

4

Aim: to practise an exam-type task

- Students now do sentence transformations which are designed to practise what they have learned from exercises 1, 2 and 3.
- Before they attempt the task, ask them to look at the word in bold in item 1.
- Based on what they have learned from exercise 3 ask them to tell you which word in the first sentence they might need to replace (*discussed*).
- Ask: *Which noun from exercise 3 could replace 'discuss'?* (*discussion*)
- Elicit the answer to number 1.
- Remind them that they will need to rewrite the first sentence using the word in bold so that the second sentence means exactly the same thing. They shouldn't change the word given and they will need to use between two and five words.
- Remind them that contractions such as *don't, doesn't, hasn't,* etc count as two words. The exception to this is *can't* which counts as one word (because it comes from *cannot*).
- Remind students that when they have completed the sentences they should read them through again to make sure they have followed the instructions properly.
- Students then work individually to complete the exercise.
- Elicit answers.

1 My parents HAD A DISCUSSION ABOUT / TALKED ABOUT where we were going to go on holiday.
2 You HAD BETTER TAKE some warm clothes in case it's cold in Poland.
3 The holiday rep IS USUALLY RESPONSIBLE FOR organising social events.
4 They didn't RECEIVE MANY APPLICATIONS for the job at the travel agent's.
5 I much PREFER STAYING IN HOTELS RATHER than going camping when I'm on holiday.
6 We had DIFFICULTY ON HOLIDAY UNDERSTANDING the local people.

Errors to watch out for

Students often follow the verb *discuss* with the preposition *about*. Remind them that it is correct to say that we *talk about something* or that people *have a discussion about something* but that the verb *discuss* is not followed by a preposition.

Suggested homework

Assign Ex. 1 and 2 – Workbook, p.55
Ex. 1 and 2 – Workbook, p.56

Writing

1

Aim: to introduce the topic of reviews

- Ask students to study page 152 of the **Writing database** either in class or at home before the lesson starts.
- Ask students to say what a review is (a description and evaluation of something). Ask them what kind of things are often reviewed (books, films, TV programmes, holidays, etc).
- Ask students to read the writing task and to tell you who is asking for reviews (a website for teenagers) and what they are asking for reviews of (a local tourist attraction).
- Put students into pairs and ask them to look at the questions. Ask them to choose one or two local attractions to discuss. Ask them to make brief notes as they discuss, and to then report back to the whole class on their discussion.
- Alternatively, do the activity as a whole class, eliciting different students' ideas.

2

Aim: to practise phrases for expressing opinion

- Explain to students that each sentence in exercise 2 comes from a different review and gives the reviewer's opinion. They need to complete each sentence with a word from the box.
- Give students some time to complete the task and then elicit the answers.

1 To　2 In　3 In　4 personally　5 As

Additional task

- Ask students to look at each sentence and decide whether it comes from a positive or a negative review.

1 positive　2 positive　3 negative　4 positive　5 negative

3

Aim: to analyse a model answer

- Ask students to read the model answer. Ask what this is a review of (Bodmin Park, a park which includes an adventure park) and whether it's a positive or a negative review (positive).

- Individually or in pairs, ask students to read the statements about the review and decide whether each one is true or false. Point out that these statements are true (or not) of reviews generally and not just this particular review.
- Give students some time to complete the task and then elicit the answers.

1 T	3 F	5 F
2 T	4 T	6 T

4

Aim: to check comprehension of the model answer

- Ask students to read the statements about the review they have just read.
- You may like to ask students to answer the questions from what they remember of the model answer, without reading it again. They could do this in pairs or individually.
- Ask students to read the model answer again to check their answers. You may like to give students a short time limit, say one minute, to encourage them to scan the model answer for the information rather than reading it in detail.
- Elicit the answers.

1 NO	3 NO	5 YES	7 YES	9 YES
2 YES	4 YES	6 YES	8 NO	10 NO

5

Aim: to prepare students for the writing task

- Tell students that they are going to write a review in answer to the task in exercise 1. Before they do so, they are going to get together the information they need and make a plan of their piece of writing.
- Ask students to work individually to complete the notes about their chosen attraction.
- Students can complete the notes from their local knowledge, or from their imagination. Alternatively, you might like to ask students to research a local attraction on the internet and to base their piece of writing on what they find out.

students' own answers

6

Aim: to encourage students to plan their writing

- This exercise is designed to ensure that all students have enough ideas before they start writing, and to ensure that they understand how to organise those ideas.
- Ask students to look at the questions and to make notes in their notebooks.
- Remind them that they should answer the questions with one or two sentences. You might also tell them that, since this is a plan, it's not necessary to write in complete sentences at this stage.
- Give students some time to complete the task, and go round the class monitoring or helping where necessary.
- At the end of the exercise, ask individual students to read out their ideas.

students' own answers

- Ask students to turn to *Writing Planner 8* on page 158. Explain that each Writing Planner gives them a simple table to complete which helps them to put the right content in the right place in their piece of writing.
- Point out to students that each row of the table refers to a different part of their piece of writing and gives its purpose, together with useful expressions. Explain to students that they should complete the 'notes' column using their own ideas.
- Give students some time to complete the table. Invite a number of students to say what they have put in the 'notes' column for each part of the piece of writing. If possible, you may like to check the notes made by all students to ensure they have enough content to base their piece of writing on. Ask students to refer to the Writing Planner as they do their piece of writing.

7

Aim: to give students the opportunity to produce a review

- This exercise can be done in class or set for homework.
- Remind students of the importance of presenting the information about the attraction clearly, and of using appropriate phrases to introduce their own opinion.

8

Aim: to encourage students to check their written work

- Draw students' attention to the checklist.
- When they have finished writing, ask them to read each statement and to tick each one that is true for them.
- Ask them to make sure that they have ticked all of the boxes before handing their letter in to be marked.
- You might consider refusing to mark any review that does not meet all the criteria in the checklist and asking the student to rewrite.

Look Back

Aim: to review the unit and to practise scanning for specific information

- Students now have the opportunity to go back through the unit to check what they have learned.
- Ask the whole class the questions from **Look Back**.
- Elicit answers from different students.
- Encourage students to scan the unit to find any information they can't remember.

1 Sydney	4 variety, variation
2 a holiday brochure	5 would better
3 suggest	

Suggested homework

Assign Ex. 1, 2 and 3 – Workbook, p.57

Webquest

- Ask students to complete the **Webquest** on page 199 of the Student's Book. You might ask students to work on this together in class if you have internet access, or you might assign it for homework.
- Explain to students that the answers to the questions are not in the Student's Book but that they need to find the answers online.
- Check the answers together and ask students to explain where they found the answers and how they found them (eg by typing terms into a search engine).

1 chopsticks
2 Giglio
3 Jamie's 30-minute Meals
4 New York (City)
5 fish
6 Edinburgh
7 (John Wheeley) Lea / (William Henry) Perrins
8 sausage(s)
9 Istanbul
10 Byzantium / Constantinople

Further material

- For further practice and consolidation, ask students to complete the Unit 8 tasks on the Student's CD-ROM.
- To test students' understanding of the material in Unit 8, you may like to administer the Unit 8 Test, which is in the Tests section of the Teacher's DVD-ROM. You may also like to construct your own test using the Test Generator material for Unit 8.

Revision Units 7-8

1

1 C	3 B	5 D	7 D	9 C
2 A	4 A	6 B	8 B	10 A

2

(2 marks for each correct answer)

1 Phillip said (that) he was meeting Mark outside the cinema.
2 As we entered the old house, Mariana said (that) she had been there before.
3 Alex suggested seeing what was on at the cinema.
4 My mum told me to put my dirty clothes in the washing basket.
5 Mrs Lewis said she was tired because she had been working all day.
6 Nancy refused to lend me any money.
7 My dad said he thought Grandma would be there at the weekend.

3

1 going	3 to be	5 to play
2 visiting	4 eating	6 to go

4

1 at	3 in	5 about
2 on	4 on	

5

1 make	3 cut	5 fall
2 run	4 turn	

6

(2 marks for each correct answer)

1 discussion	6 responsibility
2 choice	7 agreement
3 appearance	8 difficulty
4 description	9 explanation
5 variety	10 belief

9

Lab Report

Target language

Grammar:	conditionals (1): zero, first, second /*unless, in case, as long as* / word patterns
Lexis:	topic vocabulary / collocations /phrasal verbs with *off*
Reading skills:	scanning for specific information
Listening skills:	listening for specific information
Speaking skills:	talking about hopes
Writing skills:	paragraphing / informal letter/email
Pronunciation:	/s/ and /ʃ/

- A *lab report* is a written report by a scientist on the results of a particular experiment carried out in a laboratory, eg *Professor Smith has asked me to prepare a lab report on his latest experiment.*
- Write the words *lab report* on the board.
- Ask students what they think the title refers to.
- Explain the meaning of a *lab report.*
- Write the example sentence given above on the board.
- Elicit suggestions as to what the unit might be about.

ON THE BOARD

> **lab report**
>
> **Professor Smith has asked me to prepare a lab report on his latest experiment.**

Start thinking!

Aim: to introduce the topic of science and technology through personal responses

- Ask students to work in pairs to talk about the questions in the Student's Book.
- Go round the class monitoring and helping where necessary.
- If you prefer, conduct a brief discussion involving the whole class by reading the questions and inviting different students to give their answers.

Additional task

- First, write these words on the board: *science* and *technology.*
- Elicit from the students which items or subjects they would put into each category. You might need to prompt them by offering a few suggestions, eg *chemistry, the internet, jet engine, astronomy,* etc. (*Science* refers to the study of the physical world, which includes humans and animals, and its behaviour, eg medicine, human biology, physics, etc. *Technology* refers to machines and equipment which have been developed using scientific knowledge, eg computers, DVD players, telephones, etc.)

Reading CD2, Track 1

1

Aim: to read for gist

- Students are now going to read a magazine article. Begin by asking them to look at the title of the article and predict what it might be about.
- Elicit ideas.
- Ask students to read the article. This can be done individually or as a whole class activity with different students being asked to read different sections aloud to the rest of the class.
- Ask students to read the article quickly. At this stage, tell them to ignore any vocabulary they don't understand but to try to get the gist of each paragraph.
- Ask students to match a heading to each paragraph. Tell them that the heading they choose should express the gist of that paragraph.
- Give students some time to complete the task and then elicit the answers.

a 2	d 4	f 6
b 5	e 1	g 3

Heading c is not used.

2

Aim: to scan for specific information

- Ask students to look at the phrases given. Explain that they need to scan the article to find phrases that mean something similar to the phrases given.
- Encourage students not to read the article in detail from the beginning to the end, but to scan the relevant paragraph to find words that may mean the same as each phrase given. Once they've located the relevant part of the text, they should then read in detail to check that they have found the answer.
- You may like to do the first one as a whole class. If necessary, elicit the meaning of 'mobile' for any students who don't know it. Elicit that they should be looking for a word or phrase that is the opposite of 'mobile'.
- If necessary, guide students towards the first sentence, where the answer appears. Elicit the answer.
- Either continue in this way as a whole class, or give students some time to complete the exercise individually. Then elicit the answers.

1 were firmly stuck
2 on the go
3 Several key aspects had to come together
4 to do so
5 There's no point
6 extremely widespread
7 create an environment
8 it seems likely

3

Aim: to check comprehension of the article

- Explain to students that they have to find a word or short phrase from the article which completes each sentence.
- Tell them that they should read each sentence and then scan the article until they find the section that is talking about the same thing.
- They should then read in detail to find the precise word or phrase they need to complete each sentence.
- Give students some time to complete the task and then elicit the answers.

1 sending and receiving text messages
2 quality
3 long-lasting
4 large amounts of data
5 Wifi / wireless networks
6 (being) rotated
7 online banking
8 (air) sensor

WORD BOX

4

Aim: to introduce new vocabulary

- Before the students do this exercise, ask them to read the definitions.
- Remind them of the importance of deciding before they complete the definitions whether they need to look for a noun, adjective, verb or adverb in the article.
- Ask students to work individually or with a partner to do the exercise.
- Elicit answers.
- Ask students if there were any other words in the article which they didn't know the meaning of.
- Remind them to make a note of the words and to look them up in a dictionary before the start of the next lesson.
- Ask students if they enjoyed reading the article and whether they learned anything from it or not and get them to justify their answers.

1 handy	6 decrease
2 device	7 quality
3 development	8 reasonably-priced
4 improve	9 functions
5 undoubtedly	10 digital

Additional task

- Ask students to choose five words from the **WORD BOX** and to write their own sentences with the word missing.
- Students then swap their sentences with a partner and try to fill in the missing word.

Have your say!

Aim: to give students the opportunity to express their own opinions

- Put the students in pairs and get them to ask each other the questions. Ask them to make brief notes on their partner's answers. When they have finished, invite various students to tell the whole class what they discussed.
- Alternatively, you may like to do the activity as a whole class. Invite various students to give their opinions, encouraging them to agree or disagree with what other students have said. Encourage them to give reasons for their opinions.

Suggested homework

Assign Ex.1 – Workbook, p.62–63
Ex.1 – Workbook, p.63

Grammar clinic

1

Aim: to review zero, first and second conditionals

- Before students do the exercises on this page, ask them to study page 185 of the **Grammar database**, either in class or at home before the lesson starts.
- The first exercise refers back to the reading passage so that students can see the grammar in question being used in context.

- Read the sentences and ask students to tell you which conditional is being used in each sentence.
- Ask students to match each sentence to its explanation.

1 b	The zero conditional is used to talk about general truths and scientific facts.
2 a	The first conditional is used to talk about real possibilities in the present, in the future, or generally.
3 c	The second conditional is used to talk about unreal possibilities (things that are unlikely, impossible or hypothetical) in the present and in the future.

2

Aim: to practise zero, first and second conditionals

- Write this sentence on the board: *If you will go to the beach tomorrow, give me a call.*
- Ask students to explain to you what is wrong with the sentence (In a first conditional talking about the future, we use *if* … present tense, not *if* … *will* …).
- Before students do the exercise, go through the first sentence together.
- Ask: *Is this a general truth or a hypothetical situation?* (a hypothetical situation)
- Ask: *Which conditional is used to talk about a hypothetical situation?* (second conditional)
- Ask: *How do we form the second conditional?* (*if* … past tense … *would* … bare infinitive)
- Remind students that instead of *If I were* … , which is more formal, they can also say *If I was* …
- Remind students to go through this process of asking themselves questions about the sentence before they choose the answer.
- Students then work individually or with a partner to do the exercise.
- Elicit answers, asking students to give reasons for their answers from the explanations a–c in exercise 1.

1 a 2 c 3 b 4 a 5 c

ON THE BOARD

If you will go to the beach tomorrow, give me a call.

3

Aim: to further practise zero, first and second conditionals

- Before students complete the sentences, go through the first one together.
- Ask: *Is this a general truth or a hypothetical situation?* (a hypothetical situation)
- Ask: *Which conditional is used to talk about a hypothetical situation?* (second conditional)
- Ask: *How do we form the second conditional?* (*if* … past tense … *would* … bare infinitive)
- Remind students that they can also write all conditional sentences the other way round, with the *if* clause second, as in sentence 2.
- Remind students to go through this process of asking themselves questions about the sentence before they complete it.
- Ask students to work individually or with a partner.
- Elicit answers.

1 were/was / I'd get
2 you click
3 didn't exist / wouldn't be
4 make
5 you lower
6 you've used / you'll find

4

Aim: to further practise using zero, first and second conditionals

- Ask students to look at the information about a student, Richard.
- Explain that there is general information about Richard in the middle and if they follow each of the lines, they come to an action. Following the lines further leads them to a (positive or negative) result.
- Students should look at the information about Richard and write six conditional sentences as in the example.
- Ask students to work individually or with a partner to do the rest of the exercise.
- Elicit answers.

(suggested answers)
If Richard passes his chemistry exam, he will study chemistry at university.
Richard will study chemistry at university if he passes his chemistry exam.
If Richard fails his chemistry exam, he will get a job as a lab assistant.
Richard will get a job as a lab assistant if he fails in his chemistry exam.
If Richard wins the lottery, he will buy a new computer.
Richard will buy a new computer if he wins the lottery.
If Richard doesn't win the lottery, he won't feel too disappointed.
Richard won't feel too disappointed if he doesn't win the lottery.
If Richard knew how to drive, he would save up to buy a car.
Richard would save up to buy a car if he knew how to drive.

Suggested homework

Assign Ex. 1, 2 and 3 – Workbook, p.64

V Vocabulary builder

1

Aim: to focus on topic vocabulary

- Ask students to look at the pictures.
- Students use the words in the box to label the pictures.

1 h / k (in either order)
2 f
3 e
4 i
5 c / b (in either order)
6 l
7 g
8 d
9 a
10 g

2

Aim: to further develop topic vocabulary

- Ask students to work individually or with a partner to do the exercise.
- Remind students to reread the sentences when they have completed them to check for sense.
- Elicit answers.
- Encourage students to make a note of any new words or phrases that they learn in their notebooks.

1 inventions	4 research
2 theory	5 experiment
3 laboratories	6 discovery

3

Aim: to match collocations connected to technology

- Ask students to look at the words and to try and match them to make phrases.
- Elicit answers.

1 an experiment / research
2 an experiment / research
3 a memory stick / a theory / software
4 a theory / an experiment
5 software
6 software
7 a memory stick
8 a memory stick

4

Aim: to introduce phrasal verbs with *off*

- Point out to students that phrasal verbs that share the same particle *(up, down, out,* etc*)* sometimes have meanings that have something in common. All the verbs here use *off* and they all have something to do with removing, stopping or cancelling something.
- Ask: *Which phrasal verb might mean to remove an item of clothing?* (*take off*) and *Which phrasal verb might mean to stop a machine?* (*turn off*)
- Elicit any ideas they have.
- Students then work individually to match the phrasal verbs to the definitions.
- Elicit answers.
- Remind students that sometimes phrasal verbs can have more than one meaning.
- Encourage students to make a note of the different meanings of phrasal verbs in their notebooks.

1 go off	4 call off
2 take off	5 make off
3 put off	6 turn off

5

Aim: to practise using phrasal verbs with *off*

- Ask students to look at the first sentence and elicit what the burglars might have done in a white car.
- Make suggestions by substituting the phrasal verb definitions into the gap to see if it makes sense. Do this with two incorrect definitions first and then with the correct one.
- Say: *The burglars stole a flat screen TV and cancelled a planned event in a white car,* and then, *Does this make sense?* Elicit 'no'.
Then say: *The burglars stole a flat screen TV and stopped a machine in a white car,* and then ask: *Does this make sense?* Elicit 'no'. Then say: *The burglars stole a flat screen TV and escaped after a crime in a white car*, and then ask: *Does this make sense?* Elicit 'yes'.
- Encourage students to substitute the definitions first before they complete the gaps with the phrasal verbs to see which make logical sense.
- Before students attempt this task alone remind them that they might need to change the tense of the phrasal verb to the correct form.
- Students then work individually to complete the sentences.
- Elicit answers.

1 made off
2 put (the experiment) off
3 take off
4 gone off
5 called (it) off
6 turn (your computer) off

Additional task

- Elicit any other phrasal verbs the students know with *off* (Possible answers: *go off* (for food), *let off*).
- Ask individual students to give you example sentences which you can write on the board.
- Encourage students to write definitions and example sentences in their notebooks.

Suggested homework

Assign Ex. 1 – Workbook, p.64–65
Ex. 2 – Workbook, p.65

Listening

Warm up!

Aim: to introduce the topic and warm students up

- Ask students if they play computer games. Ask them to say what types of computer game they enjoy and to say which ones are their favourite games.

- Ask students to say what makes a good computer game. Encourage them to respond to each other and to agree or disagree.

1

Aim: to listen for specific information and introduce the listening task

- Students are now going to listen to five people talking about new computer games and decide which game each enjoyed the most.
- Ask students to read through the list of games.
- Remind them that each speaker will probably mention several games and they should try to listen for words or phrases which express the speaker's preference for one particular game.
- Play the listening text.
- Elicit answers, asking students to justify their answers by paraphrasing what they heard.

CD2, Track 2

Speaker 1 C: '*… so I'd rather play something like* Mad Driver City, *you know …*'
Speaker 2 A: '*Something like* Night Thief *is probably more my style … Yeah, definitely.*'
Speaker 3 B: 'Cave Warrior *is a great game, although it's not perfect.*'
Speaker 4 E: '*You can imagine how we felt when* Cup Final *came out.*'
Speaker 5 D: '*You might be able to find a better look than* Tower of Evil, *but I doubt it.*'

2

Aim: to listen for specific information

- Students now hear the extracts again.
- First, remind students of the best way to approach it so that they become familiar with exam technique.
- Remind them of the importance of listening for synonyms or similar words to any that appear in the sentences.
- Remind students that they will hear each extract twice and that they should listen to the whole of the extract before they decide on the answer.
- Play the listening text.
- Elicit answers, asking students to justify their answers by paraphrasing what they heard.

CD2, Track 2

1 B '*It can be a bit predictable, though …*'
2 B '*It all seemed to be happening a bit fast for me.*'
3 A '*… but it's a bit too much like being at criminal school for me …*'
4 C '*… but you have to take it in turns and then compare scores, which spoils it for us.*'
5 B '*You have to play quite a few to find out what your tastes are, otherwise you could waste money on a puzzle game …*'

Soundbite

Aim: to practise listening for the sounds /s/ and /ʃ/

- Students now listen for words which begin with either a /s/ and /ʃ/ sound.
- Explain that they will hear someone say four sentences and they must circle which word they hear.
- Play the listening text.
- Ask individual students to repeat the sentences that they have heard back to you, paying particular attention to the way they pronounce /s/ and /ʃ/.

CD2, Track 3

1 Only half of the people were saved.
2 Could you get me a sheet from the office, please?
3 Did you show all of them?
4 They have lots of different sorts.

Speaking

1

Aim: to talk about hopes for the future

- Students now get the chance to talk about their hopes and ambitions for the future.
- Remind students that the FCE interview begins with each candidate being asked to give some personal details about themselves.
- Direct students' attention to the example and ask students to look at the conditional sentences.
- Tell them to complete the sentences, deciding what needs to happen first before they can realise their ambitions.
- Remind them that because they are talking about the future they should use *if … present tense*, not *if … will.*
- Students then work individually to complete the sentences.
- Elicit ideas from several students.

(suggested answers)
I want to get married if I meet the right person.
I hope to have a family if I can afford to have children.
It'd be nice to work as a doctor if I manage to pass all my exams.
I'd love to visit China one day if I had enough money.
I'd like to live in New York if I had a good job.

2

Aim: to practise an exam-type task

- Before students do this exercise, ask them to study the **Speaking database** on page 165.
- Students now have the chance to practise talking about hopes for the future.

- Ask students to read the questions and the useful phrases given.
- Divide the class into pairs.
- Remind students to use the notes that they made in exercise 1 and also to expand on their ideas using the prompts from the Student's Book.
- Go round the class monitoring or helping where necessary.

Additional task

- Ask students to think of two more questions to ask and answer.
- Ask students to write out their dialogue in their notebooks.

Use of English

1

Aim: to practise using *unless, in case* and *as long as*

- Before students do these exercises, ask them to study page 186 of the **Grammar database**, either in class or at home before the lesson starts.
- First, ask students to look at the first sentence.
- Write the following sentence on the board: *You can borrow my new computer game __________ you promise to give it back tomorrow.*
- Ask students to decide whether we need *unless, in case* or *as/so long as* to complete this sentence and to justify their answer (*as/so long as* because it means *only if*).
- Remind them that in each case they will need to rewrite the first sentence using *unless, in case* or *as/so long as* so that the second sentence means exactly the same thing.
- Students then work individually or with a partner to rewrite the sentences.
- Elicit answers.

1 You can borrow my new computer game as long as you promise to give it back tomorrow.
2 I can't play on my computer unless I finish my homework.
3 Save your documents on an external hard drive or memory stick in case your computer gets a virus.

ON THE BOARD

You can borrow my new computer game __________ __________ you promise to give it back tomorrow.

2

Aim: to practise confusable word patterns

- Ask students to read each sentence, ignoring the gap.
- Students should then choose which word or phrase best completes each sentence.
- Elicit answers.
- Ask students to justify their answers. Explain the differences between the word patterns (*because* is followed by a clause, *because of* is followed by a noun; *believe* a statement or claim; *believe in* something that may or may not exist; *provide* something; *provide* something/somebody *with* something else).

1 b 2 a 3 a 4 b 5 b

3

Aim: to practise an exam-type task

- Students now do a gap-fill to practise some of what they have learned from exercises 1 and 2.
- Ask students to read through the passage and tell you what the gist is (whether time travel into the past and the future is possible).
- Explain that at this stage it is not important to understand all of the words, but draw students' attention to clues before and after the gaps that might help them find the answer. These include prepositions, articles, personal pronouns and determiners.
- Remind students that when they have completed the exercise they should read it through again to check for sense.
- Remind students that they should write only one word in each gap, and that each word should be in capital letters.
- Students may work individually or with a partner.
- Elicit answers.

1 NOT	7 BECAUSE
2 WOULD	8 IT
3 OTHERS / SOME	9 LONG
4 IF	10 WHICH
5 UP	11 TO
6 DO / CAN	12 WILL

Suggested homework

Assign Ex. 1 and 2 – Workbook, p.65
Ex. 1 and 2 – Workbook, p.66

Writing

1

Aim: to review informal letters/emails

- First, ask students to study page 154 of the **Writing database**, either in class or at home before the lesson starts.
- Ask students to read the writing task and to tell you who the email should be written to (a friend in another country).
- Elicit why the email is informal.

because it is written to someone you know personally

Additional task

- Encourage students to think about the kind of information that they could include in their email (tell her which pieces of technology we have in the house: dishwasher, computer, the internet, mobile phones, DVD player; which ones we use most often; which ones are most useful, etc).

2

Aim: to encourage students to think about the style of informal letters/emails

- Remind students that they have already written an informal letter in Unit 1 and should be familiar with the style of informal letters/emails.
- Ask students to work individually or with a partner to do the exercise.
- Elicit answers.

1 T	It's a good idea to start with a question about the person's health / news, etc.
2 F	Contractions are suitable for informal writing.
3 T	We can use shortened sentences to make our letters sound conversational.
4 F	Exclamation marks are a good way of expressing our surprise, shock or delight in an informal letter.
5 F	Every piece of writing should be divided into paragraphs.
6 F	If you don't answer the question, you will lose marks.

3

Aim: to provide a model answer for students to refer to and to practise paragraphing

- Students now read the model answer to the question in exercise 1.
- Ask them to read the email through once.
- Then ask them to read through again quickly and to underline all the informal phrases that the writer has used.
- Ask students why we use paragraphs (to make writing easier to understand because each paragraph contains one main idea).
- Students should then work individually or with a partner to decide where the paragraphs should begin.
- Elicit answers.
- Encourage students to give their opinion on whether this is a good email, whether it answers the question correctly and whether the fact that the writer hasn't used paragraphs will affect her overall mark (Yes – the email answers the question. However, the fact that the writer hasn't used paragraphs and has made some mistakes means that the email would not be given a high mark.).

To: *Miss Ashley Williams*
Sent: *18th February*
Subject: *Technology!*

Dear ~~Miss~~ Ashley ~~Williams~~,

How are you? How did your French test go? I bet you passed!

You asked me about ***technology****. Well, the first thing I should tell you is that I've got a new computer! So far, I've used it for playing games and for* ***surfing*** *the internet. It's not as complicated as I thought. I'm even teaching my dad how to use it!*

What else? Of course, we've got things like a TV and a DVD player. We watch a few hours of TV every day, and we watch a DVD once a ***week****. My brother watches more than I do. Lazy boy! My dad says he's thinking of getting* ***satellite*** *TV, so maybe I'll start watching a bit more.*

The only other thing I can think of is my mobile phone. It's a smartphone and it's really cool! I never go anywhere without it. I use it all the time and send about twenty text ***messages*** *every day! (Luckily, Mum and Dad pay the bill.)*

Got to go. Love to your sister.

Take care,
Jessica ~~Saunders~~
(answers to exercise 4: wrong names are crossed out and corrected spelling mistakes are in bold.)

4

Aim: to correct mistakes in an email

- Ask students to read the model email in exercise 3 again.
- Explain that the writer has made five spelling mistakes and mistakes with the names that she has used.
- Students then work individually or with a partner to correct the mistakes.
- Elicit answers, asking students to spell out the corrected words and to explain what is wrong with the names.

5

Aim: to prepare students for the writing task

- Ask them to look at the writing task.
- Ask: *Will you be writing to a pen friend or a member of your family?* (a pen friend)
- Then ask: *Will you be writing about your family or your pen friend's family?* (your family)
- Then ask them to look at the list of questions and to tell you which information they think their pen friend will want to know and why.

Your pen friend will want to know about:
- how much television you watch
- whether you have a computer at home
- whether your parents have mobile phones

The other points are irrelevant.

6

Aim: to encourage students to plan their writing

- This exercise is designed to encourage students to use their imagination and to make sure that all students have enough ideas before they start writing.
- Remind students that careful planning will improve their emails.
- Ask students to look at the questions and to make notes in their notebooks.
- Remind them that they should be answering the questions with one or two sentences.
- Go round the class monitoring or helping where necessary.
- At the end of the exercise, ask individual students to read out their ideas.

1 *Dear* (friend's name)
2–6 students' own answers
7 Each student should write their own first name only.

- Ask students to turn to **Writing Planner 9** on page 159. Explain that each Writing Planner gives them a simple table to complete which helps them to put the right content in the right place in their piece of writing.
- Point out to students that each row of the table refers to a different part of their piece of writing and gives its purpose, together with useful expressions. Explain to students that they should complete the 'notes' column using their own ideas.
- Give students some time to complete the table. Invite a number of students to say what they have put in the 'notes' column for each part of the piece of writing. If possible, you may like to check the notes made by all students to ensure they have enough content to base their piece of writing on. Ask students to refer to the Writing Planner as they do their piece of writing.

7

Aim: to give students the opportunity to produce an informal email

- This exercise can be done in class or set for homework.
- Remind students of the importance of using a conversational tone, of answering the question by including the information from their notes and of dividing their composition into appropriate paragraphs (Refer to Unit 1.).

8

Aim: to encourage students to check their written work

- Draw students' attention to the checklist.
- When they have finished writing, ask them to read each statement and to tick each one that is true for them.
- Ask them to make sure that they have ticked all of the boxes before handing their email in to be marked.
- You might consider refusing to mark any email that does not meet all the criteria in the checklist and asking the student to rewrite.

Additional task

- In order to monitor whether students have checked their work carefully, you could ask them to underline in pencil on their emails places where they have 'used informal phrases', for example.
- Alternatively, invite individual students to read parts of their emails to the rest of the class or get students to exchange emails with each other and to check each other's emails for mistakes before handing them in.

Look Back

Aim: to review the unit and to practise scanning for specific information

- Students now have the opportunity to go back through the unit to check what they have learned.
- Ask the whole class the questions from **Look Back**.
- Elicit answers from different students.
- Encourage students to scan the unit to find any information they can't remember.

1 Wifi/Wi-Fi
2 come up with
3 (suggested answers) mouse, monitor, keyboard, keys, modem, speakers, screen
4 *put off* means to delay something until a later time whereas *call off* means to cancel a planned event
5 as long as

Suggested homework

Assign Ex. 1, 2, 3 and 4 – Workbook, p.67

Further material

- For further practice and consolidation, ask students to complete the Unit 9 tasks on the Student's CD-ROM.
- To test students' understanding of the material in Unit 9, you may like to administer the Unit 9 Test, which is in the Tests section of the Teacher's DVD-ROM. You may also like to construct your own test using the Test Generator material for Unit 9.

10

Let Me Entertain You

Target language

Grammar:	modals (1) / parts of speech / word formation: prefixes
Lexis:	topic vocabulary / confusable words /collocations (entertainment)
Reading skills:	distinguishing fact and opinion
Listening skills:	predicting
Speaking skills:	expressing attitude and opinion
Writing skills:	cohesion / essay
Pronunciation:	/ə/

- The phrase *let me entertain you* might be familiar to your students from a recent Robbie Williams song.
- Write the phrase *let me entertain you* on the board.
- Ask students what they think the title refers to.
- Explain where they might have heard the phrase *let me entertain you* before.
- Elicit suggestions as to what the unit might be about.

ON THE BOARD

let me entertain you

Start thinking!

Aim: to introduce the topic of entertainment through personal responses

- Ask students to work in pairs to talk about the questions in the Student's Book.
- Go round the class monitoring and helping where necessary.
- If you prefer, conduct a brief discussion involving the whole class by reading the questions and inviting different students to give their answers.

Reading CD2, Track 4

1

Aim: to read for gist

- Students are now going to read a newspaper column.
- Ask students to predict the type of TV shows that the critic might review.
- Ask students to read the column. This can be done individually or as a whole class activity with different students being asked to read different sections aloud to the rest of the class.
- Remind students that at this stage they do not need to understand all of the vocabulary as items will be covered in the **WORD BOX** section.
- Elicit answers from a few students as to which programme they would most like to watch and why.

Additional task

- In order to check your students' ability to scan for specific information, elicit the answers to the questions below.
- Remind students that they don't have to reread large parts of the passage but should look for clues or key words that might help them find the answer. The key words have been underlined in each sentence in case students need help.

1. What is the name of Channel 9's new reality show? (Staff Room)
2. How long does Lucy say that television has been popular for? (50–60 years)
3. Who presents Joke-a-Cola? (Max Read)
4. Which sitcom does Lucy think is badly written? (Oh! Those Kids!)
5. How long has SuperTV been on the air? (5 years)

2

Aim: to encourage students to think about the difference between fact and opinion

- Explain that in any piece of writing, but particularly journalistic writing, there will be a mix of facts which are true and the writer's own opinions. In order to help them distinguish between the two, remind students to look out for opinion markers. These are usually phrases which express opinion, such as: *I believe ...* , *In my opinion ...* , *I think that ...* , etc. They also need to be aware that factual information may consist of numbers or figures.

- Ask students to read the statements 1–6 and underline the part of the text which refers to them.
- Ask students to decide whether each statement 1–6 is a fact or an opinion.
- Elicit answers, asking for justification.

1 fact	3 fact	5 opinion
2 opinion	4 fact	6 fact

Additional task

- Ask students to underline other examples in the passage where the writer has expressed her own opinion or given factual information.
- Go round the class asking individual students to give you one piece of factual information and an opinion on television programmes that they watch.

3

Aim: to practise an exam-type task

- First, remind students of the best way to approach it so that they become familiar with exam technique.
- Remind them of the importance of looking for sentences from the passage which explain one of the four options A–D. It is also possible that they might be able to work out from the passage which three options could not be the answer.
- Direct students' attention to the first question.
- Ask: *Where does the writer mention something about a certain time of year?*
- Elicit the answer (the first paragraph *'I always look forward to this time of year ...'*).
- Ask: *What does the writer say about this time of year?*
- Elicit the answer (*'It's the time of year ... and every year I tell myself that it might be different. It never is.'*).
- Ask: *What would the writer like to be different and why is she disappointed?* (She would like the programmes to be better and she is disappointed because they never are.)
- Elicit the answer to question 1, asking students to explain whether this refers to the writer's opinion or a fact.
- Remind students of the importance of underlining where they found the answer within the passage, as this makes it much quicker and easier for them to be able to justify their answers.
- Ask students to work individually or with a partner to do the rest of the exercise.
- Elicit answers, asking for justification from the passage.

1 C	*'It's the time of year ... and every year I tell myself that it might be different. It never is.'*
2 A	*'This channel ... broadcasts a depressing mix of game shows ... They're also planning to repeat ...'*
3 A	*'It should be the hit of the summer ... Great stuff!'*
4 C	*'The first series was slightly amusing, the second hilarious.'*
5 D	*'What they should be doing is making new, exciting programmes.'*
6 C	*'... but it might not be popular forever.'*

WORD BOX

4

Aim: to introduce new vocabulary

- Before the students do this exercise, ask them to read the sentences.
- Remind them of the importance of looking back at the passage for clues if they are not sure of the meaning of any words.
- Ask students to work individually or with a partner to do the exercise.
- Elicit answers.
- Ask students if there were any other words in the passage which they didn't know the meaning of.
- Remind them to make a note of the words and to look them up in a dictionary before the start of the next lesson.
- Ask students if they enjoyed reading the TV review and whether they learned anything from it or not and get them to justify their answers.

1 Music videos	5 hilarious
2 entertaining	6 cast
3 hit	7 script
4 amusing	8 leisure time

Additional task

- Ask students to choose five words from the **WORD BOX** and to write their own sentences with the word missing.
- Students then swap their sentences with a partner and try to fill in the missing word.

Have your say!

Aim: to give students the opportunity to express their own opinions

- Put the students in pairs and get them to ask each other the questions. Ask them to make brief notes on their partner's answers. When they have finished, invite various students to tell the whole class what they discussed.

- Alternatively, you may like to do the activity as a whole class. Invite various students to give their opinions, encouraging them to agree or disagree with what other students have said. Encourage them to give reasons for their opinions.

Suggested homework

Assign Ex. 1 – Workbook, p.68–69
Ex. 1 – Workbook, p.69

G Grammar clinic

1

Aim: to review modals

- Before students do the exercises on this page, ask them to study pages 187–188 of the **Grammar database**, either in class or at home before the lesson starts.
- The first exercise refers back to the reading passage so that students can see the grammar in question being used in context.
- Read the sentences and ask students to tell you which modal is used in each sentence.
- Ask students to match each sentence to what it expresses.
- Point out to students that these are only examples of the meanings of these modals and that modals can often be used in two or three different ways.

1 c *Might* is used to talk about possibilities in the present, the future and generally.
2 b *Can't* is used to express an inability to do something.
3 a *Should* is used to say that something is probably true or will probably happen.
4 e *Must* is used here to draw a conclusion about other people.
5 d *Should* is used to ask for and give advice about now, the future, or generally.
6 f *Have (got) to* is used for obligation.

Additional task

- Ask students to write six sentences of their own which can be matched to the list of explanations in a–f.

2

Aim: to choose the correct meaning of modal verbs

- First, write this sentence on the board: *You can go to the cinema if you promise to be home by 11.*
- Ask students to tell you what the modal verb is in the sentence (*can*).
- Ask: *Is 'can' used here to say that someone is allowed to do something or that someone is capable of doing something?* (someone is allowed to do something)
- Ask: *So, is it used to express ability or to give permission in this sentence?* (to give permission)
- Go through the first sentence together.
- Ask: *What is the modal verb in the sentence?* (*should*)
- Ask: *Is 'should' used here to say that someone is allowed to do something or someone should do something because it's a good idea?* (someone should do something because it's a good idea)
- Elicit the answer to item 1.
- Remind students to go through this process of asking themselves questions about the sentence before they decide on the meaning of the verb.
- Ask students to work individually or with a partner to do the rest of the exercise.
- Elicit answers.

1 a	2 b	3 b	4 a

ON THE BOARD

You can go to the cinema if you promise to be home by 11.

3

Aim: to practise using modal verbs

- Before students circle the best verb to complete the sentence, go through the first one together.
- Ask: *What is the person doing in the sentence?* (giving advice)
- Ask: *Which of the modal verbs in a–c is used for giving advice?* (*should*)
- Ask: *Which other modal verb could be used in this sentence?* (*ought to*)
- Remind students to go through this process of asking themselves questions about the sentence before they choose the best verb.
- Ask students to work individually or with a partner to do the exercise.
- Elicit answers.

1 b	2 c	3 a	4 a	5 b

4

Aim: to practise rewriting sentences

- Students now rewrite sentences which are designed to practise what they have learned from exercises 1, 2 and 3.
- Before they attempt the task, ask them to look at the modal verb given in item 1.
- Based on what they have learned ask them to tell you which words in the first sentence they might need to replace (*will probably*).
- Elicit the answer to item 1.
- Remind students that when they have completed the sentences they should read them through again to make sure they make sense.
- Students then work individually to complete the exercise.
- Elicit answers.

1 Justin Bieber's new song should win an award.
2 Madonna might be recording a new album.
3 Listening to very loud music can damage people's ears.
4 You can get me a CD if you like, but you don't have to.
5 We ought to check to see if there are any tickets left.
6 I might go to the theatre while I'm in London.

Additional task

- Give students the following sentences and ask them to tell you what they would do in these situations using modal verbs.
  1 I've been getting really bad headaches lately.
  2 It's my brother's birthday next week and I want to buy him a present. He really loves listening to music.
  3 My mum has told me that I'm not allowed to stay out later than midnight.
  4 I'm having problems with my maths homework.

Suggested homework

Assign Ex.1 and 2 – Workbook, p.70

V Vocabulary builder

1

Aim: to focus on vocabulary connected to entertainment

- This exercise is probably best done as a whole class. If time allows however, divide the class into small groups and encourage them to use a dictionary in order to find the meaning of any unknown words.
- First, ask students to read through the questions 1–7 and underline any words which might act as clues.
- Elicit the clues and ask if there were any which they could do given the clues in the definition.
- As an example of this you could direct students' attention to question 3. The word *actors* suggests that the answer may be the verb *act*. Even if students don't know the words, searching for clues can sometimes help them to make an educated guess.
- Elicit answers.
- Encourage students to make a note of any new words or phrases that they learn in their notebooks.

1 stage	4 audition	6 review
2 play	5 critic	7 rehearsal
3 act		

Errors to watch out for

Students often make mistakes when talking about what actors do. You might hear them say things like *'My favourite actor, Brad Pitt, plays in this film.'* Remind them that it is more natural to say that someone *'plays the role of…' (Brad Pitt plays the role of the gangster in this film.)* or *'stars in a film' (Brad Pitt stars in the film* Seven.*)*.

2

Aim: to practise using vocabulary connected to entertainment

- Remind students that they need to use a word from exercise 1 to complete the sentences. They may have to change the word slightly.
- Remind students to reread the sentences when they have completed them to check for sense.
- Ask students to work individually or with a partner to do the exercise.
- Elicit answers.

1 reviews	4 critics	6 audition
2 play	5 stage	7 act
3 rehearsal		

3

Aim: to practise using words which are easily confused

- Before students attempt this task, write on the board: *famous* and *popular.* Ask students to explain the difference between them (*Famous* means known by a lot of people and *popular* means liked by a lot of people.).
- Ask students to look at the first item and decide which meaning is required (popular).
- Ask students to do the remaining items.
- Elicit answers, asking students to give you a definition of the words and an example sentence.
- Encourage students to learn these definitions by heart.

1 popular
2 famous
3 listen to (listen to = make an effort to follow or understand - hear = experience sound or noise)
4 hear
5 speak (tell = give information to sb - say = express in words – speak to = talk to sb)
6 tell
7 say
8 reading (read = get information from written words - study = concentrate on to learn or understand)
9 studying

ON THE BOARD

famous popular

Errors to watch out for

Students often make the mistake of omitting the word *to* from the phrase *'listen to music.'* Remind students that *listen* is followed by *to.*

4

Aim: to focus on collocations connected to entertainment

- Ask students to match the words and phrases to make collocations connected to entertainment and humour.
- Elicit answers.

1 b	2 a	3 e	4 c	5 d

5

Aim: to further practise collocations

- Ask students to quickly read the text and say what it's about (someone who can't tell jokes and doesn't get jokes).

- Ask students to complete the text by writing one word in each gap. Explain that students should use the phrases from exercise 4 to help.
- Give students some time to complete the task and then elicit the answers.

1 tell	3 finds	5 fun
2 have	4 get	6 of

Suggested homework

Assign Ex. 1 – Workbook, p.70
Ex. 2 – Workbook, p.71

Listening

Warm up!

Aim: to introduce the topic and warm students up

- Ask students if any of them have a video camera, or have video cameras on their phones. Ask what they use them for.
- Ask if students think it would be interesting to make a short film. Encourage them to say what they would like to make a film about if they had the chance.

1

Aim: to practise predicting

- Tell students that they are going to listen to a woman being interviewed on an online radio station.
- Before the students do this exercise, remind them of the best way to approach it so that they become familiar with exam technique.
- Remind them of the importance of listening for key words or phrases which could fit the gaps.
- Look at the first gap together. Elicit suggestions for what words could possibly complete the sentence (eg *in the holidays, after school, with their friends,* etc).
- Make a list of all the suggestions, including incorrect suggestions, on the board. Ask students to comment on whether all the suggestions are possible. Remove any suggestions the students identify as incorrect.
- Do not at this stage confirm any correct suggestions. Put the students into pairs and ask them to continue in the same way.
- Ask them to read through the sentences in exercise 2 and talk together about the kind of information that they think they might hear.
- Elicit their suggestions, asking for justification.

2

Aim: to practise an exam-type task

- Students now listen to the whole of the interview with the woman.
- Remind them that they will hear the interview twice. The first time they listen they should take notes and the second time they listen they should check their answers.
- Encourage students to complete all of the gaps. If they are not certain of an answer, they should make an educated guess.
- Finally, remind students that they only need to write a word or a short phrase.
- Play the listening text.
- Elicit answers, asking students to justify their answers by paraphrasing what they heard.

CD2, Track 5

1 in their free time
2 satisfying
3 (any) preparation (at all) / (quite a lot of) planning
4 expensive equipment
5 sound
6 full script
7 the director
8 wear their own clothes

3

Aim: to allow students to evaluate their predictions

- Ask students if any of their predictions turned out to be correct or nearly correct.
- Ask students if they think that predicting answers in this way is a useful strategy.

Soundbite

Aim: to practise listening for the sound /ə/

- Write these words on the board: *doctor, alive, photograph*
- Explain that the sound /ə/ is one of the most common sounds in English and appears in these words. Underline the appropriate syllable in each word.
- Model the sound for your students and invite students to repeat.
- Explain that students will hear someone read the sentence from their Student's Book and that they should pay particular attention to the way the underlined syllables are pronounced.
- Play the first part of the listening text.

CD2, Track 6

- Ask individual students to repeat the sentence that they have heard back to you, paying particular attention to the way they pronounce /ə/.
- Ask students to look at the list of words and to underline the syllable which they think contains the sound /ə/.
- Play the second part of the listening text and ask students to listen to check their answers.

CD2, Track 6

ON THE BOARD

doctor, alive, photograph

letter leisure about exercise entertain occur teacher

Speaking

1

Aim: to practise expressing attitude and opinion

- Ask students to decide what they like and dislike about the activities and to make notes in their notebooks.
- Remind students that they must be able to give reasons for their opinions.

Additional task

- You could extend this exercise by dividing the class into pairs and encouraging students to talk about their opinions together.

2

Aim: to practise an exam-type task

- Before students do this exercise, ask them to study the **Speaking database** on page 165.
- Divide the class into pairs. You could also do this exercise in groups of three, one student taking the role of the interlocutor, students then swapping roles.
- Remind students that the second part of the FCE interview requires them to be able to talk about the similarities and differences between two photographs for one minute.
- Explain to students that they will need to compare the photographs and explain what they like and dislike about each form of entertainment.
- Remind students that the questions they should answer will be printed above the pictures.
- Remind students that they can use the prompts in exercise 1 to help them and that they should be able to expand on these.
- Go round the class monitoring or helping where necessary.
- You might wish to set a time limit of three or four minutes for this.
- Elicit ideas.

Use of English

1

Aim: to practise identifying parts of speech

- Before students attempt this task, write this sentence on the board: *John walked _________ to the front of the class to collect his marks.*
- Elicit which part of speech would complete the sentence and why (an adverb, because it follows the verb and explains how the action was performed).
- Ask individual students round the class to come up with as many adverbs which could complete the sentence on the board as they can (eg *quickly, slowly, nervously*, etc).
- Remind students to look at words which come before and after the gap.
- Ask students to work individually or with a partner to do the exercise.
- Elicit answers.

1 a	2 b	3 a	4 b	5 a

ON THE BOARD

John walked _______________ to the front of the class to collect his marks.

2

Aim: to further practise parts of speech

- Students now look at the list of words in the box and decide which parts of speech they are.
- Ask students to use five of the words from the list to complete the sentences in exercise 1.
- Ask students to work individually or with a partner to do the exercise.
- Elicit answers.

loud - adjective loudness - noun
sizeable – adjective
decide - verb enjoyable - adjective
exciting - adjective
excited - adjective decision - noun
decisive - adjective
size - noun loudly - adverb enjoyment - noun
indecisive – (negative) adjective enjoy – verb

1 loudly 3 exciting 5 enjoyment
2 size 4 decide

Additional task

- After students have completed the exercise, draw a four-column table on the board with the following headings: *verb, noun, adjective* and *adverb.*
- Ask students to look at the words from exercise 2 and brainstorm any other forms of the words which they might know already and write them on the board in the appropriate column.
- Encourage students to copy the table into their notebooks. Remind them that these tables will help them when doing word formation exercises.

3

Aim: to practise writing example sentences using different parts of speech

- Ask students to choose two words from exercise 2 that they didn't know before and to write example sentences using those words.
- Divide the class into pairs.

- Students then compare their sentences to their partner's.
- Ask individual students to read their sentences to the rest of the class.

4

Aim: to practise using prefixes

- Ask students to look at the prefixes and to form the negative of the adjectives, nouns and the verb in the list. Stress that in exam-type word formation exercises students will need to work out for themselves whether the word required should be positive or negative.
- Ask students to work individually or with a partner to do the exercise.
- Elicit answers.

> unable (There is also the verb *disable* = cause something not to work)
> disability, inability (*disability* = physical or mental problem, such as not being able to walk; *inability* = lack of ability to do something)
> disadvantage / disapprove / disbelief / unbelievable / unclear / discomfort / uncomfortable / unemployed / unexpected / unlucky / disorganised / unsuitable

5

Aim: to practise an exam-type task

- First, remind students of the best way to approach it so that they become familiar with exam technique.
- Remind them of the importance of reading for gist.
- Ask students to read through the passage and tell you what the gist of it is (busking or street performance).
- Explain the importance of reading whole sentences rather than just single lines.
- Remind students, too, that they will need to think about not only whether the word should be a verb, noun, adjective or adverb but whether the word is plural or singular or positive or negative.
- Emphasise that spelling is extremely important.
- Remind them that the first word is given as an example.
- Once they have finished the exercise remind them to read the passage again to check for sense.
- Remind students that they should write only one word in each gap, and that each word should be in capital letters.
- Finally, remind students that they should always fill in an answer, even if they are not sure it is correct.
- Ask students to work individually or with a partner to do the rest of the exercise.
- Elicit answers.

1 ENTERTAINMENT	6 UNEXPECTED
2 UNEMPLOYED	7 UNABLE
3 SUITABLE	8 UNCOMFORTABLE
4 DISAPPROVE	9 UNLUCKY
5 ENJOYABLE	10 DISADVANTAGE

Suggested homework

Assign Ex.1 and 2 – Workbook, p.71
Ex. 1 and 2 – Workbook, p.72

Writing

1

Aim: to encourage students to think about the subject of the writing task

- Before students do the exercises on this page, ask them to study page 153 of the **Writing database**, either in class or at home before the lesson starts.
- Ask students to read the list of questions.
- Conduct a class discussion on the questions. Encourage students to justify their answers with reasons and examples.
- Encourage students to make a note of their opinions in their notebooks.

Additional task

- If time allows, organise a more formal debate on the question, 'Should children's TV educate or entertain?'. Divide students into those 'for' and those 'against' and allow them time to prepare their arguments as groups. Chair the debate.

2

Aim: to review essays

- Ask students to read the writing task and to tell you what kind of style would be appropriate and why.
- Elicit their ideas, asking for justification.

> This writing task is an essay, so it should be formal.

Additional task

- Encourage students to think about the kind of points that they could include in their essay (the type of programmes that children watch, which ones are popular, which type of programmes there should be more (or less) of, personal opinion on whether children's TV should educate or entertain, etc).
- Remind them that they need to be able to justify or give reasons for their opinions.

3

Aim: to provide a model answer for students to refer to

- Students now read the model answer to the question in exercise 2.
- Ask them to read the essay through once to get the gist.
- Then ask them to read through again quickly and to write one sentence which summarises each paragraph. Point out that that is the essay plan that the writer used.

> Paragraph 1: Children should be entertained because they work hard.
> Paragraph 2: Children's TV should be like TV for adults.
> Paragraph 3: All programmes teach us something.
> Paragraph 4: Children should be given quality entertainment.

4

Aim: to practise expressing opinion of a model essay

- Encourage students to give their opinion on whether this is a good essay, whether it answers the question correctly and whether they agree or disagree with the writer's main arguments (Yes – this essay would be given a high mark in the exam.).
- Remind students that they need to be able to give reasons for their opinions.

5

Aim: to raise awareness of grammatical cohesion

- This exercise is probably best done as a class.
- Before students attempt this task, write this paragraph on the board: *Some students prefer watching reality shows. For some students, reality shows are the most entertaining because reality shows feature real people and real people's lives can be fascinating.*
- Ask students to tell you which words can replace the underlined phrases to make the paragraph sound more natural (*them*, *they*, *their*).
- Point out to students that words like these that refer to things in other sentences help to hold the essay together.
- Direct students' attention to the words in red in the text.
- Ask them to read through the first paragraph and elicit what the words refer to.
- Go through the model essay paragraph by paragraph, asking students to tell you what the words in red refer to.
- Remind students that they might need to refer back to previous paragraphs in order to find the answer.

1 children
2 relax
3 watching television
4 game shows and drama series
5 game shows and drama series
6 children's
7 children's television
8 children

ON THE BOARD

Some students prefer watching reality shows. For some students, reality shows are the most entertaining because reality shows feature real people and real people's lives can be fascinating.

6

Aim: to review phrases used in essays

- Ask students to look at the words and phrases in blue.
- Ask them to match each of the phrases to what the phrase is used for.
- Remind students that these are words and phrases that they can learn and use in appropriate essays.
- Elicit answers.

1 for instance	4 First of all
2 To sum up	5 Secondly
3 Although / Despite	

7

Aim: to prepare students for the writing task

- Ask students to look at the writing task and to tell you the subject that they will be writing about (whether children today watch too much television).
- Elicit whether students agree or disagree with the statement that children nowadays watch too much TV, asking them to provide justification for their answers.

8

Aim: to encourage students to plan their writing

- Remind students that one of the things that examiners are looking for in essays is evidence of organisation and that careful planning can make an essay 'flow'. The better organised an essay, the higher the mark.
- This exercise is designed to encourage students to focus their attention on paragraphing, which aids cohesion.
- Ask students to think about the kind of information that they want to include in each paragraph and to make notes in their notebooks.
- Remind them that they can look back at the way their ideas were organised in exercise 8 of Unit 2 on page 21 if they need any guidance.
- Go round the class monitoring or helping where necessary.
- At the end of the exercise, ask individual students to read out their ideas.
- Encourage students to make a note of good ideas they hear.
- Ask students to turn to **Writing Planner 10** on page 159. Explain that each Writing Planner gives them a simple table to complete which helps them to put the right content in the right place in their piece of writing.
- Point out to students that each row of the table refers to a different part of their piece of writing and gives its purpose, together with useful expressions. Explain to students that they should complete the 'notes' column using their own ideas.
- Give students some time to complete the table. Invite a number of students to say what they have put in the 'notes' column for each part of the piece of writing. If possible, you may like to check the notes made by all students to ensure they have enough content to base their piece of writing on. Ask students to refer to the Writing Planner as they do their piece of writing.

9

Aim: to give students the opportunity to produce an essay

- This exercise can be done in class or set for homework.
- Remind students of the importance of using *it, this, them,* etc, to connect phrases and of answering the question by including the information from their essay plan in exercise 8.

10

Aim: to encourage students to check their written work

- Draw students' attention to the checklist.
- When they have finished writing, ask them to read each statement and to tick each one that is true for them.
- Ask them to make sure that they have ticked all of the boxes before handing their essay in to be marked.
- You might consider refusing to mark any essay that does not meet all the criteria in the checklist and asking the student to rewrite.

Look Back

Aim: to review the unit and to practise scanning for specific information

- Students now have the opportunity to go back through the unit to check what they have learned.
- Ask the whole class the questions from **Look Back**.
- Elicit answers from different students.
- Encourage students to scan the unit to find any information they can't remember.

1 hit
2 should
3 reviews
4 popular
5 a person who performs on the streets for money, by either singing, playing an instrument, juggling or doing magic tricks

Suggested homework

Assign Ex. 1, 2 and 3 – Workbook, p.73

Webquest

- Ask students to complete the **Webquest** on page 200 of the Student's Book. You might ask students to work on this together in class if you have internet access, or you might assign it for homework.
- Explain to students that the answers to the questions are not in the Student's Book but that they need to find the answers online.
- Check the answers together and ask students to explain where they found the answers and how they found them (eg by typing terms into a search engine).

1 2008
2 *Home and Away*
3 read-only memory (meaning that computers can read the data but can't write new data on the CD)
4 *My World*
5 Madonna Louise Ciccone
6 (29th June) 2007
7 Broadway
8 1960s
9 Stephenie Meyer
10 1879–1955

Further material

- For further practice and consolidation, ask students to complete the Unit 10 tasks on the Student's CD-ROM.
- To test students' understanding of the material in Unit 10, you may like to administer the Unit 10 Test and Term Test 2, which are in the Tests section of the Teacher's DVD-ROM. You may also like to construct your own test using the Test Generator material for Unit 10.

Revision Units 9-10

1

1 C	3 A	5 D	7 C	9 D
2 B	4 C	6 A	8 A	10 B

2

1 f	3 a	5 b
2 d	4 e	6 c

3

1 uncomfortable	5 unable
2 disorganised	6 disapprove
3 inability, disability	7 unsuitable
4 discomfort	8 unemployed

4

1 have gone off	4 made off
2 put off	5 call off
3 take off	6 turn off

5

1 popular	6 are saying / say
2 famous	7 hear
3 tell	8 read
4 speak	9 study
5 listen	

6

1 loudness	4 enjoyably
2 decision	5 sizeable
3 enjoyable	

7

(2 marks for each correct answer)

1 A	3 A	5 B	7 D
2 C	4 C	6 D	8 C

11

The Learning Curve

Target language

Grammar:	relative clauses / relative pronouns and prepositions / word patterns
Lexis:	topic vocabulary / phrasal verbs with *over* / metaphors (the mind)
Reading skills:	lexical referencing
Listening skills:	predicting
Speaking skills:	prioritising
Writing skills:	selecting correct register / informal letter/email
Pronunciation:	stress (1)

- The phrase *the learning curve* is the rate at which you learn something, eg *My first term at university was a steep learning curve, as I had never lived away from home before.* (The phrase *steep learning curve* suggests that you are forced to learn something very quickly.)
- Write the phrase *the learning curve* on the board.
- Ask students what they think the title refers to.
- Explain the meaning of the phrase *the learning curve.*
- Write the example sentence given above on the board.
- Elicit suggestions as to what the unit might be about.

ON THE BOARD

the learning curve

My first term at university was a steep learning curve, as I had never lived away from home before.

Start thinking!

Aim: to introduce the topic of education through personal responses

- Ask students to work in pairs to talk about the questions in the Student's Book.
- Go round the class monitoring and helping where necessary.
- If you prefer, conduct a brief discussion involving the whole class by reading the questions and inviting different students to give their answers.

Reading CD2, Track 7

1

Aim: to read for gist

- Students are now going to read a newspaper article. Begin by asking them to look at the title of the article and predict what it might be about.
- Elicit ideas.
- Ask students to read the article. This can be done individually or as a class activity with different students being asked to read different sections aloud to the rest of the class.
- Remind students that at this stage they do not need to understand all of the vocabulary as items will be covered in the **WORD BOX** section.
- Elicit answers from a few students as to how Abbot Hill School has changed since Elaine Atkins became head teacher.

Background information

- *The title 'Top Marks!' refers to the fact that Elaine Atkins improved her school.*

> Abbot Hill School has become one of the best schools in Britain. (*'Elaine Atkins, head teacher … into one of the best.'*)

Additional task

- In order to check your students' ability to scan for specific information from the passage, elicit the answers to the questions below.

- Remind students that they don't have to reread large parts of the passage but should look for clues or key words that might help them find the answer. The key words have been underlined in each sentence.

1 When <u>did Elaine Atkins</u> come to Abbot Hill School? (three years ago)
2 <u>Name a student of Abbot Hill</u>. (Sharon Tucker)
3 What is a <u>symbol of community</u> in the school? (the uniform)
4 Do Abbot Hill students have to do <u>after-class activities</u>? (No, they are not compulsory.)

2

Aim: to practise lexical devices

- Ask students to quickly scan the text to find the words listed in numbers 1–6.
- Remind them that the position of a word within a sentence can often help them to understand the meaning or the function of the word.
- Ask them to look at the sentence *So how has she achieved the impossible?* (after the first gap) and to tell you what the *she* and *the impossible* refers to (*She* refers to Elaine Atkins and *the impossible* to her achievements at Abbot Hill School).
- Go through the rest of the words in the same way, asking students to tell you what the words refer to.
- Point out to students that these linking devices can often help them to identify the missing sentence.

1 b	3 a	5 b
2 a	4 b	6 a

3

Aim: to practise an exam-type task

- Before the students do this exercise, remind them of the best way to approach it so that they become familiar with exam technique.
- Remind students of the importance of looking for lexical linking devices, which they practised in exercise 2.
- Encourage students to approach each of the sentences in the same way.
- Remind students of the importance of underlining key words or sentences which helped them find the answer within the passage, as this makes it much quicker and easier for them to be able to justify their answers in class and check their work in the exam.
- Ask students to work individually or with a partner to do the exercise.
- Elicit answers, asking students to indicate the words or phrases which helped them choose the answer.

1 G *'It was a failing school, and a school failing the community. Then, Elaine …' 'Today, the main problem she faces is a waiting list of parents …'*
2 A *'No, we're not going to do it like that anymore.' 'We're going to do it differently.'*
3 D *'I wanted them to feel they were part of what was going to happen.' '… will you support me?'*
4 H *'Children were being bullied, and no-one stopped the bullies.' 'The students thought they could get away with anything.'*
5 B *'… chaos in the classroom?' 'The teacher has to be in control.'*
6 F *'They can choose from sports, aerobics, … ' 'You name it – we offer it!'*
7 E *'Now, I look forward to coming.' 'I have a great time while I'm here … '*

WORD BOX

4

Aim: to introduce new vocabulary

- Before the students do this exercise, ask them to read the sentences.
- Remind them of the importance of deciding before they complete the sentence whether they need to look for a noun, adjective, verb or adverb in the passage.
- Ask students to work individually or with a partner to do the exercise.
- Elicit answers.
- Ask students if there were any other words in the passage which they didn't know the meaning of.
- Remind them to make a note of the words and to look them up in a dictionary before the start of the next lesson.
- Ask students if they enjoyed reading the article and whether they learned anything from it or not and get them to justify their answers.

1 school uniform	4 in trouble
2 bullied	5 compulsory
3 qualifications	6 school trips

Additional task

- Ask students to choose five words or phrases from the **WORD BOX** and to write a short paragraph about their school containing those words.

Suggested homework

Assign Ex.1 – Workbook, p.76–77
Ex. 1 – Workbook, p.76

Have your say!

Aim: to give students the opportunity to express their own opinions

- Put the students in pairs and get them to ask each other the questions. Ask them to make brief notes on their partner's answers. When they have finished, invite various students to tell the whole class what they discussed.
- Alternatively, you may like to do the activity as a whole class. Invite various students to give their opinions, encouraging them to agree or disagree with what other students have said. Encourage them to give reasons for their opinions.

G Grammar clinic

1

Aim: to focus on relative clauses

- Before students do the exercises on this page, ask them to study pages 189–190 of the **Grammar database**, either in class or at home before the lesson starts.
- The first exercise refers back to the reading passage so that students can see the grammar in question being used in context.
- Read the first sentence and ask students to tell you which relative pronoun is used (*which*).
- Ask: *If we remove the relative clause, does the sentence make sense?* (no)
- Explain that this is a defining relative clause. The relative clause that starts with *which* tells us exactly which things we are talking about and it can't be removed from the sentence.
- Ask students to tell you if *which* can be replaced by *that* and if so, why (Yes – because *that* can be used instead of *who* or *which* in defining relative clauses).
- Remind students that using *that* is more informal.
- Read the second sentence and ask students to tell you which relative pronoun is used (*which*).
- Ask: *If we remove the relative clause, does the sentence make sense?* (yes)
- Explain that this is a non-defining relative clause. It just gives us extra information and so isn't necessary.
- Ask students to tell you if *which* could be replaced by *that* and if so, why (No – because we do not use *that* in non-defining relative clauses).
- Point out that non-defining relative clauses are separated from the rest of the sentence by commas, whereas defining relative clauses aren't.
- Ask students to look through the article and the removed sentences and underline other sentences which contain relative clauses.
- Ask students to work individually or with a partner to do the exercise.
- Elicit answers, asking whether the sentences are like sentences 1 or 2.

1a F	1b T	2a T	2b F

'... the number of children who regularly played truant from school ...' (1)
'She told them some of the things which she wanted to change ...' (1)
'Now, there are a huge number of things which the students can choose from.' (1)
'Sharon Tucker, 16, who I met outside the school gates, summed up ...' (2)
'Today, the main problem she faces is a waiting list of parents who are desperate to get their children into the school.' (1) (*which* has been omitted)

2

Aim: to help students understand the difference between defining and non-defining relative clauses

- Ask students to look at the first sentence. Elicit whether the relative clause (*who went to the same school as me*) tells us who we are talking about or gives us extra information about someone (it gives us extra information; we know who we are talking about: '*my dad*'). Elicit that that means that the relative clause is non-defining.
- Put students in pairs and ask them to work through the rest of the sentences, in each case deciding whether the relative clause is defining or non-defining. Alternatively, you could do the task as a whole class or ask students to work individually.
- Give students some time to complete the task and then elicit the answers.

1 N	3 D	5 D
2 N	4 N	6 D

3

Aim: to practise relative clauses in context

- Remind students that they can't use *that* as a relative pronoun in non-defining relative clauses and that they can't leave out the relative pronoun.
- Ask students to work individually or with a partner to do the exercise.
- Elicit answers, asking whether each relative clause is defining or non-defining.

1 b	3 b	5 a
2 b	4 b	6 c

Suggested homework

Assign Ex. 1, 2 and 3 – Workbook, p.78

V Vocabulary builder

1

Aim: to focus on vocabulary connected to education

- This exercise is probably best done as a whole class. If time allows however, divide the class into small groups and encourage them to use a dictionary in order to find the meaning of any unknown words.

- First, ask students to read through the sentences 1–8 and underline any key words or phrases. These might be useful as clues to help them do the exercise.
- Go through the first sentence as an example.
- Elicit the key phrases *period of time, 45 minutes* and *students learn in a classroom.*
- Ask: *Which word describes the 45 minutes when students learn in a classroom?* (lesson)
- Elicit the key words or phrases for the rest of the sentences and ask if there were any which they could do given the clues in the sentence.
- Remind students that even if they don't know the words, searching for clues can sometimes help them to make an educated guess.
- Elicit answers.

1 lesson	5 suspend
2 play truant	6 subject
3 term	7 prefect
4 break up	8 expel

Additional task

- Have a class discussion about whether truancy is a problem at their school and what can be done to stop students playing truant.

2

Aim: to practise using vocabulary connected to education

- Ask students to complete the sentences with one of the words or phrases from exercise 1.
- Remind students that they might need to change the form of the word so that it makes grammatical sense.
- You might ask students to work with a partner to do the exercise.
- Elicit answers.

1 lessons	5 suspended
2 playing truant	6 expelled
3 prefects	7 break up
4 term	8 subject

3

Aim: to introduce phrasal verbs with *over*

- Point out to students that phrasal verbs that share the same particle *(up, down, out,* etc*)* sometimes have meanings that have something in common. All the verbs here use *over* and they all have something to do with movement or control.
- Ask students to speculate about what the car might have almost done to the cat.
- Elicit that the missing phrasal verb must mean something like *hit, hurt* or *injure.*
- Ask: *Why does the phrasal verb that completes the sentence not mean 'kill'?* (because the second sentence tells us that the cat was okay)
- Students then work individually to complete the sentences.
- Elicit answers.
- Remind students that sometimes phrasal verbs can have more than one meaning.
- After students have completed this task, write on the board: *The documentary about Russian wildlife was really boring so I ________.*
- Elicit which of the phrasal verbs from exercise 3 could fit this sentence. (*turned over*)
- Encourage students to make a note of the different meanings of phrasal verbs in their notebooks.

1 a	2 b	3 c	4 c	5 a

ON THE BOARD

The documentary about Russian wildlife was really boring so I ______________ .

Additional task

- Ask students to look up in a dictionary the other phrasal verbs from exercise 3 which weren't used to complete any of the sentences.
- Ask individual students to give you example sentences which you can write on the board.

4

Aim: to introduce students to metaphorical words and phrases used for talking about the mind

- Explain that when we talk about the mind we sometimes describe it as a container, like a box.
- Ask students to look at the phrases in the box and speculate on the meaning of any of them.
- Students then work individually or with a partner.
- Elicit answers.

1 in your mind
2 filled with
3 out of my mind
4 an open mind
5 at the back of my mind

Suggested homework

Assign Ex.1 – Workbook, p.78
Ex.2 – Workbook, p.79

Listening

Warm up!

Aim: to introduce the topic and warm students up

- Ask students to think about different schools in their area and to comment on differences between them. They may like to talk about differences in facilities, in size, in subjects offered, in amount of homework set, etc.

- Ask students what they think are the best two aspects of their school and what they think are the worst two aspects. You may like to put them in pairs to discuss this and then get students to share their ideas with the whole class.

1

Aim: to encourage anticipation and introduce the listening task

- Students are going to listen to five different people talking about a school.
- Before they listen, ask students to predict what they might hear the first speaker talk about.
- Ask the same question and elicit suggestions for the other four speakers.

(suggested answers)
The head teacher: good/bad exam results, better/worse results than previous years, school achievements in sporting events / extracurricular activities, etc
A pupil: subjects which they enjoy/dislike, their favourite teacher, what makes a good/bad lesson, etc
A teacher: size of classes, long hours, the different subjects that they teach, etc
The caretaker : difficulties of the job, litter, broken windows, graffiti, etc
A parent: good/bad exam results, feeling proud/ disappointed, etc

2

Aim: to practise listening to deduce meaning

- Students now listen to five people talking about a school.
- Before the students do this exercise, remind them of the best way to approach it so that they become familiar with exam technique.
- Remind them of the importance of listening for synonyms.
- Ask: *What words or phrases might someone use if they were talking about the school not having a very good sports team?* (poor performance, do badly, missed a goal, lost a game, etc)
- Ask students to read through the sentences A–F. Remind them that they will need to match one of the five speakers to one of the sentences and that there is an extra sentence which they will not need to use.
- Remind them that they will hear the piece twice. The first time they listen they should fill in any answers they hear and the second time they listen they should check their answers.
- Play the listening text.
- Elicit answers, asking students to justify their answers by paraphrasing what they heard.
- Ask students if they can tell you what each person liked or disliked about the school.

CD2, Track 8

Speaker 1 E: *'... I never really have a chance to speak to the teachers, apart from when they send for me when something is broken.'*
Speaker 2 B: *'Unfortunately, the head of English, Mrs Drinkwater, is retiring this year ...'*
Speaker 3 F: *'I've been in a number of schools, and none of them are quite as good as St George's.'*
Speaker 4 C: *'... and the students don't get hours and hours of homework, which is good.'*
Speaker 5 D: *'It's quite a traditional school, so we do things like Latin and we don't really do computers very much.'*

Soundbite

Aim: to practise correct stress in opinion phrases

- Divide the class into pairs.
- Ask students to work together to decide which of the words in the prompts in the Student's Book are stressed the most.
- Ask students to underline the words.
- Explain that students will now hear the sentences and they should listen and check their answers.
- Play the listening text.
- Elicit answers, making sure that students repeat the sentences back to you with the stress placed on the correct word.
- Remind students that these are phrases that they can use when they are expressing their opinion on a subject in Part 3 of the FCE Speaking paper.

CD2, Track 9

As far as <u>I'm</u> concerned, ... In <u>my</u> opinion, ... If you ask <u>me</u> ... To <u>my</u> mind, ... From <u>my</u> point of view,...

Speaking

1

Aim: to practise phrases used for prioritising ideas

- Remind students that in Part 3 of the FCE Speaking paper, they will be asked to make suggestions and discuss an issue with another student for three minutes.
- Elicit from students the phrases that they can use to make suggestions and write these on the board.
- Explain that when they make suggestions they should be thinking of how to prioritise their ideas. This means that they should be able to talk about why certain ideas are better or worse than others.
- Direct students' attention to the phrases in exercise 1.
- Explain that these are phrases that they can learn by heart and use to make suggestions during an interview.
- Ask them to complete the phrases using the words in the box.

- Students then work individually or in pairs to make phrases.
- Elicit answers.

X is not <u>as</u> useful <u>as</u> Y because …
The most useful <u>of</u> all is Z because …
<u>Out</u> of these ideas, X is most useful because …
After X,Y is the <u>second</u> best idea because …
Z is probably the <u>least</u> useful idea because …

2

Aim: to practise prioritising ideas

- Before students do this exercise, ask them to study the **Speaking database** on page 165.
- Divide the class into pairs. Read the instructions to the class.
- Remind students that the questions they should answer will be printed above the pictures.
- Explain that students should discuss how popular they think these after-class activities would be and which one they would recommend setting up.
- Go round the class monitoring and helping where necessary.
- You might wish to set a time limit of three or four minutes.
- Elicit ideas. After students have completed the task, discuss as a class which three ideas were the most popular.

Use of English

1

Aim: to practise using relative clauses with prepositions

- First, ask students to study page 190 of the **Grammar database**, either in class or at home before the lesson starts.
- Before students attempt this task, write this sentence on the board: *The hotel that we stayed had just been built.*
- Ask students to tell you what is wrong with the sentence (We need the preposition *in* at the end of the clause.).
- Ask individual students to come up to the board and rewrite the sentence using *where* and then *in which* (*The hotel where we stayed had just been built. / The hotel in which we stayed had just been built.*).
- Remind students that there are other prepositions that they can use, but that when they use *where* and *when* they don't need a preposition.
- Ask students to look at number 1.
- Ask students to tell you what they think corporal punishment is (physical punishment).
- Explain that it was common in the past for children to be physically punished at school for doing something wrong, but that this doesn't happen any more.
- Elicit the answer to number 1.
- Students then work individually or with a partner to complete the exercise.
- Elicit answers.

1 c	3 a	5 b
2 f	4 e	6 d

ON THE BOARD

The hotel that we stayed had just been built.

2

Aim: to practise using prepositional phrases

- Ask students to complete each prepositional phrase.
- Elicit answers.
- After checking the answers, write on the board: *Helen said that she was keen ___ horse-riding.*
- Elicit from students which is the correct preposition (*on*).
- Remind students that sometimes a different preposition can follow a verb and change the meaning.
- Write on the board: *Helen was keen for her brother to get married.*
- Explain that if you are *keen <u>on</u> something* you like doing it and if you are *keen <u>for</u> someone <u>to do</u> something* you want them to do it.

1 fond <u>of</u>
2 keen <u>on</u> something (keen <u>for</u> someone to do something)
3 aware <u>of</u>
4 concentrate <u>on</u>
5 refer <u>to</u>
6 complain <u>about</u> something (<u>to</u> someone)
7 interested <u>in</u>

ON THE BOARD

Helen said that she was keen ______ horse-riding.
Helen was keen for her brother to get married.

3

Aim: to practise an exam-type task

- Ask students to read through the passage and tell you what is unusual about Summerhill School (students do not have to attend lessons if they don't want to).
- Explain that at this stage it is not important to understand all of the words in the passage but draw students' attention to clues before and after the gaps that might help them find the answer. These include prepositions, articles, personal pronouns and determiners.
- Remind students that when they have completed the exercise they should read it through again, inserting the missing word in the gap to check for sense.
- Students then work individually or with a partner to complete the exercise.
- Elicit answers.

1 B	3 D	5 C	7 D	9 B
2 C	4 A	6 B	8 A	10 D

4

Aim: to encourage students to express their opinions

- Ask students to tell you what they think of Summerhill School and why.
- Encourage students to talk about whether they would like to go to a school like that and why / why not.

Suggested homework

Assign Ex.1 and 2 – Workbook, p.79
Ex. 1 – Workbook, p.80

Writing

1

Aim: to review informal letters/emails and develop awareness of register

- First, ask students to study page 154 of the **Writing database**, either in class or at home before the lesson starts.
- Ask students to read the writing task and to tell you who the letter should be written to (a female pen friend).
- Elicit why the letter is informal.

> because it is written to someone you know personally

Additional task

- Encourage students to think about the kind of information that they have to include in their letter to their pen friend (kind of schools there are – nursery, primary and secondary – and how old we are when we go there, education is free but there are some private schools, take exams every year, take important exams at 18 for university, etc).

2

Aim: to focus on aspects of informal letters

- Explain to students that they have already written informal letters/emails earlier in the course and so they should be familiar with the style.
- Ask them to read the statements and decide whether each one is correct or incorrect. They should tick the correct statements. You might put them in pairs to do this exercise.
- Give students some time to complete the task and then elicit the answers.

> 2 ✓ 6 ✓ 7 ✓ 8 ✓

3

Aim: to provide a model answer for students to refer to

- Students now read the model answer to the question in exercise 1.
- Ask them to read the letter through once.
- Then ask them to read it again quickly and to underline all the information from the notes that the writer has included in the letter.

> *Dear Andrea,*
> *Thanks for your letter! How was your party? You asked about the educational system here. <u>Well, most people go to nursery school between two and six years old</u>. I went when I was four and I loved it! <u>Then, from six onwards, education is compulsory and everyone goes to primary school</u>. The schools are usually quite small and <u>you stay there until you're 10. From 11 to 14, we go to secondary school. At 15, we move to another school – a bit like senior high in America. We stay there till 18</u> and then either get a job or go to university.*
> *<u>We take exams at school every year but the really important ones come at the age of 18. You have to get good grades to get into university</u>.*
> *I have to go shopping with my mum now. I hope that was useful! Write soon!*
> *Best wishes,*
> *Paul*

4

Aim: to encourage students to think about the style of informal letters/emails

- Ask students to decide whether the statements are true or false for the model.
- Elicit answers.
- Encourage students to give their opinion on whether this is a good letter, whether it answers the question correctly and whether Paul has included all of the information he should have (Yes – this letter would be given a high mark in the exam.).
- In particular, ask students to comment on how formal or informal the letter is, giving examples.

> 1 T
> 2 T The style of the composition is conversational or 'chatty'.
> 3 F Paragraphs are an essential part of any written work.
> 4 T Paul starts his letter by asking, *'How was your party?'*

5

Aim: to introduce students to American and British words for different schools

- Explain to students that there are differences between the vocabulary that Americans use to talk about the schools they go to and the vocabulary that British people use. Explain that the education system is different in each country so they shouldn't expect to find words that exactly describe their own school.
- Ask students to look at the words and phrases in the box and to read the text once to get the gist.
- Then ask students to read again, this time completing the passage using the words given.
- Elicit answers.

- Remind students that they can use British or American vocabulary for the schools they go to but that it's usually a good idea to try to be consistent.
- Ask students to make a note in their notebooks of the words that they are going to use.

1 nursery	5 elementary
2 primary	6 junior high
3 secondary	7 senior high
4 sixth form	

6

Aim: to encourage students to plan their writing

- Explain to students that they are going to write a letter in response to the writing task in exercise 1, describing the education system in their own country.
- Ask them to read the questions and to make notes in their notebooks of the information they are going to include about each aspect of the topic.
- Give students some time to complete the task and then elicit from different students the ideas they plan to include in their letter.

> 1 *Dear Andrea,*
> 2–6 students' own answers
> 7 Suggested answers: *Love; Lots of love; All my love; Write to me soon.*
> 8 Each student should write their own first name only.

- Ask students to turn to **Writing Planner 11** on page 160. Explain that each Writing Planner gives them a simple table to complete which helps them to put the right content in the right place in their piece of writing.
- Point out to students that each row of the table refers to a different part of their piece of writing and gives its purpose, together with useful expressions. Explain to students that they should complete the 'notes' column using their own ideas.
- Give students some time to complete the table. Invite a number of students to say what they have put in the 'notes' column for each part of the piece of writing. If possible, you may like to check the notes made by all students to ensure they have enough content to base their piece of writing on. Ask students to refer to the Writing Planner as they do their piece of writing.

7

Aim: to give students the opportunity to produce an informal letter

- This exercise can be done in class or set for homework.
- Remind students of the importance of using the correct vocabulary and of answering the question by including the information from their paragraph plan in exercise 6.

8

Aim: to encourage students to check their written work

- Draw students' attention to the checklist.
- When they have finished writing, ask them to read each statement and to tick each one that is true for them.
- Ask them to make sure that they have ticked all of the boxes before handing their letter in to be marked.
- You might consider refusing to mark any letter that does not meet all the criteria in the checklist and asking the student to rewrite.

Additional task

- In order to monitor whether students have checked their work carefully, you could ask them to underline in pencil on their letters places where they have 'used informal phrases', for example.
- Alternatively, invite individual students to read parts of their letter to the rest of the class or get students to exchange letters with each other and to check each other's letters for mistakes before handing them in.

Look Back

Aim: to review the unit and to practise scanning for specific information

- Students now have the opportunity to go back through the unit to check what they have learned.
- Ask the whole class the questions from **Look Back**.
- Elicit answers from different students.
- Encourage students to scan the unit to find any information they can't remember.

> 1 school uniform
> 2 school trip
> 3 yes
> 4 not go to school / attend lessons when you should
> 5 attendance is voluntary / not compulsory

Suggested homework

Assign Ex. 1, 2 and 3 – Workbook, p.81

Further material

- For further practice and consolidation, ask students to complete the Unit 11 tasks on the Student's CD-ROM.
- To test students' understanding of the material in Unit 11, you may like to administer the Unit 11 Test, which is in the Tests section of the Teacher's DVD-ROM. You may also like to construct your own test using the Test Generator material for Unit 11.

12

Fighting Fit

Target language

Grammar:	result clauses: *so, such, too, enough* / infinitives of purpose / word patterns
Lexis:	topic vocabulary / collocations: *make/do* / metaphors (problems)
Reading skills:	scanning for specific information
Listening skills:	listening for gist
Speaking skills:	discourse management
Writing skills:	awareness of purpose / report
Pronunciation:	/ɑː/, /ɔː/ and /uː/
Exam skills:	Reading Part 3; Listening Part 4; Speaking Part 4; Use of English Part 2; Writing Part 2 (report)

- The phrase *fighting fit* means that someone is very healthy, usually because they have been doing a lot of exercise or training hard, eg *After being in training for two years for this race, Paul Ratcliffe is fighting fit.*
- Write the phrase *fighting fit* on the board.
- Ask students what they think the title refers to.
- Explain the meaning of the phrase *fighting fit.*
- Write the example sentence given above on the board.
- Elicit suggestions as to what the unit might be about.

ON THE BOARD

> *fighting fit*
>
> *After being in training for two years for this race, Paul Ratcliffe is fighting fit.*

Start thinking!

Aim: to introduce the topic of health and fitness through personal responses

- Ask students to work in pairs to talk about the questions in the Student's Book.
- Go round the class monitoring and helping where necessary.
- If you prefer, conduct a brief discussion involving the whole class by reading the questions and inviting different students to give their answers.

Additional task

- Elicit from the students which items of food and drink they would consider to be healthy and unhealthy. You might need to prompt them by offering a few suggestions, eg pasta, chicken, cheese, hamburger, apples, etc.

Reading CD2, Track 10

1

Aim: to read for gist

- Students are now going to read information about a local fitness centre. Begin by asking them to look at the headings of the paragraphs and to say which of the activities on offer interests them the most.
- Ask them to read the article quickly to get the gist. Remind students that at this stage they do not need to understand all of the vocabulary as items will be covered in the **WORD BOX** section.
- Ask them to say whether places like this are popular in their country. Encourage them to expand on their answers.

2

Aim: to scan for specific information

- Remind students that they can look at the passage but they don't need to read it in detail again.
- Remind students of the importance of underlining where they find the answer in the passage.
- Ask students to work individually or with a partner to do the exercise.
- Elicit answers, asking for justification from the passage.

1 from Wednesday to Saturday, 1–2pm
2 on weekdays, 10–11am
3 from 7am–7pm, seven days a week
4 on the first Saturday of each month
5 on Friday at 12pm

3

Aim: to practise an exam-type task

- First, remind students of the best way to approach it so that they become familiar with exam technique.
- Remind them of the importance of looking for key words or phrases which are synonymous or similar in meaning to the words in the question.
- Remind them, too, of the importance of underlining where they found the answer within the passage, as this makes it much quicker and easier for them to be able to justify their answers in class and check their work in the exam.
- Finally, remind them that the activities may be chosen more than once and that some questions have more than one answer.
- Ask students to work individually or with a partner to do the exercise.
- Elicit answers, asking for justification from the passage.

1 D
2, 3, 4 A / B / D (in any order)
5, 6 B / C (in any order)
7 E
8 A
9, 10 A / C (in any order)

Additional task

- Ask students to write a short paragraph of 50 words explaining which activities they would prefer to do and why.

WORD BOX

4

Aim: to introduce new vocabulary

- First, ask students to read the sentences.
- Remind them of the importance of deciding before they complete the sentences whether they need to look for a noun, adjective, verb or adverb in the passage.
- Ask students to work individually or with a partner to do the exercise.
- Elicit answers.
- Ask students if there were any other words in the passage which they didn't know the meaning of.
- Remind them to make a note of the words and to look them up in a dictionary before the start of the next lesson.
- Ask students if they enjoyed reading the passage and whether they learned anything from it or not and get them to justify their answers.

1 in shape	4 aerobics classes
2 work out	5 muscles
3 trainer	6 body building

Additional task

- Ask students to choose five words or phrases from the **WORD BOX** and to jumble up the letters to create an anagram.
- Students then swap their anagrams with a partner who must try to find the word.

Have your say!

Aim: to give students the opportunity to express their own opinions

- Put the students in pairs and get them to ask each other the questions. Ask them to make brief notes on their partner's answers. When they have finished, invite various students to tell the whole class what they discussed.
- Alternatively, you may like to do the activity as a whole class. Invite various students to give their opinions, encouraging them to agree or disagree with what other students have said. Encourage them to give reasons for their opinions.

Suggested homework

Assign Ex. 1 – Workbook, p.82–83
Ex. 1 – Workbook, p.83

G Grammar clinic

1

Aim: to focus on result clauses

- First, ask students to study pages 191–192 of the **Grammar database**, either in class or at home before the lesson starts.
- The first exercise refers back to the reading passage so that students can see the grammar in question being used in context.
- Read the sentences and ask students to tell you which result clause is being used in each sentence (*so … that, enough … to, such … that, too … to*).
- Ask students to decide if the statements are true or false.

1 T: *'Racket sports are so popular that the courts…'*
2 F: *enough* comes after an adjective or adverb: *'It's big enough to keep…'*
3 F: *such* is followed by *a/an* + adjective + singular noun, adjective + plural noun or *a lot of* + noun and then *that*: *'Dance classes are such a great way to exercise that…'*
4 T: *'It's never too late to start!'*

2

Aim: to practise using result clauses

- Before students attempt this task, write this sentence on the board: *I'd put on some weight so that I decided to go on a diet.*
- Ask students to tell you what is wrong with the sentence (When *so* is used to mean *as a result,* it isn't followed by *that.*).

- Then write this sentence on the board: *I'd put on so much weight that I decided to go on a diet.*
- Elicit from students how they would rewrite the underlined part of the sentence using the word 'such' (*I'd put on such a lot of weight that I decided to go on a diet.*).
- Go through the first sentence together.
- Tell them to ignore the missing clause for the moment.
- Ask: *Which word in the sentence acts as a clue?* (*that*)
- Ask: *Why can't 'such' fit this gap?* (because *such* is followed by *a* or *an* and the adjective)
- Ask: *Why can't 'enough' fit this gap?'* (because *enough* comes after an adjective or adverb, not before it)
- Remind students to go through this process of asking themselves questions about the sentence before they fill in the gaps.
- Ask students to work individually or with a partner to do the rest of the exercise.
- Elicit answers.

1 so	3 such	5 enough
2 enough	4 too	6 so

ON THE BOARD

I'd put on some weight so that I decided to go on a diet.
I'd put on so much weight that I decided to go on a diet.

3

Aim: to practise using result clauses

- Before students attempt this task, ask them to look at the first sentence.
- Based on what they have learned from exercise 1, ask them to tell you what can follow *so* (an adjective/adverb and a *that* clause).
- Ask: *Which word from the first sentence do you need to replace?* (*very*)
- Ask: *Which is the adjective from the sentence that we need to use with 'so'?* (*unhealthy*)
- Elicit the answer to number 1.
- Remind them that they will need to rewrite the first sentence using the word given without changing it so that the sentence means exactly the same thing.
- Students then work individually or with a partner to rewrite the sentences.
- Elicit answers.

1 Fried food is so unhealthy that it can lead to a heart attack.
2 Some people take such a lot of pills that it must be bad for them.
3 My grandma isn't well enough to leave the house.
4 There are so many people who don't do enough exercise.
5 I'm too clumsy to be a surgeon.

4

Aim: to practise using result clauses

- Ask students to write four true sentences about themselves using result clauses: *so, such, too* and *enough.*
- Ask individual students to read out their sentences to the rest of the class.
- Students compare their sentences.

Suggested homework

Assign Ex. 1 and 2 – Workbook, p.84

V Vocabulary builder

1

Aim: to focus on vocabulary connected to medicine and health

- This exercise is probably best done as a whole class. If time allows however, divide the class into small groups and encourage them to use a dictionary in order to find the meaning of any unknown words.
- Before students attempt this exercise, ask them to read through the definitions 1–8 and underline any key words or phrases. These might be useful as clues to help them do the exercise.
- Go through the first definition as an example.
- Elicit the key words and phrases *spots, cough* and *shows you are ill.*
- Ask: *Which word describes the things that show you are ill?* (*symptom*)
- Elicit the key words or phrases for the rest of the definitions and ask if there were any which they could do given the clues in the sentence.
- Remind students that even if they don't know the words, searching for clues can sometimes help them to make an educated guess.
- Elicit answers.

1 symptom
2 GP (pronounced: 'jee-pee', with stress on the second syllable)
3 surgery
4 prescription
5 diagnosis
6 cure
7 injection
8 allergy

2

Aim: to practise collocations with *make* / *do*

- Before students attempt this task, write this sentence on the board: *I get home from school at 3.30 and make my homework before I go to basketball practice.*
- Elicit what is wrong with the sentence (you *do* homework, not *make* it).
- Explain that there are many collocations in English that use the verbs *make* and *do.*
- Ask students to tell you as many of the collocations they know with *make* or *do* and write them on the board.
- Students then work individually or with a partner to complete the phrases.
- Elicit answers.

- Encourage students to make a note of collocations that they learn in their notebooks.

make an appointment	do your homework
make a complaint	make the bed
do some exercise	make friends
do the housework	make a mistake
make a noise	make sure
make up your mind	do well at something
do your best	make a decision
make a fuss	make an effort
make a mess	do you good
make a phone call	make money
do the washing-up	do the shopping
make a suggestion	make a meal

ON THE BOARD

I get home from school at 3.30 and make my homework before I go to basketball practice.

3

Aim: to practise using collocations with *make / do*

- Ask students to write three example sentences in their notebooks using three collocations from exercise 2.
- Divide the class into pairs.
- Ask students to swap their notebooks and to compare their sentences with their partner's.
- Ask a few students to read out their sentences to the rest of the class.

4

Aim: to introduce students to metaphorical words and phrases used for talking about problems

- Explain that when we talk about problems, we often use words or phrases connected to illness.
- Students then work individually or with a partner to complete the sentences.
- Elicit answers.

1 get over	3 unhealthy
2 headache	4 recover

Suggested Homework

Assign Ex. 1 – Workbook, p.84
Ex. 2 – Workbook, p.85

Listening

Warm up!

Aim: to introduce the topic and warm students up

- Ask students if they think that people worry too much about what they eat, or perhaps don't worry enough about what they eat.
- Ask if they try to eat healthily. Ask what they think constitutes a healthy diet.

1

Aim: to practise listening for gist

- Students are going to listen to an interview with a woman who is on a diet.
- Remind students that they need to decide whether the answer is true or false based on what the speaker says.
- Before they listen, ask them to read questions 1–4, and ask them to make notes about the kind of information and the vocabulary that they might hear for each of the four questions.
- Play the listening text.
- Elicit answers, asking students to justify their answers by paraphrasing what they heard.

CD2, Track 11

1 F *'It's just to get healthy, really. I've been feeling a bit down recently, so I thought I'd try to get a bit fitter.'*
2 T *'The first thing is that you can eat whatever you want.'*
3 T *'The idea is that you have to have a balanced diet, you know, with a bit of everything in it, even fast food.'*
4 F *'When you eat something from each group, that's one point, and you have to count your points each day. You have to have two points from each group.'*

2

Aim: to further practise listening for gist

- Students now hear the same interview again.
- Before they listen, ask them to read questions 1–5 and to see if they can answer any of the questions based on what they heard the first time.
- Play the listening text.
- Elicit answers, asking students to justify their answers by paraphrasing what they heard.

CD2, Track 11

1 B *'… I just felt like I didn't have any energy.'*
2 A *'The first thing you have to do is learn a lot about how healthy different kinds of food are and why.'*
3 B *'The idea is that you have to have a balanced diet, you know, with a bit of everything in it.'*
4 C *'Dairy products. You know, eggs …'*
5 B *'… there are five basic kinds of food.' 'You have to have two points from each group, apart from the 'Enjoyment' group, where you can have one point.'*

Soundbite

Aim: to practise listening for the sounds /ɑː/, /ɔː/ and /uː/

- Ask students to look at the vowels that are underlined in each of the words and to circle which word in each group of four has a different vowel sound.
- Play the listening text.
- Students check their answers as they listen.
- When they have finished ask a few students to say the words to you, making sure that they pronounce the words correctly.

CD2, Track 12

1 car fat father can't
2 word sword court bored
3 boot look too shoot

Additional task

- Divide the class into pairs.
- Ask students to write three sentences which include at least two of the words from each group of four in their notebooks.
- Students then swap their notebooks with their partner, who must read the sentences aloud.
- Go round the class monitoring and helping, where necessary.
- Elicit some sentences from individual students.

Speaking

1

Aim: to practise phrases used for discourse management

- Remind students that in many exams, including Cambridge FCE, they are asked to give their opinion on a topic of general interest.
- Explain that they will need to use phrases to organise their ideas and opinions and to introduce any examples they want to make.
- Read the question to the students and ask them to look at the phrases.
- Students then work individually or with a partner to complete the text.
- Elicit answers.

Yes, we are. To begin with, we have a better diet. For example, people today eat more fruit and vegetables. Of course, we also eat more fast-food, but generally our diet is better. Secondly, doctors can cure more illnesses, so we live longer. Yes, we're definitely healthier today.

2

Aim: to practise an exam-type task

- Before students do this exercise, ask them to study the **Speaking database** on page 165.
- Students now work in pairs to discuss their opinions.
- Ask students to read the questions and prompts given.
- Ask students to discuss the questions with their partner.
- Remind them to use the phrases from exercise 1 when giving examples and to use the prompts from the Student's Book.
- Go round the class monitoring and helping, where necessary.
- Elicit ideas from individual students.

Use of English

1

Aim: to practise using infinitives of purpose

- Before students do the exercises on this page, ask them to study page 192 of the **Grammar database**, either in class or at home before the lesson starts.
- Before students attempt this task, write this sentence on the board: *I watched the weather forecast for to see if it would rain.*
- Elicit what is wrong with the sentence (We use a full infinitive to refer to someone's purpose but we don't need to use the preposition *for* as well.).
- Remind students that they can also use the phrase *in order* before the full infinitive but, in general, *in order* is more formal than the full infinitive on its own.
- Then, write this sentence on the board: *I took an umbrella in order not to get wet.*
- Ask students to tell you what can replace the underlined words (*so as not*).
- Remind students that with a negative infinitive and with stative verbs, we normally use *in order not* or *so as not*. The full infinitive is not normally used on its own.
- Students then work individually or with a partner to rewrite the sentences.
- Elicit answers.

2 I went on a strict diet in order to lose some weight. / In order to lose some weight, I went on a strict diet.
3 My mum takes vitamin tablets in order not to get ill. / In order not to get ill, my mum takes vitamin tablets.
4 Many people take up sports so as to keep fit. / So as to keep fit, many people take up sports.
5 I try to eat lots of fruit in order to stay healthy. / In order to stay healthy, I try to eat lots of fruit.
6 I wore a warm coat and a scarf in order not to catch a cold. / In order not to catch a cold, I wore a warm coat and a scarf.

ON THE BOARD

I watched the weather forecast for to see if it would rain.
I took an umbrella in order not to get wet.

2

Aim: to practise word patterns

- Before students attempt this task, write on the board: *'Congratulations about/on winning the lottery,' said Kevin.*
- Elicit from students which is the correct preposition (*on*).
- Remind them that the preposition which follows a gap often acts as a clue.
- Ask students to look at the words in the box.
- Ask students to underline the prepositions in each of the sentences and to see if they can match each of the prepositions to one of the verbs.
- Do the first one together.
- Students then work individually or with a partner to complete the exercise.
- Elicit answers.

1 approve	5 congratulate
2 capable	6 succeed
3 manage	7 afraid
4 prevent	8 objected

ON THE BOARD

'Congratulations about/on winning the lottery,' said Kevin.

3

Aim: to practise using word patterns

- Ask students to write three example sentences in their notebooks using three words from exercise 2.
- Divide the class into pairs.
- Ask students to swap their notebooks and to compare their sentences with their partners.
- Ask a few students to read out their sentences to the rest of the class.

4

Aim: to practise an exam-type task

- Students now do a gap-filling exercise which is designed to practise what they have learned from exercises 1 and 2.
- Ask students to read through the passage and tell you what the gist of it is (what alternative medicine is).
- Explain that at this stage it is not important to understand all of the words but draw students' attention to clues before and after the gaps that might help them find the answer. These include prepositions, articles, personal pronouns and determiners.
- Remind students that when they have completed the exercise they should read it through again to check for sense.
- Remind students that they should write only one word in each gap, and that each word should be in capital letters.
- Students then work individually or with a partner to complete the exercise.
- Elicit answers.

1 A	6 ON
2 WHETHER/IF	7 SO
3 TO	8 INTO
4 ORDER	9 WHICH
5 OF	10 FROM

Suggested homework

Assign Ex. 1 and 2 – Workbook, p.85
Ex. 1 and 2 – Workbook, p. 86

Writing

1

Aim: to encourage students to think about the purpose for writing

- First, ask students to study page 151 of the **Writing database**, either in class or at home before the lesson starts.
- Remind students that one of the things they need to think about in any type of written work is the purpose for writing, because often the purpose will dictate the kind of style, language and level of formality.
- As an example, focus their attention on the list of purposes a–h.
- Ask: *Which of these is the main purpose for writing an informal letter?* (to gossip and swap news)
- Students then work in pairs to match the types of writing to the purposes.
- Elicit answers.

1 f	3 c	5 g	7 h
2 e	4 a	6 b	8 d

2

Aim: to review report writing

- Ask students to read the writing task and to tell you who is going to read the report and what it should be about. (the report is about health facilities for tourists coming to the local area)
- Elicit why the report should be formal (because it is written to be read by your manager).

> The manager of a local tourist office is going to read the report.

Additional task

- Encourage students to think about the kind of information that they could include in their report (describe the kind of health facilities there are, the cost, whether tourists are treated at the doctor's for free, etc).

3

Aim: to provide a model answer for students to refer to

- Ask them to read the model answer through once.
- Then ask them to read it again quickly and to underline all the information that the writer has included about health facilities.
- Encourage students to give their opinion on whether this is a good report, whether it answers the question correctly and whether the writer has included all of the information they should have (Yes – this is a good report, although the writer has made some mistakes at the beginning.).

> *To:* ***My manager***
> *From:* ***Me***
> *Subject:* ***What you asked me to do***
> ***Introduction***
> *As requested, I have done some research into health facilities in this area. There is a hospital, an eye clinic and a large number of doctors' surgeries. This is very good for such a small town.*
> ***Westford hospital***
> *Westford hospital is modern, with beds for about 1,000 patients. They deal with illnesses and accidents, although people who are seriously ill are moved to Pentonfield, 20 miles away. Tourists are treated at the hospital for free.*
> ***Westford Eye Clinic***
> *Westford has very good facilities for eye problems. The eye clinic takes patients from all over the world and the doctors and surgeons are very highly trained. It is unlikely that tourists would need the eye clinic.*
> ***Doctors' surgeries***
> *There are about thirty GPs' surgeries in Westford. They deal with minor illnesses and accidents. Most of them charge for treating people who are not local residents.*
> ***Conclusion***
> *In conclusion, it is clear that Westford has excellent medical facilities for a small town. Tourists are welcome at the hospital and eye clinic, although they may have to pay to see a local GP.*

Additional task

- Ask students to work together in pairs to come up with alternative headings for each of the three main paragraphs.

4

Aim: to encourage students to think about the style of reports

- Elicit from students what is wrong with the beginning of the model report.
- Remind students that they can use their own names after the word *From* but that they will need to think of an imaginary name to write after *To.*
- Explain that they will also need to think of a suitable subject for their report, which should be short and clear.
- Elicit how the model report should have started, asking for a few different suggestions on the subject of the report.
- Decide as a class which subject is the most suitable.
- You might like to point out to students that they could also add *Date* at the start of the report.

> ***To:*** *Elizabeth Watson*
> ***From:*** *Sharon Gilmore*
> ***Subject:*** *Health facilities in the area / Health facilities in the area for tourists*

5

Aim: to encourage students to think about the style of reports

- Remind students to look back at the model report in exercise 3 to help them with the true or false statements.
- Ask students to work individually or with a partner to do the exercise.
- Elicit answers, asking for justification from the model report.

> 1 F: The language is generally formal. For example: *As requested*
> 2 T
> 3 T: Each piece of information is dealt with separately under a different heading.

6

Aim: to prepare students for the writing task

- First, remind students of the importance of identifying who they are writing to.
- Then ask: *Will you be writing about which gym you belong to or about gyms in the local area?* (about gyms in the local area)
- Then ask: *Do you need to make any suggestions?* (Yes – in the last paragraph students can make suggestions about which gym they would recommend.)
- Elicit who will be reading the report.

> the manager of the sports shop

7

Aim: to encourage students to plan their writing

- This exercise is designed to encourage students to use their imagination and to make sure that all students have enough ideas before they start writing.
- Ask students to look at the questions and to make notes in their notebooks.
- Remind them that they will need to think of the names of three gyms. You might like to encourage them to use their imagination.
- Students should be answering the questions with one or two sentences.
- Go round the class monitoring or helping where necessary.
- At the end of the exercise, ask individual students to read out their ideas.

- If you have time, check that all students have completed the questions with appropriate information.

1	***To:*** *Mr* [name of manager] ***From:*** [student's first and second names] ***Subject:*** *Gym facilities in our area / Recommendations on gym facilities in our area,* etc
2–6	students' own answers

- Ask students to turn to **Writing Planner 12** on page 160. Explain that each Writing Planner gives them a simple table to complete which helps them to put the right content in the right place in their piece of writing.
- Point out to students that each row of the table refers to a different part of their piece of writing and gives its purpose, together with useful expressions. Explain to students that they should complete the 'notes' column using their own ideas.
- Give students some time to complete the table. Invite a number of students to say what they have put in the 'notes' column for each part of the piece of writing. If possible, you may like to check the notes made by all students to ensure they have enough content to base their piece of writing on. Ask students to refer to the Writing Planner as they do their piece of writing.

8

Aim: to give students the opportunity to produce a report

- This exercise can be done in class or set for homework.
- Remind students of the importance of keeping their purpose in mind, of using formal language and of answering the question by including the information from their notes in exercise 7.

9

Aim: to encourage students to check their written work

- Draw students' attention to the checklist.
- When they have finished writing, ask them to read each statement and to tick each one that is true for them.
- Ask them to make sure that they have ticked all of the boxes before handing their report in to be marked.
- You might consider refusing to mark any report that does not meet all the criteria in the checklist and asking the student to rewrite.

Additional task

- In order to monitor whether students have checked their work carefully, you could ask them to underline in pencil on their reports places where they have 'used formal language', for example.
- Alternatively, invite individual students to read parts of their report to the rest of the class or get students to exchange reports with each other and to check each other's reports for mistakes before handing them in.

Look Back

Aim: to review the unit and to practise scanning for specific information

- Students now have the opportunity to go back through the unit to check what they have learned.
- Ask the whole class the questions from **Look Back**.
- Elicit answers from different students.
- Encourage students to scan the unit to find any information they can't remember.

1 work out	4 do a suggestion
2 a bad thing	5 on
3 a prescription	

Suggested homework

Assign Ex. 1 and 2 – Workbook, p.87

Webquest

- Ask students to complete the **Webquest** on page 200 of the Student's Book. You might ask students to work on this together in class if you have internet access, or you might assign it for homework.
- Explain to students that the answers to the questions are not in the Student's Book but that they need to find the answers online.
- Check the answers together and ask students to explain where they found the answers and how they found them (eg by typing terms into a search engine).

1 Coventry
2 Doctor of Philosophy
3 maths/mathematics
4 GCSEs
5 O-levels
6 pharmacist
7 J. M. Barrie
8 Great Ormond Street Hospital
9 Peter Pan
10 shoulder blade

Further material

- For further practice and consolidation, ask students to complete the Unit 12 tasks on the Student's CD-ROM.
- To test students' understanding of the material in Unit 12, you may like to administer the Unit 12 Test, which is in the Tests section of the Teacher's DVD-ROM. You may also like to construct your own test using the Test Generator material for Unit 12.

Revision Units 11-12

1

1 D	3 A	5 B	7 A	9 D
2 C	4 C	6 C	8 C	10 B

2

1 A	2 C	3 C	4 A	5 B

3

1 make	5 make	8 make
2 do	6 make	9 do
3 make	7 make	10 make
4 do		

4

1 broke up	4 take over
2 working out	5 got over
3 run over	

5

1 of	5 on	8 in
2 about	6 of	9 from
3 of	7 on	10 to
4 of		

6

1 prevent (it) from	6 aware of
2 complained about	7 capable of
3 concentrate on	8 approve of
4 afraid of	9 keen on
5 referring to	10 succeed in

7

1 enough	3 so	5 too
2 so	4 such	

8

1 compulsory	4 muscles
2 surgery	5 qualifications
3 trainer	

13

Art Attack

Target language

Grammar:	the causative / gradable and ungradable adjectives and adverbs / synonyms
Lexis:	topic vocabulary / word formation (suffixes) / metaphors (description)
Reading skills:	understanding main points
Listening skills:	identifying relationships
Speaking skills:	talking about interests
Writing skills:	making recommendations / review
Pronunciation:	silent letters (2)

- The title *art attack* suggests a sudden desire to produce or create something artistic and is a play on the phrase *heart attack*. It was also the title of a popular children's TV show about art.
- Write the words *art attack* on the board.
- Ask students what they think the title refers to.
- Explain the meaning of an *art attack*.
- Elicit suggestions as to what the unit might be about.

ON THE BOARD

art attack

Start thinking!

Aim: to introduce the topic of art and music through personal responses

- Ask students to work in pairs to talk about the questions in the Student's Book.
- Go round the class monitoring and helping where necessary.
- If you prefer, conduct a brief discussion involving the whole class by reading the questions and inviting different students to give their answers.

Reading CD2, Track 13

1

Aim: to read for gist

- Students are now going to read a short story about an art competition. Begin by asking them to look at the title of the short story and elicit what the story is about.
- Ask students to read the short story. This can be done individually or as a class activity with different students being asked to read different sections aloud to the rest of the class.
- Remind students that at this stage they do not need to understand all of the vocabulary as items will be covered in the **WORD BOX** section.
- Ask a few students to describe briefly what happens in the story.

> Sadie took part in a painting competition and won; as a result her painting was displayed in an art gallery in London.

Additional task

- In order to check your students' ability to scan for specific information, elicit the answers to the questions below.
- Remind students that they don't have to reread large parts of the text but should look for clues or key words that might help them find the answer. The key words have been underlined in each sentence.

> Which paragraph refers to:
> 1 Somebody thinking about what she could paint? (paragraph 3)
> 2 Someone believing that she hadn't won? (paragraph 6)
> 3 Drawing a picture of someone in her family? (paragraph 9)
> 4 A telephone call? (paragraph 6)
> 5 Someone's friends being away? (paragraph 2)

2

Aim: to practise understanding the main points of a text

- Ask students to read the list of things that the writer has mentioned in each of the paragraphs.
- Remind students that they don't have to reread large parts of the story, but that they should look for clues or key words that might help them find the answer.
- Elicit answers, asking for justification.

1 d	*'Not that,' said her mum. 'This!'*
2 b	*'Sadie read it aloud.'*
3 g	*'For hours, she ran through the options.'*
4 a	*'She spent hours each day up in her room.'*
5 e	*'Don't worry, love, … I've got my fingers crossed for you.'*
6 f	*'… and I'm very pleased to tell you that your painting has been selected.'*
7 c	*'Sadie and her mum were standing on the pavement outside the Shoreham Gallery.'*

3

Aim: to practise an exam-type task

- Before students do this exercise, remind them of the best way to approach it so that they become familiar with exam technique.
- Ask them to read sentence A. Elicit which word or phrase might act as a clue to which gap the sentence fits (*They might look good*).
- Remind students that they need to look for information before or after the gap.
- Remind them also of the importance of looking for discourse markers such as relative and personal pronouns, defining and non-defining clauses and determiners.
- Elicit suggested answers but do not negate or confirm them at this stage.
- Encourage students to approach each of the sentences in the same way.
- Remind students of the importance of underlining the words which helped them find the answer within the passage, as this makes it much quicker and easier for them to be able to justify and check their answers.
- Finally, remind them that there is one extra sentence which they do not need to use.
- Ask students to work individually or with a partner.
- Elicit answers, asking students to indicate the words or phrases which helped them choose the answer.

1 D	*'That gives me three weeks.' 'All my friends are on holiday.'*
2 A	*'I'm not doing an abstract …' 'It's got to be something with detail.'*
3 G	*'If I win …' 'If I don't, then it's not worth seeing anyway.'*
4 B	*'… no news from the competition …' 'It'll take them a bit of time to choose the winners.' 'You'll hear one way or the other in time.'*
5 C	*'I'm calling about the painting competition you entered.'*
6 F	*'… standing on the pavement outside …' '… before entering …'*

Additional task

- Ask students to suggest headings for each of the paragraphs.

WORD BOX

4

Aim: to introduce new vocabulary

- Before the students do this exercise, ask them to read the definitions.
- Remind them of the importance of deciding before they complete the definitions whether they need to look for a noun, adjective or verb from the words in the box.
- Ask students to work individually or with a partner to do the exercise.
- Elicit answers.
- Ask students if there were any other words in the passage which they didn't know the meaning of.
- Remind them to make a note of the words and to look them up in a dictionary before the start of the next lesson.
- Ask students if they enjoyed reading the story and whether they learned anything from it or not and get them to justify their answers

1 talent	5 sketch
2 art gallery	6 abstract
3 work of art	7 genius
4 portrait	8 creative

Additional task

- Ask students to choose five words or phrases from the **WORD BOX** and to write their own sentences with the word missing.
- Students then swap their sentences with a partner and try to fill in the missing word.

Have your say!

Aim: to give students the opportunity to express their own opinions

- Put the students in pairs and get them to ask each other the questions. Ask them to make brief notes on their partner's answers. When they have finished, invite various students to tell the whole class what they discussed.
- Alternatively, you may like to do the activity as a whole class. Invite various students to give their opinions, encouraging them to agree or disagree with what other students have said. Encourage them to give reasons for their opinions.

Suggested homework

Assign Ex. 1 – Workbook, p.90–91
Ex. 1 – Workbook, p.90

G Grammar clinic

1

Aim: to review the causative

- First, ask students to study page 193 of the **Grammar database**, either in class or at home before the lesson starts.
- Read the sentence in italics and ask students to tell you who is going to paint the portrait.
- Ask students to answer questions 2 and 3.
- Elicit answers.
- Remind students that the causative is formed by using the verb *have* + object + past participle, but that they can also use the verb *get*, which is less formal. As with the passive voice, they can use *by* when they want to say who does the action.

> 1 b 2 b 3 have
> *Get* can also be used

Additional task

- Ask students to write three sentences of their own which use the causative and which describe things that they have done for them by someone else.
- You might like to write the example sentence: *I have my teeth checked by the dentist every six months.* on the board.

ON THE BOARD

> *I have my teeth checked by the dentist every six months.*

2

Aim: to practise using the causative

- Before students attempt this task, write this sentence on the board: *Mum's new washing machine is being put in at the moment.*
- Ask students to explain to you whether Mum is putting in the washing machine or whether someone else is doing it for her (someone else is doing it for her).
- Ask a volunteer to write a causative sentence on the board that means the same as the sentence above (*Mum is having her new washing machine put in at the moment.*).
- Remind students to go through this process of asking themselves questions about the sentence before they choose the answer.
- Students then work individually or with a partner to do the exercise.
- Elicit answers.

> 1 b 2 a 3 b 4 a

ON THE BOARD

> *Mum's new washing machine is being put in at the moment.*

3

Aim: to practise using the causative

- Go through the first one together.
- Explain that there are two objects in this sentence because there are two different actions taking place.
- Ask: *What are the two objects of the sentence?* (*your hair* and *your photo*)
- Ask: *Should the objects come after or before the verb 'have'?* (after)
- Elicit the answer to number 1.
- Remind students to go through this process of asking themselves questions about the sentence before they correct it.
- Ask students to work individually or with a partner to do the exercise.
- Elicit answers, asking students to tell you which sentence is correct.

> 1 Why don't you have your hair cut before you have your photo taken?
> 3 Not many people have had their portrait painted by a famous artist.
> 4 My dad has had a book published about the history of art.
> 5 Many companies have new works of art created for them.
> Sentence 2 is correct.

4

Aim: to practise an exam-type task

- Students now do sentence transformations which are designed to practise what they have learned from exercises 1, 2 and 3.
- First, ask students to look at the word in bold in number 1.
- Based on what they have learned from exercise 2 ask them to tell you the object of the first sentence (the new gallery).
- Ask: *What verb do we need to use before the object?* (*have*)
- Ask: *And which verb do we need to use after the object?* (the past participle of the verb *open*)
- Elicit the answer to number 1, reminding students that the person who is doing the action is important information so we use *by*.
- Remind students to go through this process of asking themselves questions about the sentence before they rewrite it.
- Remind them that they will need to rewrite the first sentence using the word in bold so that the second sentence means exactly the same thing. They shouldn't change the word given and they will need to use between two and five words.
- Remind them that contractions such as *don't, doesn't, hasn't,* etc count as two words. The exception to this is *can't* which counts as one word (because it comes from *cannot*).

- Remind students that when they have completed the sentences they should read them through again to make sure they have followed the instructions properly.
- Students then work individually to complete the exercise.
- Elicit answers.

1 They hope to <u>have the new gallery opened</u> by the Queen.
2 The museum <u>has had ten paintings stolen</u> in the last four months.
3 We are going to <u>have a school wall painted</u> by a famous graffiti artist.
4 We are <u>having some music written</u> especially for our wedding.
5 Jen <u>got her poster designed by</u> a friend.
6 They <u>were having their/the hall redecorated</u> when I went round.

Suggested homework

Assign Ex. 1, 2 and 3 – Workbook, p.92

V Vocabulary builder

1

Aim: to focus on topic vocabulary

- Ask students to look at the pictures.
- Elicit from individual students what each of the pictures is.
- You could extend this exercise by asking students to write their own definitions for each of the words.

2

Aim: to practise using topic vocabulary

- Ask students to complete the sentences using words from exercise 1 in the correct form.
- Remind students to reread the sentences when they have completed them to check for sense.
- Ask students to work individually or with a partner to do the exercise.
- Elicit answers.

1 composers	3 sculptor	5 brushes
2 frame	4 statues	6 easel

3

Aim: to practise forming adjectives by adding a suffix

- Encourage students to copy the table into their notebooks. Remind them that these tables will help them when doing word formation exercises in Part 3 of the FCE Use of English paper.
- Remind students that spelling is very important in word formation exercises and if the word is spelled incorrectly, they will lose marks.
- Students then work individually or with a partner to make the adjectives using the suffixes that they are given and write them in the table in their notebooks.
- Remind them that they should also write the negative adjectives where appropriate.
- Elicit answers and encourage individual students to come up and write the words on the board, checking that the words are spelled correctly.

-ous	**-ful**	**-less**
anxious famous industrious	harmful helpful useful	endless harmless useless valueless
-al	**-able**	**-ive**
additional industrial (un)professional	(un)believable (un)comfortable (un)reasonable (un)recognisable (un)usable valuable	(in)active creative (in)effective successive

Additional task

- Ask students to choose five adjectives from the table on the board and write a short paragraph about someone they know using those adjectives.

4

Aim: to introduce students to metaphorical words used for talking about descriptions

- Explain that words connected to descriptions are often associated with painting and drawing, as if we draw a picture using words.
- Students then work individually or with a partner to complete the sentences.
- Elicit answers.

1 colourful	3 picture
2 image	4 outline

Suggested homework

Assign Ex. 1 and 2 – Workbook, p.93

Listening

Warm up!

Aim: to introduce the topic and warm students up

- Ask students if they have ever been to an art gallery or a museum. Ask them to explain what it was like, what they did and how they felt.
- Ask students what they think makes a good picture. Encourage them to explain what kind of art they like and why.

1

Aim: to practise identifying relationships

- Before students attempt this task, explain that they are going to hear five different conversations which are taking place in an art gallery.
- Ask them to read the relationships between the different people in a–e.
- Elicit the type of conversations that they might expect to hear being used between these people.
- Ask: *What might two friends who are at college talk about in an art gallery?* (doing research, studying, working on a project, lesson, lectures, etc)
- Elicit their suggestions for each of the conversations.
- Remind students that they should also be listening for the tone and style of the extract. Explain that a conversation between an artist and a gallery owner is likely to be more formal than one between two friends.
- Play the listening text.
- Elicit answers, asking students to justify their answers by paraphrasing what they heard.

CD2, Track 14

Conversation 1 e
Conversation 2 d
Conversation 3 b
Conversation 4 a
Conversation 5 c

2

Aim: to practise an exam-type task

- Students now hear the extracts again.
- Before the students do this exercise, remind them of the best way to approach it so that they become familiar with exam technique.
- Remind them of the importance of listening for synonyms or similar words to any that appear in the sentences.
- Remind students that they will hear each extract twice and that they should listen to the whole of the extract before they decide on the answer.
- Play the listening text.
- Elicit answers, asking students to justify their answers by paraphrasing what they heard.

1 A *'... the art world went through some dramatic changes in the first quarter of the twentieth century, led by Pablo Picasso.'*
2 C *'You've seen what he's got in his office, all that old-fashioned stuff.'*
3 B *'Hmm. I'm not sure. I liked his other stuff, but this one ...'*
4 B *'We don't want to do the same thing, do we? No, I just need to get a few ideas.'*
5 C *'We thought there was a good contrast, you know. She's so ... well ... so bright and confident, whereas your work is a little quieter, more understated, isn't it?'*

CD2, Track 14

Soundbite

Aim: to listen to identify silent letters

- Before students do this exercise write this sentence on the board: *Henry said 'Hello' to the heir of the handkerchief factory during his lunch hour.*
- Explain that in some words, the 'h' at the beginning of the word is silent and in some it is pronounced.
- Ask students to tell you which letters in this sentence are silent letters.
- Elicit answers and ask individual students to come up to the board to underline the letters but don't negate or acknowledge them at this stage.
- Ask students to look at the list of words in the Student's Book and circle the words where they think the 'h' is silent.
- Play the listening text.
- Students check their answers as they listen.
- Elicit the answers, making sure that students pronounce the words correctly.

CD2, Track 15

hour hello himself heir handkerchief
honour heel humour

ON THE BOARD

Henry said 'Hello' to the heir of the handkerchief factory during his lunch hour.

Speaking

1

Aim: to practise phrases connected to free time

- Ask students to look at the phrases and to circle the word or words which complete the phrase.
- Remind students that these are useful phrases for them to learn by heart and that they can use them when talking about their hobbies in Part 1 of the FCE Speaking paper.
- Elicit answers, asking for students to give you an example sentence which uses the phrase correctly.

spend time doing
make time to do
spend time on
waste time doing
be short of free time
have enough time to do

Additional task

- Divide the class into pairs.
- Student A asks Student B to talk about what they would like to do if they had more free time.

- Students then swap roles.
- Remind students to use the phrases from exercise 1.
- Go round the class monitoring and helping where necessary.

2

Aim: to practise an exam-type task

- Before students do this exercise, ask them to study the **Speaking database** on page 165.
- Remind students that they are often asked to talk about their hobbies and free-time activities in Part 1 of the interview.
- Divide students into pairs and ask them to interview each other, using the questions given in the Student's Book.
- Monitor the pairwork.
- Ask students to report back to the whole class on what they discussed.

Use of English

1

Aim: to focus on gradable and ungradable adjectives and adverbs

- First, ask students to study page 193 of the **Grammar database**, either in class or at home before the lesson starts.
- Before students attempt this task, write this sentence on the board: *The art gallery is absolutely interesting but the restaurant there is very awful.*
- Elicit what is wrong with the sentence (*interesting* is a gradable adjective so it can't be used with *absolutely*; *awful* is an ungradable adjective so it can't be used with *very*).
- Remind students that *quite* with a gradable adjective means *fairly* and *quite* with an ungradable adjective means *completely*.
- Students then work individually or with a partner to circle the correct answer.
- Elicit answers.

1 really	3 absolutely	5 totally
2 a little	4 a bit	6 quite

ON THE BOARD

The art gallery is absolutely interesting but the restaurant there is very awful.

2

Aim: to match synonymous words and expressions

- Students now match words and expressions which mean the same thing.
- Encourage students to make notes in their notebooks of these words and expressions and any other synonyms they come across.
- Elicit answers.
- Remind students that they can use these words and expressions to help them with the next exercise.

1 e	3 a	5 g	7 f
2 c	4 b	6 d	

Additional task

- Divide the class into pairs.
- Student A writes five short sentences from the words or expressions 1–7. Student B writes five sentences from the words or expressions a–g.
- Students then swap their sentences and rewrite their partner's sentences using the appropriate verb or phrase.
- Ask individual students to read their sentences out to the rest of the class.

3

Aim: to practise using synonyms

- Ask students to read each sentence. Explain that the words in bold all appear in exercise 2, together with synonyms.
- Ask students to identify the correct synonym, and then to put it in the correct form to replace the words in bold in the sentence.
- Give students some time to do the exercise and then elicit the answers.

1 pulled down	5 succeeded in creating
2 took a look at	6 did you work for
3 took you for	7 put up with
4 turned down	

4

Aim: to practise an exam-type task

- Students now do sentence transformations which are designed to practise what they have learned from exercise 2.
- Before they attempt the task, ask them to look at the word in bold in number 1.
- Based on what they have learned from exercise 2 ask them to tell you which words in the first sentence they might need to replace (*works for*).
- Ask: *Which phrase from exercise 2 means 'works for'?* (*be employed by*)
- Elicit the answer to number 1.
- Remind them that they will need to rewrite the first sentence using the word in bold so that the second sentence means exactly the same thing. They will need to use between two and five words, including the word given.
- Remind students that they should write the missing words in capital letters.
- Remind them that contractions such as *don't, doesn't, hasn't,* etc count as two words. The exception to this is *can't* which counts as one word (because it comes from *cannot*).
- Remind students that when they have completed the sentences they should read them through again to make sure they have followed the instructions properly.

- Students then work individually to complete the exercise.
- Elicit answers.

> 1 I have a cousin who IS EMPLOYED BY a local record company.
> 2 We WERE EXHAUSTED after walking round museums all day.
> 3 *U2* TURNED DOWN THE FEE they were offered to perform a concert.
> 4 I'm hoping that I can afford TO HAVE MY PORTRAIT PAINTED by a professional artist.
> 5 The school has decided TO PUT UP WITH graffiti art on certain walls.
> 6 I suggest HAVING/GETTING YOUR LIVING ROOM DECORATED by a professional decorator.

Suggested homework

Assign Ex. 1 and 2 – Workbook, p.93
Ex. 1 and 2 – Workbook, p.94

Writing

1

Aim: to practise the topic of reviews

- First ask students to study page 152 of the **Writing database**, either in class or at home before the lesson starts.
- Ask students to read the writing task and to tell you who is going to read the review (people who would like to find a nice book on art to read).
- Ask students to read the book types in the box and discuss which types would be suitable for reviewing.

> The following types would be suitable: autobiography, biography, fiction, handbook, history.
> Students might also review other non-fiction books, such as an encyclopaedia, but this would be slightly more unusual.

Additional task

- Encourage students to think about the type of details they could include in this review (the name of the author, the title of the book, the name of the publisher, etc).

2

Aim: to practise using words which are easily confused

- Before students attempt this task, write on the board *advice* and *advise*. Ask students to explain to you the difference between them and to give you an example sentence for each of the words (*Advice* is a noun meaning an opinion given on something whereas *advise* is a verb meaning to give advice.).
- Encourage students to learn collocations or phrases which will help them to remember how the words are used, such as *If you take my advice, you'll listen to him.* or *I would advise you to go.*
- Elicit answers to numbers 1 and 2.
- Ask students to look at numbers 3–5 and elicit the answers.

1 strongly	3 miss	5 make
2 advise	4 do	

3

Aim: to provide a model answer for students to refer to

- Students now read the model answer to the question in exercise 1.
- Ask them to read the review through once.
- Then ask them to read it again quickly and to underline all the descriptive adjectives and adverbs that the writer has included.
- Encourage students to give their opinion on whether this is a good review, whether it answers the question correctly and whether the writer has used appropriate descriptive language (Yes – this review would be given a high mark in the exam).

> ***Art for Teenagers***
> *'Art for teenagers', written by Sharon Bollinger and published by Teenlearn Books, is a wonderful handbook with over two hundred different activities for teenagers interested in art. From doing a simple sketch to making a mask out of newspaper, 'Art for Teenagers' shows you how to do it.*
> *The book is divided into four sections: 'Drawing things', 'Painting things', 'Making things' and 'Know your materials'. This final section shows things like the difference between oil paints and water-based paints, and the different kinds of pencils available. For each activity, Sharon Bollinger takes us step-by-step through the process. There are full-colour photos of actual teenagers doing the activities, and the results are impressive. I've already tried several of them, and they're as easy to do as she says. I can't wait to do more of them!*
> *I'd strongly recommend this book to any teenager who is creative and likes painting, drawing or making things. It would make the perfect Christmas or birthday present too!*

Additional task

- In order to check students' understanding of reviews, ask them to paraphrase the main points of the review.

4

Aim: to encourage students to think about the structure of a review

- Remind students to look back at the model review in exercise 3 to help them with the true or false statements.
- Elicit answers.

1 T	The title is *'Art for Teenagers.'*
2 F	
3 T	The review contains the name of the book, its author and publisher.
4 F	The writer expresses his/her opinion in other paragraphs.
5 F	He/She uses some contractions *(I've, I'd).*

5

Aim: to help students write a review

- Explain that students are going to answer the writing task in exercise 1.
- Ask them to read the notice again.
- Ask students to think of a book about art, imaginary or not, and complete the chart.
- At the end of the exercise, ask individual students to read out the information about their book.

6

Aim: to encourage students to plan their writing

- This exercise is designed to encourage students to use their imagination and to make sure that all students have enough ideas before they start writing.
- Remind students that careful planning will improve their reviews.
- Ask students to look at the questions and to make notes in their notebooks.
- Remind them that they should be answering the questions with one or two sentences.
- Go round the class monitoring or helping where necessary.
- At the end of the exercise, ask individual students to read out their ideas.
- If you have time, check that all students have completed the questions with appropriate information.

1–4 students' own answers

- Ask students to turn to **Writing Planner 13** on page 161. Explain that each Writing Planner gives them a simple table to complete which helps them to put the right content in the right place in their piece of writing.
- Point out to students that each row of the table refers to a different part of their piece of writing and gives its purpose, together with useful expressions. Explain to students that they should complete the 'notes' column using their own ideas.
- Give students some time to complete the table. Invite a number of students to say what they have put in the 'notes' column for each part of the piece of writing. If possible, you may like to check the notes made by all students to ensure they have enough content to base their piece of writing on. Ask students to refer to the Writing Planner as they do their piece of writing.

7

Aim: to give students the opportunity to produce a review

- This exercise can be done in class or set for homework.
- Remind students of the importance of including all the information that is contained in their table.

8

Aim: to encourage students to check their written work

- Draw students' attention to the checklist.
- When they have finished writing, ask them to read each statement and to tick each one that is true for them.
- Ask them to make sure that they have ticked all of the boxes before handing their review in to be marked.
- You might consider refusing to mark any review that does not meet all the criteria in the checklist and asking the student to rewrite.

Additional task

- In order to monitor whether students have checked their work carefully, you could ask them to underline in pencil on their reviews 'their recommendations', for example.
- Alternatively, invite individual students to read parts of their review to the rest of the class or get students to exchange reviews with each other and to check each other's reviews for mistakes before handing them in.

Look Back

Aim: to review the unit and to practise scanning for specific information

- Students now have the opportunity to go back through the unit to check what they have learned.
- Ask the whole class the questions from **Look Back**.
- Elicit answers from different students.
- Encourage students to scan the unit to find any information they can't remember.

1	a portrait
2	have / get
3	(un)reasonable
4	an handkerchief
5	because *perfect* is an ungradable adjective. You are either perfect or you aren't.

Suggested homework

Assign Ex. 1, 2 and 3 – Workbook, p.95

Further material

- For further practice and consolidation, ask students to complete the Unit 13 tasks on the Student's CD-ROM.
- To test students' understanding of the material in Unit 13, you may like to administer the Unit 13 Test, which is in the Tests section of the Teacher's DVD-ROM. You may also like to construct your own test using the Test Generator material for Unit 13.

14

Game, Set and Match

Target language

Grammar:	modals (2): modal perfect / the unreal past
Lexis:	topic vocabulary / collocations / phrasal verbs with other particles
Reading skills:	understanding text structure
Listening skills:	listening for specific information
Speaking skills:	comparing
Writing skills:	selecting correct register / article
Pronunciation:	stress (2)

- The phrase *game, set and match* is used by an umpire at the end of a game of tennis to indicate who has won, eg *'And it's game, set and match to Venus Williams, who wins Wimbledon yet again'.*
- Write the phrase *game, set and match* on the board.
- Ask students what they think the title refers to.
- Explain where they might have heard the phrase *game, set and match* before.
- Write the example sentence given above on the board.
- Elicit suggestions as to what the unit might be about.

ON THE BOARD

> game, set and match
>
> 'And it's game, set and match to Venus Williams, who wins Wimbledon yet again.'

Start thinking!

Aim: to introduce the topic of sports through personal responses

- Ask students to work in pairs to write down as many Olympic® events as they can.
- Go round the class monitoring and helping where necessary.
- If you prefer, conduct a brief discussion involving the whole class by inviting different students to give their answers.
- Explain any of the sports to the students that they might not have heard about before.

> **Olympic® sports:**
> athletics events: 100/200/400/800/1,500/5,000/10,000 metres, marathon, 110/400 metres hurdles, 3,000 metre steeplechase, 20,000/50,000 metre walk, decathlon, pentathlon, heptathlon, high jump, pole vault, long jump, triple jump, shot put, discus, hammer, javelin, archery, baseball, basketball, boxing, canoeing, cycling, diving, equestrian, fencing, football, gymnastics, handball, hockey, judo, rowing, sailing, shooting, softball, swimming, synchronised swimming, table tennis, taekwondo, tennis, triathlon, volleyball, water polo, weightlifting, wrestling.

Reading CD2, Track 16

1

Aim: to read for gist

- Students are now going to read a magazine article about the decathlon.
- Explain that the decathlon is considered to be one of the most difficult Olympic® sports because athletes need to be experts in 10 different events.
- Ask students to predict which 10 events make up the decathlon.
- Elicit ideas.
- Ask students to read the article. This can be done individually or as a class activity with different students being asked to read different sections aloud to the rest of the class.
- Remind students that at this stage they do not need to understand all of the vocabulary as items will be covered in the **WORD BOX** section.

- Elicit answers from a few students as to which sports mentioned they prefer watching and why.

Background information

- *An 'all-round champion' is one who is an expert in several different sporting events.*

2

Aim: to encourage students to think about text structure

- Ask students to read the information contained in each paragraph as set out in the sentences.
- Elicit from students any details that they remember about what they have read and ask them to tell you which paragraph those details appeared in.
- Remind students of the importance of underlining where they found the answer within the passage, as this makes it much quicker and easier for them to be able to justify their answers in class and check their work in the exam.
- Ask students to work individually or with a partner to do the exercise.
- Elicit answers, asking for justification.

a 2	b 4	c 7	d 3	e 6

3

Aim: to practise an exam-type task

- First, remind students of the best way to approach it so that they become familiar with exam technique.
- Remind them of the importance of looking for sentences from the passage which explain one of the four options A–D. It is also possible that they might be able to work out from the passage which three options could not be the answer.
- Direct students' attention to the first question.
- Ask: *Where does the writer mention something about today's athletes?* (the first paragraph – 'Today, athletes from countries all over the world …')
- Ask: *What does the writer say about these athletes?* ('The athletes then could make a lot of money from winning, just like today's competitors.')
- Elicit the answer to question 1.
- Remind students of the importance of underlining where they found the answer within the passage, as this makes it much quicker and easier for them to be able to justify their answers in class and check their work in the exam.
- Ask students to work individually or with a partner to do the rest of the exercise.
- Elicit answers, asking for justification from the passage.

1 D	*'The athletes then could make a lot of money from winning, just like today's competitors.'*
2 B	*'This consisted of the long jump, the discus, the javelin, a running race and wrestling.'*
3 D	*'… with the heptathlon … for women being introduced later.'*
4 A	*'At the end of the two days, the person with the most points is the champion …'*
5 C	*'All the other events demand speed or strength. With the long race, it's stamina.'*
6 A	*'… you need expert help.'*

WORD BOX

4

Aim: to introduce new vocabulary

- Before students do this exercise, ask them to read the sentences.
- Remind them of the importance of deciding before they complete the sentences whether they need to look for a noun, adjective, verb or adverb in the passage.
- Ask students to work individually or with a partner to do the exercise.
- Elicit answers.
- Ask students if there were any other words in the passage which they didn't know the meaning of.
- Remind them to make a note of the words and to look them up in a dictionary before the start of the next lesson.
- Ask students if they enjoyed reading the article and whether they learned anything from it or not and get them to justify their answers.

1 athletics	4 Stamina
2 competitor	5 club
3 opponents	

Additional task

- Ask students to choose five words from the **WORD BOX** and to write their own sentences with the word missing.
- Students then swap their sentences with a partner and try to fill in the missing word.

Have your say!

Aim: to give students the opportunity to express their own opinions

- Put the students in pairs and get them to ask each other the questions. Ask them to make brief notes on their partner's answers. When they have finished, invite various students to tell the whole class what they discussed.
- Alternatively, you may like to do the activity as a whole class. Invite various students to give their opinions, encouraging them to agree or disagree with what other

students have said. Encourage them to give reasons for their opinions.

Suggested homework

Assign Ex. 1 – Workbook, p.96–97
Ex. 1 and 2 – Workbook, p.97

G Grammar clinic

1

Aim: to review the modal perfect

- First, ask students to study page 194 of the **Grammar database**, either in class or at home before the lesson starts.
- The first exercise refers back to the reading passage so that students can see the grammar in question being used in context.
- Read the sentence and ask students to tell you which modal is used.
- Elicit answers to questions 1 and 2.
- Ask students to work individually or with a partner to look back at the article and find four other examples of the modal perfect.
- Elicit answers, asking students whether the examples refer to the past or present and express certainty or possibility.

1 the past
2 certainty

'*... a great champion might have received ...*' (the past, possibility)
'*... who must have been a great athlete ...*' (the past, certainty)
'*... he must have been crazy to take up the decathlon.*' (the past, certainty)
'*I could have done lots of different sports ...*' (the past, possibility)

2

Aim: to choose the correct meaning of modal verbs

- Before students attempt this task, write this sentence on the board: *I'm not sure where Karen is. She ________ have gone to volleyball practice.*
- Ask students to tell you what the missing modal verb is in the sentence (*might/may/could*).
- Ask: *Does the modal verb mean that this is a certainty or a possibility?* (a possibility)
- Elicit from students how the modal perfect is formed (modal + *have* + past participle).
- Go through the first sentence together.
- Ask: *What is the modal verb in the sentence?* (*should*)
- Ask: *Does the sentence refer to the past or the present?* (the past)
- Ask: *Is 'should' used here to say that someone did something or that they didn't do something?* (they didn't do something and it was wrong of them not to)
- Elicit the answer to number 1.
- Remind students to go through this process of asking themselves questions about the sentence before they decide on what the sentence expresses.
- Ask students to work individually or with a partner to do the rest of the exercise.
- Elicit answers.

1 b	3 b	5 b
2 a	4 b	6 b

ON THE BOARD

I'm not sure where Karen is. She ________ have gone to volleyball practice.

3

Aim: to practise using the modal perfect

- Before students correct the mistakes, go through the first one together.
- Ask: *Does this sentence refer to the present or the past?* (the past)
- Ask: *What is the modal verb in the sentence?* (*might*)
- Ask: *What follows a modal verb when we use the modal perfect?* (the perfect infinitive)
- Elicit the answer to the first sentence.
- Remind students to go through this process of asking themselves questions about the sentence before they correct it.
- Ask students to work individually or with a partner to do the exercise.
- Elicit answers, asking students to tell you which sentence is correct.

1 Britney might have heard about the competition from Sarah last week.
2 Look out! You could have killed someone playing like that!
3 Oh, he's missed! He really should have scored from that position!
4 Thinking about it now, we could have played better in last week's match.
Sentence 5 is correct.

4

Aim: to practise using the modal perfect in transformations.

- Before they attempt the task, ask them to look at the verb in brackets in number 1.
- Ask: *Does the first sentence express possibility or certainty?* (certainty – the only explanation is that he forgot his football)
- Ask: *Which modal verb do we use to express certainty about the past?* (*must*)
- Elicit the answer to number 1.
- Remind students that they will need to use the modal perfect and the verb in brackets in the correct form.
- Remind students that when they have completed the sentences they should read them through again to make sure they make sense.

- Students then work individually to complete the exercise.
- Elicit answers.

1 'Will must have forgotten his football.'
2 'George can't have scored a goal!'
3 'She must have been playing volleyball when you called.'
4 'You shouldn't have complained during the match.'

Suggested homework

Assign Ex. 1, 2 and 3 – Workbook, p.98

V Vocabulary builder

1

Aim: to focus on vocabulary connected to sport

- This exercise is probably best done as a whole class. If time allows however, divide the class into small groups and encourage them to use a dictionary in order to find the meaning of any unknown words.
- Before students attempt this exercise, ask them to read through sentences 1–10 and underline any words which might act as clues.
- Elicit the clues and ask if there were any which they could do given the clues in the sentences.
- As an example of this you could direct students' attention to number 1. The pronoun *his* tells us that this is a person and that this person *starts a football game.* Even if students don't know the words, searching for clues can sometimes help them to make an educated guess.
- Elicit answers.

1 referee	5 medal	8 umpire
2 victory	6 trainers	9 individual
3 spectator	7 team	10 defeat
4 trainer		

2

Aim: to develop vocabulary connected to sports

- Students now work to match each sport to the correct picture.
- You might wish to set a time limit of two or three minutes for this. You might like to get students to do the activity in pairs.
- Elicit answers.

(from left to right) basketball, football, hockey, rugby, squash, tennis, volleyball, cricket, badminton

Additional task

- You might like to set your students a task of finding out as much as they can about these sports from an encyclopaedia or the internet and reporting back to the class on what they learned.
- You might like to ask them to research:
  1 How many players play these games?
  2 Where do they usually play? (indoors, outside, on a pitch/court, etc)
  3 Are there any world champions from your country in these sports?
  4 What are the basic rules of each sport?

3

Aim: to practise sport collocations

- Ask students to decide whether each sport in exercise 2 is played on a court or a pitch.
- Explain that a court is usually smaller than a pitch. A court is often indoors, while a pitch is usually outdoors. Individual sports are often played on a court, while team games are often played on a pitch.
- Encourage students to make a note of these collocations in their notebooks and to learn them by heart.
- Elicit answers.
- When students have completed the exercise you could also explain that sometimes the word *pitch* is replaced by the word *field,* especially when the game is being played between amateurs rather than in a big stadium.

court: basketball, volleyball, tennis, squash, badminton
pitch: cricket, rugby, football, hockey

Errors to watch out for

Students may tend to over-generalise and may refer to *a golf pitch*, etc. Encourage students to learn collocations for individual sports, like *golf course, race course, skating rink,* etc.

4

Aim: to introduce phrasal verbs with other particles

- Ask students to read the first sentence and to speculate about what the phrasal verb *put through* could possibly mean.
- Elicit any ideas they have.
- Students then work individually or with a partner.
- Elicit answers.
- Remind students that sometimes phrasal verbs can have more than one meaning.
- Encourage students to make a note of the different meanings of phrasal verbs in their notebooks.

1 put through = to connect somebody on the phone
2 turn into = to become
3 take after = to be like an older relative
4 bring forward = to move to an earlier date or time
5 get away with = to escape
6 look into = to investigate
7 look after = to keep in good condition

Suggested homework

Assign Ex. 1 and 2 – Workbook, p.99

Listening

Warm up!

Aim: to introduce the topic and warm students up

- Ask students if they recognise the game in the photograph (It is snooker – a game played on a large table with a white ball, 15 red balls and 6 coloured balls. Players hit the white ball to knock the other balls into the pockets ('pot the balls'). Players must pot a red, then a colour, then a red, then a colour, and continue in this way until they miss a ball. They score points for potting balls. Students may say the game is 'pool', which is a similar game played on a smaller table. They may also say 'billiards', which is an old-fashioned game that is rarely played today.)
- Ask students if they have ever played this game or other similar games and what skills they think you need to be successful at this type of game.

1

Aim: to introduce the listening task and to listen for specific information

- Students now listen to an extract from an interview with a sportswoman.
- Ask them to read questions 1–5 so that they are aware of the kind of information that they will need to listen for.
- Play the listening text.
- Elicit answers, asking students to justify their answers by paraphrasing what they heard.

CD2, Track 17

1 Women In Sport
'Welcome back to another edition of Women In Sport.'
2 15/fifteen
'...Angela Oliver, who's 15 years old...'
3 6/six
'...and has been playing snooker since she was six.'
4 last month
'Last month, Angela became the first teenage girl ever to win the Lancashire Amateur Snooker Championship...'
5 a professional (player)
'...she hopes when she's older to become a professional player.'

2

Aim: to practise listening for specific information and to practise an exam-type task

- Tell students that they are going to listen to the complete interview.
- Remind them of the best way to approach it so that they become familiar with exam technique.
- Remind them of the importance of listening for key words or phrases which could fit the gaps.
- Remind them that they will hear the whole interview twice. The first time they listen they should take notes and the second time they listen they should check their answers.
- Encourage students to complete all of the gaps. If they are not certain of an answer, they should make an educated guess.
- Finally, remind students that they only need to write a word or a short phrase.
- Play the listening text.
- Elicit answers, asking students to justify their answers by paraphrasing what they heard.
- Ask students if any of their guesses were right or nearly right.

CD2, Track 18

1 (very) proud
'Your dad must have felt very proud, too.'
2 15/fifteen red balls
'There are 15 red balls,...'
3 blue
'Yellow's worth two points, green three points, then brown, blue, pink and black, each going up by one point each time.'
4 in order of points
'Then you try to pot the coloured balls in order of points, so you start with the lowest first, and finish with the black.'
5 seven points
'So if you incorrectly pot the black, that's seven to the other side!'
6 directly hit
'If you can't directly hit the ball you need to hit because there's another ball in the way, that's a "snooker",...'
7 the cushion
'The cushion is what we call the inside side of the table, right?'

Soundbite

Aim: to practise stress

- Ask students to work together and underline the stressed syllables.
- Explain that students will now hear the words and they should listen and check their answers.
- Play the listening text.
- Elicit answers, making sure that students repeat the words back to you with the stress placed on the correct syllable.

CD2, Track 19

athlete	athletic	victory	victorious
famous	infamous	science	scientific
concentrate	concentration		

Speaking

1

Aim: to prepare for comparing

- Read the example to students and ask them to make notes in their notebooks about three things that football and the high jump have in common.
- Go round the class monitoring and helping where necessary.
- You might wish to set a time limit of three or four minutes for this.
- Elicit ideas.

(suggested answers)
You have to train hard to be good at these sports.
They can both be done indoors or outdoors.
They are both Olympic® events.

2

Aim: to further practise comparing

- Read the example and ask students to make notes about three differences between football and the high jump.
- Go round the class monitoring and helping where necessary.
- You might wish to set a time limit of three or four minutes for this. Elicit ideas.

(suggested answers)
Speed and stamina are the skills needed to be a good footballer whereas you need to be agile and quite tall to be a good high jumper.
Football is more popular than high jumping as a spectator sport.
The high jump is an athletic event whereas football is a team sport.

3

Aim: to practise expressing preference

- Ask students whether they prefer watching football or the high jump.
- Elicit ideas, asking for justification.

4

Aim: to practise an exam-type task

- Before students do this exercise, ask them to study the **Speaking database** on page 165.
- Divide the class into pairs.
- Remind students to use the notes they made in exercises 1 and 2 and that they should be able to expand on their notes to add some details of their own based on what they can see in the photographs.
- Remind students that the questions they should answer will be printed above the pictures.
- Go round the class monitoring or helping where necessary.
- Students report back on what they have discussed.

Use of English

1

Aim: to focus on the unreal past

- Before students do the exercises on this page, ask them to study page 194 of the **Grammar database**, either in class or at home before the lesson starts.
- Before students attempt this task, write this sentence on the board: *Suppose you won the lottery! What would you spend the money on?*
- Ask: *Look at the verb 'won'. What tense is it in?* (past simple)
- Ask: *Does it refer to the past?* (no – present or future possibility)
- Remind students that the past tense doesn't always refer to the past, but may refer to other things, such as a hypothetical situation.
- Ask students to complete the exercise, choosing the correct word to complete each sentence.
- Elicit answers.

1 started	3 had	5 took
2 watch	4 played	6 didn't

ON THE BOARD

Suppose you won the lottery!
What would you spend the money on?

2

Aim: to practise using the unreal past

- Before students complete the notes, go through the first one together.
- Tell them to ignore the missing words for the moment.
- Ask: *Is this a real or a hypothetical situation?* (a hypothetical situation)
- Ask: *Which verb tells us that it's hypothetical?* (*wish*)
- Ask: *Which tense do we use for the unreal past?* (past simple)
- Elicit the answer to number 1.
- Remind students to go through this process of asking themselves questions about the sentence before they complete the notes.
- Students then work individually or with a partner to do the exercise.
- Elicit answers.

- 1 I wish I were/was better at football.
- 2 Laurence would rather you didn't come to/and watch him play this weekend.
- 3 It is about time we got ready for the match.
- 4 Joanne wishes she didn't have to play handball this weekend.
- 5 Instead of a theatre, I'd rather the town spent the money on a new stadium.

3

Aim: to raise awareness of common mistakes

- Before students attempt this task, explain to them what a phrasal verb is (*A phrasal verb consists of a verb and a preposition.*). Write *to look forward* on the board and ask if it is a phrasal verb (*No, it needs a preposition to have meaning.*). Then elicit which preposition does *to look forward* take (*to*).
- Remind students to go through this process of asking themselves questions about the sentence before they circle the correct word.
- Encourage students to learn collocations, phrases or phrasal verbs, which will help them to remember how the words are used.
- Ask students to look at the remaining questions and elicit the answers.

1 to	3 rather	5 joined
2 both	4 wish	

ON THE BOARD

to look forward

4

Aim: to practise an exam-type task

- Before the students do this exercise, remind them of the best way to approach it so that they become familiar with exam technique.
- Remind them of the importance of reading through the passage once before they start to get an idea of the gist of it.
- Explain that at this stage it is not important to understand all of the words, but draw students' attention to clues before and after the gaps that might help them find the answer. These include prepositions, articles, personal pronouns and determiners.
- Remind students that when they have completed the exercise they should read it through once to check for sense.
- Remind students that each answer should be written in capital letters.
- Finally, remind students that they should always fill in an answer, even if they are not sure it is correct.
- Ask students to work individually or with a partner to do the rest of the exercise.
- Elicit answers, asking for justification from the passage.

1 LOOKS	5 WHICH	9 BEEN
2 EVEN	6 AND	10 FOR
3 SPEND	7 CAME	11 TOOK
4 PART	8 HAVE	12 WOULD

Suggested homework

Assign Ex. 1 and 2 – Workbook, p.99
Ex. 1 and 2 – Workbook, p.100

Writing

1

Aim: to review article writing

- First, ask students to study page 153 of the **Writing database**, either in class or at home before the lesson starts.
- Ask students to read the writing task and to tell you who is going to read the article (pupils at their school).
- Ask students what the article should be about (encouraging students to join their school athletics club).
- Elicit why the report should be quite informal (because it is written to be read by other young people).

Although the editor of the school magazine will read the article, the article will eventually be read by the pupils at the school who read the school magazine.

Additional task

- Encourage students to think about the kind of information that they could include in their article (why students should join the athletics club – to meet new friends and get fit, the sports that are available, details about when the club meets, opinions about the club from someone who is already a member, how to get further information, etc).

2

Aim: to encourage students to think about the style of an article

- Ask students to work in pairs to decide whether the statements are true or false.
- Elicit answers, asking for justification based on what they have learned about articles from the **Writing database**.

1 F The article should be quite informal because it is written to be read by young people.
2 F The article should be quite informal because it is going to be read by young people.
3 T
4 F Contractions are acceptable in informal writing.
5 F The main aim should be to try to encourage all students to join the athletics club.
6 T
7 F Direct speech, where relevant, is acceptable in an article.
8 F Exclamation marks can be used to emphasise a point in an article.

3

Aim: to provide a model answer for students to refer to

- Students now read the model answer to the question in exercise 1.
- Ask them to read the article through once.
- Then ask them to read it again quickly and to underline all the phrases that the writer has used which are informal.
- Encourage students to give their opinion on whether this is a good article, whether it answers the question correctly and whether the writer has used a conversational style. (Yes – this article would be given a high mark in the exam, although the title could be much better.)

> *WHY YOU SHOULD THINK ABOUT JOINING*
> ***THE SCHOOL ATHLETICS CLUB***
> *WHICH IS RUN BY MR RICHARDS*
> *We all know that we should get more exercise. We all know that sport is a great way to enjoy yourself and meet new friends. We all know that winning is a great feeling. So why aren't we all in the athletics club?*
> *'It's perfect for students who want to take up a new sport,' says Mr Richards, the teacher in charge, and he's right! You can do almost anything at the club, including running, the pole vault and the javelin. In fact, there's everything you need to become the next Olympic® decathlon champion!*
> *The members of the club meet every Monday and Thursday evening between 5pm and 7pm. I spoke to one of them to find out what she gets out of being a member. 'Well, it's a lot of fun,' says Tracy Jones, who's been a member for two years, 'It can be hard work but you see your friends and you keep in shape. Oh, and it's completely free!'*
> *Why not try it? If you're interested, ask Mr Richards for more details.*

4

Aim: to further analyse the model

- First, remind students that punctuation can often help them to understand someone's intention in an article.
- Ask students to read the model answer in exercise 3 again and underline where the writer does these things.
- Elicit answers.

> 1 So why aren't we all in the athletics club?
> 2 'It's perfect for students who want to take up a new sport,' says Mr Richards, the teacher in charge …
> 3 … and he's right!
> 4 Why not try it?
> 5 If you're interested, ask Mr Richards for more details.

5

Aim: to think of an appropriate title for the model article

- Remind students that articles should have a title as they do in magazines and newspapers.
- Brainstorm with students alternative titles for the model article in exercise 3, asking students to justify their suggestions with examples from the article.
- Remind students that a better title should probably be shorter and less descriptive. An exclamation mark will also attract the reader's attention.

> No. Something like *'Come on, join today!'* or *'The athletics club needs YOU!'* would be more appropriate as a title for a magazine article.

6

Aim: to prepare students for the writing task

- First, remind students of the importance of identifying what they are writing about and who they are writing for.
- Ask students to read the writing task.
- Ask: *Will you be writing about your experience of the athletics club or to encourage other students to join the athletics club?* (to encourage other students to join the athletics club)
- Then ask: *Will you be writing an article or an informal letter?* (an article)
- Then ask: *Should you give your article a title*? (yes)
- Elicit who the editor suggests students could speak to (to James Edwards).

7

Aim: to encourage students to plan their writing

- This exercise is designed to encourage students to use their imagination and to make sure that all students have enough ideas before they start writing.
- Remind students that careful planning will improve their articles.
- Ask students to look at the questions and to make notes in their notebooks.
- Remind them that they should be answering the questions with one or two sentences.
- Go round the class monitoring or helping where necessary.
- At the end of the exercise, ask individual students to read out their ideas.
- Encourage students to make a note of any good ideas they hear.
- If you have time, check that all students have completed the questions with appropriate information.

> 1–7 students' own answers

- Ask students to turn to **Writing Planner 14** on page 161. Explain that each Writing Planner gives them a simple table to complete which helps them to put the right content in the right place in their piece of writing.
- Point out to students that each row of the table refers to a different part of their piece of writing and gives its purpose, together with useful expressions. Explain to students that they should complete the 'notes' column using their own ideas.

- Give students some time to complete the table. Invite a number of students to say what they have put in the 'notes' column for each part of the piece of writing. If possible, you may like to check the notes made by all students to ensure they have enough content to base their piece of writing on. Ask students to refer to the Writing Planner as they do their piece of writing.

8

Aim: to give students the opportunity to produce an article

- This exercise can be done in class or set for homework.
- Remind students that they should start their article with a question and use at least one example of direct speech and that they should include the information from their notes in exercise 7.

9

Aim: to encourage students to check their written work

- Draw students' attention to the checklist.
- When they have finished writing, ask them to read each statement and to tick each one that is true for them.
- Ask them to make sure that they have ticked all of the boxes before handing their article in to be marked.
- You might consider refusing to mark any article that does not meet all the criteria in the checklist and asking the student to rewrite.

Additional task

- In order to monitor whether students have checked their work carefully, you could ask them to underline in pencil on their articles places where they have 'used direct speech', for example.
- Alternatively, invite individual students to read parts of their article to the rest of the class or get students to exchange articles with each other and to check each other's articles for mistakes before handing them in.

Look Back

Aim: to review the unit and to practise scanning for specific information

- Students now have the opportunity to go back through the unit to check what they have learned.
- Ask the whole class the questions from **Look Back**.
- Elicit answers from different students.
- Encourage students to scan the unit to find any information they can't remember.

1 the heptathlon
2 a bronze medal
3 the long jump
4 past simple
5 an umpire

Suggested homework

Assign Ex. 1, 2 and 3 – Workbook, p.101

Webquest

- Ask students to complete the **Webquest** on page 201 of the Student's Book. You might ask students to work on this together in class if you have internet access, or you might assign it for homework.
- Explain to students that the answers to the questions are not in the Student's Book but that they need to find the answers online.
- Check the answers together and ask students to explain where they found the answers and how they found them (eg by typing terms into a search engine).

1 Leonardo da Vinci / the Louvre, Paris
2 1984, Los Angeles, USA
3 9
4 1890s
5 Pablo Picasso
6 7,000m
7 He killed / shot himself.
8 Uruguay
9 A Christmas Carol
10 Wimbledon

Further material

- For further practice and consolidation, ask students to complete the Unit 14 tasks on the Student's CD-ROM.
- To test students' understanding of the material in Unit 14, you may like to administer the Unit 14 Test, which is in the Tests section of the Teacher's DVD-ROM. You may also like to construct your own test using the Test Generator material for Unit 14.

Revision Units 13-14

1

1 A	3 D	5 C	7 C	9 B
2 B	4 C	6 B	8 D	10 D

2

(2 marks for each correct answer)

1 We're thinking of having our new house done by a professional decorator.
2 Mike suggested getting/having my car cleaned before I sold it.
3 You should get your eyes tested if you can't read that sign.
4 Megan couldn't speak properly because she had had a tooth removed.
5 I am having/getting my hair cut tomorrow morning, so I can't meet you at nine.
6 Why don't you get/have your bike fixed so we can go for a ride?

3

1 write	3 that	5 swimming
2 who	4 learned	

4

1 must have forgotten
2 shouldn't have said
3 couldn't have killed
4 might have met
5 can't have cleaned
6 ought to have called

5

1 absolutely	5 absolutely
2 absolutely	6 very
3 very	7 absolutely
4 absolutely	

6

(2 marks for each correct answer)

1 successful	6 expensive
2 recognisable	7 valuable
3 desirable	8 unbelievable
4 endless	9 famous
5 financial	10 creations

15

Up in Smoke

Target language

Grammar:	the future (2): future perfect (simple and continuous), future continuous / transferred negation / word formation
Lexis:	topic vocabulary / confusable words / metaphors (ideas)
Reading skills:	grammatical referencing
Listening skills:	understanding purpose
Speaking skills:	expressing attitude and opinion
Writing skills:	using prompts / formal letter/email
Pronunciation:	/ɒ/ and /əʊ/

- The phrase *up in smoke* means to vanish, leaving nothing behind. It is always preceded by the verb *go*, eg *Melanie's plans to go to university have gone up in smoke.* Here it refers to rainforests disappearing.
- Write the phrase *go up in smoke* on the board.
- Ask students what they think the title refers to.
- Write the example sentence given above on the board.
- Elicit suggestions as to what the unit might be about.

ON THE BOARD

> *go up in smoke*
> *Melanie's plans to go to university have gone up in smoke.*

Start thinking!

Aim: to introduce the topic of the environment through personal responses

- Ask students to work in pairs to talk about the questions in the Student's Book.
- Go round the class monitoring and helping where necessary.
- If you prefer, conduct a brief discussion involving the whole class by inviting different students to give their answers.

Reading CD2, Track 20

1

Aim: to read for gist

- Students are now going to read an article. Begin by asking them to look at the title of the article and predict what it might be about.
- Elicit ideas.
- Ask students to read the article. This can be done individually or as a class activity with different students being asked to read different sections aloud to the rest of the class.
- Remind students that at this stage they do not need to understand all of the vocabulary as items will be covered in the **WORD BOX** section.
- Elicit answers from a few students as to why we should care about the rainforests.

> We should care about rainforests because they help to keep the Earth's climate balanced. They are also a vital source of new medicines.

Additional task

- In order to check your students' ability to scan for specific information from the article elicit the answers to the questions below.
- Remind students that they don't have to reread large parts of the article but should look for clues or key words that might help them find the answer. The key words have been underlined in each sentence.

> 1 Where do one third of the world's animals live? (the Amazon rainforest in South America)
> 2 Who can you contact to help prevent the cutting down of the rainforest? (environmental organisations)
> 3 What's ten times the size of France? (the Amazon rainforest)
> 4 How much forest was cut down in 2006? (13,000 square kilometres)
> 5 What do most scientists see as a great danger? (deforestation)

2

Aim: to practise grammatical referencing

- Ask students to quickly scan the article to find the words listed in numbers 1–6 and to underline them.
- Remind them that the position of a word within a sentence can often help them to understand the meaning or the function of the word.
- Ask them to tell you what the word *it* refers to in the sentence '*It couldn't happen, could it?*' (the animals/birds/insects losing their homes)
- Go through the rest of the words in the same way, asking students to tell you what the words refer to and whether they refer to information in a sentence which is missing.
- Remind students that these grammatical markers can often help them to identify the missing sentence.

1 the animals / birds / insects losing their homes
2 deforestation
3 the animals / birds / fish and plants that live in the Amazon rainforest
4 species
5 more species becoming extinct
6 trees and plants

3

Aim: to practise an exam-type task

- First, remind students of the best way to approach it so that they become familiar with exam technique.
- Ask them to read sentence A. Elicit which word or phrase might act as a clue to which paragraph the sentence fits ('*not enough*').
- Remind students that they need to look for information before or after the gap where a process, or change, has been described which affects the habitats of plants or animals.
- Remind them of the importance of looking for grammatical markers such as relative and personal pronouns, defining and non-defining clauses and determiners.
- Elicit the answer but do not negate or acknowledge it at this stage.
- Encourage students to approach each of the sentences in the same way.
- Remind students of the importance of underlining the words which helped them find the answer within the passage, as this makes it much quicker and easier for them to be able to justify their answers in class and check their work in the exam.
- Finally, remind them that there is one extra sentence which they do not need to use.
- Ask students to work individually or with a partner to do the exercise.
- Elicit answers, asking students to indicate the words or phrases which helped them choose the answer.

1 G *'Scientists have discovered thousands of types of plant and animal that can only be found there.' 'There are thousands … we haven't discovered yet.'*
2 B *'… mainly to make room for cows.' 'These provide meat … for their owners.'*
3 A *'The good news is that it is slowing down.' 'The bad news is …'*
4 E *'… thousands of the animals, birds, fish and plants …' 'Some of them …'*
5 C *'… the trees and plants are burnt' 'This sends gases …' 'That then leads to the temperature here on the ground going up.'*
6 D *'A number of environmental organisations are campaigning to get the deforestation stopped.' '… have been partly successful.' 'The deforestation has decreased.'*

WORD BOX

4

Aim: to introduce new vocabulary

- First, ask students to read the sentences.
- Remind them of the importance of deciding before they complete the sentences whether they need to look for a noun, adjective, verb or adverb in the passage.
- Ask students to work individually or with a partner to do the exercise.
- Elicit answers.
- Ask students if there were any other words in the passage which they didn't know the meaning of.
- Remind them to make a note of the words and to look them up in a dictionary before the start of the next lesson.
- Ask students if they enjoyed reading the article and whether they learned anything from it or not and get them to justify their answers.
- As well as the words in the Student's Book, you might also like to ask students to speculate about the meaning of *atmosphere, extinct, recycled* and *protest.*

1 species
2 tropical
3 habitat
4 vital
5 Global warming

Additional task

- Ask students to choose five words from the **WORD BOX** and to write a short paragraph with the title 'The Environment' containing those words.

Have your say!

Aim: to give students the opportunity to express their own opinions

- Put the students in pairs and get them to ask each other the questions. Ask them to make brief notes on their partner's answers. When they have finished, invite various students to tell the whole class what they discussed.
- Alternatively, you may like to do the activity as a whole class. Invite various students to give their opinions, encouraging them to agree or disagree with what other students have said. Encourage them to give reasons for their opinions.

Suggested homework

Assign Ex.1 – Workbook, p.104–105
Ex. 1 – Workbook, p.105

G Grammar clinic

1

Aim: to review the *future perfect*

- First, ask students to study page 195 of the **Grammar database**, either in class or at home before the lesson starts.
- The first exercise refers back to the reading passage so that students can see the grammar in question being used in context.
- Read the sentence and ask students which tense is being used (*future perfect*).
- Remind students that they need to think about the order of events and that the *future perfect* is used to show that an action will happen at some point between now and a time in the future.
- Ask students to work individually or with a partner to find another example of the *future perfect* in the article and to write down the events that the sentence refers to in the correct order.
- Elicit answers.

1 b

Scientists predict that by 2030, the rainforest will have become smaller by 40%.
now → the rainforest will have become smaller → 2030

2

Aim: to practise identifying the order of events using the *future perfect*

- Ask students to look at the first sentence.
- Ask: *Which tense is being used here?* (*future perfect*)
- Ask: *Which happens first – the year 2150 comes and then we solve the problems of the rainforest, or we solve the problems of the rainforest and then the year 2150 comes?* (we solve the problems of the rainforest)
- Remind students that other modals such as *might, may* and *should* can be used with the *future perfect*.
- Ask students to work individually or with a partner to do the rest of the exercise.
- Elicit answers, asking for students to justify their answers with grammatical rules.

1 b 2 a 3 a 4 b

3

Aim: to practise using the *future continuous*

- Ask students to look at the diary of a student, Jack. Explain that it shows what Jack has arranged to do at different times of the day.
- Draw students' attention to the example. Point out that the *future continuous* is used for an action in progress at a particular moment in the future.
- Ask students to complete the remaining sentences in the same way. Point out that they may need to add some words or phrases of their own.
- Give the students some time to complete the exercise and then elicit the answers.

1 Jack/he will be having a meeting with Charlie.
2 Jack/he will be attending a lecture on the rainforest.
3 Jack/he will be having lunch with Kate.
4 Jack/he will be writing an essay on the rainforest.
5 Jack/he will be having dinner with Harry.

4

Aim: to practise using the *future perfect* and the *future continuous*

- Remind students that in exercise 3 Jack was planning to attend a lecture at 11am. The dialogue they are about to read takes place later that day, after Jack has attended the lecture. He is talking to a friend about it.
- Explain to students that they should read the dialogue and for each gap decide whether the verb given should be in the *future perfect* or *future continuous* tense.
- Students can do the exercise either individually or in pairs. Give the students some time to complete the exercise and then elicit the answers.

1 will have disappeared
2 will have lost
3 will have solved
4 will be meeting
5 will be working
6 will have finished

Suggested homework

Assign Ex. 1, 2 and 3 – Workbook, p.106

V Vocabulary builder

1

Aim: to focus on vocabulary connected to the environment

- This exercise is probably best done as a whole class. If time allows however, divide the class into small groups and encourage them to use a dictionary in order to find the meaning of any unknown words.

- Before students attempt this exercise, ask them to read through the sentences 1–9 and underline any words which might act as clues.
- Elicit the clues and ask if there were any which they could do given the clues in the definition.
- Remind students that even if they don't know the words, searching for clues can sometimes help them to make an educated guess.
- Elicit answers.

1 survive	6 farmland
2 endangered	7 extinct
3 countryside	8 pollution
4 fumes	9 litter
5 green	

2

Aim: to further develop vocabulary connected to the environment

- Ask students to work individually or with a partner to do the exercise.
- Encourage students to make a note of any new words or phrases that they learn in their notebooks.
- Elicit answers.

1 bottle bank
2 endangered species
3 environmentally friendly
4 nature lover
5 acid rain
6 litter bin

3

Aim: to practise using words which are easily confused

- Before students attempt this task, write on the board: *clear* and *clean*. Ask students to explain to you the difference between the words and to give you an example sentence for each of them (*Clean* means that something has been washed and is not dirty. *Clear* means easily seen, or transparent, or easily understood.).
- Encourage students to learn collocations which will help them to remember how the words are used, such as *clean clothes, clear day* or *clear argument.*
- Elicit answers to numbers 1 and 2.
- Ask students to look at numbers 3 and 4 and elicit the answers. Don't negate the answers but encourage all students to either agree or disagree with the answers given and to justify whether *bring* or *take* is used in each sentence.
- Remind them that *take* means to move something or someone from one place to another and *bring* means to take someone or something with you to a place and have them with you when you arrive somewhere else.
- Ask students to look at numbers 5 and 6 and elicit the answers. Don't negate the answers but encourage all students to either agree or disagree with the answers given and to justify whether *give, take* or *pass* is used in each sentence.
- Remind them that you *take* or *sit* an exam and if you are successful you *pass* it. A teacher can *give* his/her students a test or exam.
- Encourage students to learn these definitions by heart.

1 clean	3 take	5 taking
2 clear	4 bring	6 pass

ON THE BOARD

clear *clean*

4

Aim: to introduce students to metaphorical words and phrases used for talking about ideas

- Explain that when we talk about ideas we sometimes use words or phrases connected to plants.
- Students then work individually or with a partner to complete the sentences.
- Elicit answers.

1 grow on	3 fruitful
2 roots	4 grow

Suggested homework

Assign Ex. 1 and 2 – Workbook, p.107

Listening

Warm up!

Aim: to introduce the topic and warm students up

- Ask students what they think the biggest threats are to the environment in their area / their country / in the world.
- Ask students what they think we might do to help the environment (eg recycle as much as we can, consume less, drive less, fly less, etc).

1

Aim: to introduce the listening task and to understand purpose

- Students are now going to listen to five people talking about the environment.
- Ask students to read through the multiple-choice options for each speaker.
- Elicit the kind of vocabulary that they might hear if someone is explaining something (*so, then, what you do is, let me explain*, etc).
- Elicit the kind of vocabulary that they might hear if someone is denying something (*no, not, it wasn't me*, etc).
- Ask students to listen to decide what each speaker's purpose is.
- Play the listening text.
- Elicit answers, asking students to justify their answers by paraphrasing what they heard.

CD2, Track 21

Speaker 1 is explaining something: *'Let me try to make this a little clearer. What happens is …'*
Speaker 2 wants to entertain people: *'… you'll never guess. One of them was wearing a Coca-Cola® T-shirt and they were all smoking cigarettes.'*
Speaker 3 is complaining about something: *'It's just not good enough, really.'*
Speaker 4 is trying to persuade people: *'Why not join the campaign and start raising money to help protect this valuable natural resource?'*
Speaker 5 wants to deny something: *'The idea that this government is responsible for the levels of pollution in this country is just not true.'*

2

Aim: to practise listening for attitude and to practise an exam-type task

- Students now listen to the same five people talking but in a different order.
- Before students do this exercise, remind them of the best way to approach it so that they become familiar with exam technique.
- Remind them of the importance of listening for synonyms or similar words to any that appear in the statements.
- Ask students to read through the sentences A–F and to speculate about the vocabulary they might hear.
- Elicit their suggestions.
- Remind them that they will need to match one of the five speakers to one of the statements and that there is an extra statement which they will not need to use.
- Remind them that they will hear the piece twice. The first time they listen they should fill in any answers they hear and the second time they listen they should check their answers.
- Play the listening text.
- Elicit answers, asking students to justify their answers by paraphrasing what they heard.
- Ask students if they can tell you what aspect of the environment each speaker was talking about.

CD2, Track 22

Speaker 1 D: *'With a little time and effort, we can make a real difference to our world.'*
Speaker 2 B: *'One of them was wearing a Coca-Cola® T-shirt and they were all smoking cigarettes.'*
Speaker 3 E: *'Just because you can't see the smoke once the wind has blown it away doesn't mean that it isn't still there.'*
Speaker 4 C: *'It was the previous government that caused this situation by introducing new regulations that allowed factories to pump chemicals into our rivers and our atmosphere.'*
Speaker 5 F: *'There just aren't enough litter bins.'*

Soundbite

Aim: to practise listening for the sounds /ɒ/ and /əʊ/

- Students now listen to hear the difference between the pronunciation of the sound /ɒ/ in words such as *hot* and the sound /əʊ/ in words such as *hope*.
- Explain that they need to decide before they listen whether the underlined syllable in each of the words is pronounced /ɒ/ or /əʊ/.
- Students should write the word in the correct column.
- Explain that students will now hear the words and they should listen and check their answers.
- Play the listening text.
- Elicit answers, making sure that students pronounce the words correctly.

CD2, Track 23

like *hot*: not forgotten shopping lock stop bomb
like *hope*: hotel woke boat wrote hole comb

Speaking

1

Aim: to develop awareness of phrases which express opinion

- Students now work individually to match phrases which express opinion.
- Elicit answers, asking students to give you an example sentence which expresses their view on an environmental issue using the phrases.
- Remind students that they must be able to give reasons for their opinions.

1 c	3 e	5 f
2 a	4 d	6 b

2

Aim: to practise an exam-type task

- Before students do this exercise, ask them to study the **Speaking database** on page 165.
- Divide the class into pairs.
- Remind students to use the prompts in exercise 1 to help them express their opinions and think about ways of agreeing and disagreeing (See Unit 7).
- Remind students that there are two parts to the task. They need to discuss each of the threats and then decide which one is the biggest threat.
- Go round the class monitoring or helping where necessary.
- You might wish to set a time limit of three or four minutes for this.

- Ask students to report back on what they have discussed.

Use of English

1

Aim: to focus on transferred negation

- First, ask students to study page 195 of the **Grammar database**, either in class or at home before the lesson starts.
- Before students attempt this task, write this sentence on the board: *Peter says he thinks he doesn't have enough money to go on holiday this year.*
- Elicit what is wrong with the sentence (When we want to express a negative idea using *think, suppose, believe* or *imagine,* we normally make these verbs negative and not the second verb. Here the verb *think* should be negative and not the verb *have.*).
- Elicit the correct answer (*Peter says he doesn't think he has enough money to go on holiday this year.*).
- Then, write this sentence on the board: *Come on – we're late. I don't hope we miss the bus.*
- Ask students to tell you what is wrong with the sentence.
- Elicit that we don't make *hope* negative but make the second verb negative.
- Elicit the correct answer (*Come on – we're late. I hope we don't miss the bus.*).
- Ask students to look at the example sentence.
- Remind them that they need to use the word in brackets in each of their sentences.
- Students then work individually or with a partner to complete the exercise.
- Elicit answers.

2 Jacob doesn't think he is going to join Greenpeace.
3 Mr Hussain doesn't believe that the rainforests are his problem.
4 I don't imagine that environmental problems will be solved easily.
5 My parents don't think that recycling is such a good idea.
6 People in the Amazon hope that the rainforest won't be completely destroyed.
7 Local people don't believe that the council will solve the litter problem.

ON THE BOARD

Peter says he thinks he doesn't have enough money to go on holiday this year.
Come on – we're late. I don't hope we miss the bus.

2

Aim: to practise word formation

- Direct your students' attention to the example.
- Ask: *What is the person noun from 'inspect'?*
- Elicit the answer.
- Remind students that a person noun is often formed by adding either an *-or, -er* or *-ist* to the noun.
- Remind students that spelling is extremely important.
- Encourage students to think about the people formed from nouns and remind them that in Part 3 of the FCE Use of English paper they will be expected to work out for themselves whether the word required should be plural or singular.
- Ask students to work individually or with a partner to do the rest of the exercise.
- Elicit answers, asking individual students to spell out the words as they give them to you.

inspector / inspection	campaigner
creator / creation	protester
protector / protection	voter
scientist	visitor
biologist	politician
environmentalist	survivor / survival

3

Aim: to practise an exam-type task

- First, remind students of the best way to approach it so that they become familiar with exam technique.
- Remind them of the importance of reading through the passage once before they start to get an idea of the gist of it.
- Direct students' attention to the first sentence.
- Explain the importance of reading whole sentences rather than just single lines, as there may be additional information given on the following line or lines which affect how the word should be changed.
- Remind students, too, that they will need to think about not only whether the word should be a verb, noun, adjective or adverb but whether the word is plural or singular or positive or negative.
- Emphasise that spelling is extremely important and that words which are spelled incorrectly will be marked as wrong.
- Remind them that the first word is given as an example.
- Once they have finished the exercise remind them to read the passage again to check for sense.
- Remind students that they should write only one word in each gap, and that each word should be in capital letters. They should always fill in an answer, even if they are not sure it is correct.
- Ask students to work individually or with a partner to do the rest of the exercise.
- Elicit answers.

1 PROTESTERS	6 EXTINCTION
2 POLITICIANS	7 SCIENTISTS
3 ENVIRONMENTALISTS	8 SURVIVAL
4 PROTECTION	9 DESTRUCTION
5 ENDANGERED	10 GLOBAL

Suggested homework

Assign Ex. 1 – Workbook, p.107
Ex. 1 and 2 – Workbook, p.108

Writing

1

Aim: to encourage students to think about relevant and irrelevant information

- First, ask students to study page 150 of the **Writing database**, either in class or at home before the lesson starts.
- This exercise is probably best done as a whole class.
- Remind students that in order to support their opinions in a formal letter, they can also include information which is not necessary but which is relevant.
- Explain that they need to try to avoid making comments which are irrelevant to the subject and that they must include all the information from their notes.
- Ask students to read the points 1–6.
- Elicit answers, asking students to justify their opinions.

1 necessary
2 irrelevant
3 not necessary but relevant
4 necessary
5 necessary
6 not necessary but relevant

2

Aim: to review formal letters/emails

- Ask students to read the writing task and to tell you who the letter should be written to (the editor of a newspaper).
- Elicit why the letter is formal.

This letter should be formal because it is being written to a local newspaper and is about serious political and environmental issues. The writer also disagrees with his local MP and needs to do this in a formal but polite way.

Background information

- *An MP is a Member of the British Parliament and represents the people of a particular area.*

Additional task

- Encourage students to think about the kind of information that must be included in the letter (the river is not cleaner than it was two years ago – in fact it is dirtier than it was, the council haven't supported local environmental groups because they didn't help Greenpeace with its advertising costs, and tourism is actually falling because the sea is so dirty that tourists don't want to use the local beaches, etc).

3

Aim: to provide a model answer for students to refer to

- Students now read the model answer to the question in exercise 2.
- Ask them to read the letter through once.
- Then ask them to read it again quickly and to put the parts in the correct order.
- Encourage students to give their opinion on whether this is a good letter, whether it answers the question correctly and whether the writer has included all of the information he should have (Yes – this letter would be given a high mark in the exam.).

1 G	3 E	5 A	7 B
2 F	4 H	6 D	8 C

4

Aim: to read for specific words and phrases

- Before students attempt this task, remind them that these are informal phrases and that in a formal letter they should be using formal phrases.
- Ask students to read the model answer in exercise 3 again and underline the formal (and appropriate) phrases.
- Elicit answers.

Dear Sir/Madam,

I am writing (1) in response to an article in your newspaper on 25th February, in which my local MP, Patricia Collins, was interviewed. (2) She made a number of statements which (3) I would like to disagree with.

Firstly, it is not true that the river is cleaner than it was two years ago. Local factories are still polluting the river.

Secondly, the sea is also badly polluted. (4) Contrary to what Mrs Collins claims, tourism is falling because of this problem. Tourists and local people have also complained about the park, which is often full of litter.

Finally, I would like to point out that the local council has not always supported environmental groups. When Greenpeace requested help with advertising costs, the request was turned down.

(5) Could I suggest you interview local people to discover the truth about the environmental problems facing our area?

(6) Yours faithfully,
George Lennon

5

Aim: to prepare students for the writing task

- Before students begin these exercises, remind them of the importance of identifying who they are writing to.
- Ask them to look at the writing task and to tell you who they will be writing to.

- Ask: *Will you be writing to a person you know or don't know?* (a person I don't know)
- Then ask: *Will you be writing to express your opinions or to ask for information?* (to express opinions)
- Then ask: *Do you need to include all of the information from your notes?* (yes)
- Elicit what information students have to include in their letter.

> The information to be included here should be expanded from the students' own notes. Students will lose marks for failing to include all of the information that they have made in their notes. In this letter they need to mention that the local council haven't done a very good job of cleaning because the city centre is still full of litter, that they haven't done all of the things they promised because they didn't build a new youth club and that they haven't worked closely with the local community because they have only organised one meeting.

6

Aim: to encourage students to plan their writing

- This exercise is designed to encourage students to use their imagination and to make sure that all students have enough ideas before they start writing.
- Remind students that careful planning will improve their letters.
- Ask students to look at the questions and to make notes in their notebooks.
- Remind them that they should be answering the questions with one- or two-sentence answers.
- Go round the class monitoring or helping where necessary.
- At the end of the exercise, ask individual students to read out their ideas.
- If you have time, check that all students have completed the questions with appropriate information.

> 1 *Dear Sir/Madam*
> 2–6 students' own answers
> 7 *Yours faithfully,*
> 8 their full name

- Ask students to turn to **Writing Planner 15** on page 162. Explain that each Writing Planner gives them a simple table to complete which helps them to put the right content in the right place in their piece of writing.
- Point out to students that each row of the table refers to a different part of their piece of writing and gives its purpose, together with useful expressions. Explain to students that they should complete the 'notes' column using their own ideas.
- Give students some time to complete the table. Invite a number of students to say what they have put in the 'notes' column for each part of the piece of writing. If possible, you may like to check the notes made by all students to ensure they have enough content to base their piece of writing on. Ask students to refer to the Writing Planner as they do their piece of writing.

7

Aim: to give students the opportunity to produce a formal letter

- This exercise can be done in class or set for homework.
- Remind students of the importance of using formal language and of answering the question by including all the information from their notes.

8

Aim: to encourage students to check their written work

- Draw students' attention to the checklist.
- When they have finished writing, ask them to read each statement and to tick each one that is true for them.
- Ask them to make sure that they have ticked all of the boxes before handing their letter in to be marked.
- You might consider refusing to mark any letter that does not meet all the criteria in the checklist and asking the student to rewrite.

Additional task

- In order to monitor whether students have checked their work carefully, you could ask them to underline in pencil on their letters places where they have 'used formal language', for example.
- Alternatively, invite individual students to read parts of their letter to the rest of the class or get students to exchange letters; with each other and to check each other's letters for mistakes before handing them in.

Look Back

Aim: to review the unit and to practise scanning for specific information

- Students now have the opportunity to go back through the unit to check what they have learned.
- Ask the whole class the questions from **Look Back**.
- Elicit answers from different students.
- Encourage students to scan the unit to find any information they can't remember.

> 1 Brazil
> 2 in a bottle bank
> 3 extinct

Suggested homework

Assign Ex. 1 and 2 – Workbook, p.109

Further material

- For further practice and consolidation, ask students to complete the Unit 15 tasks on the Student's CD-ROM.
- To test students' understanding of the material in Unit 15, you may like to administer the Unit 15 Test, which is in the Tests section of the Teacher's DVD-ROM. You may also like to construct your own test using the Test Generator material for Unit 15.

16

On the Run

Target language

Grammar:	conditionals (2): third / wishes and regrets / parts of speech
Lexis:	topic vocabulary / word formation (irregular forms) / word patterns
Reading skills:	scanning for specific information
Listening skills:	listening for specific information
Speaking skills:	seeking clarification
Writing skills:	paragraphing / story
Pronunciation:	weak forms (2)

- The phrase *on the run* means trying to hide or escape from someone, especially the police, eg *The gang of four robbers has been on the run from the police for four days.*
- Write the phrase *on the run* on the board.
- Ask students what they think the title refers to.
- Write the example sentence given above on the board.
- Elicit suggestions as to what the unit might be about.

ON THE BOARD

> ***on the run***
>
> ***The gang of four robbers has been on the run from the police for four days.***

Start thinking!

Aim: to introduce the topic of crime through personal responses

- Ask students to work in pairs to talk about the questions in the Student's Book.
- Go round the class monitoring and helping where necessary.
- If you prefer, conduct a brief discussion involving the whole class by inviting different students to give their answers.

Reading CD2, Track 24

1

Aim: to read for gist

- Students are now going to read a magazine article. Begin by asking them to look at the title of the article and predict what it might be about.
- Elicit ideas.
- Ask students to read the article. This can be done individually or as a class activity with different students being asked to read different sections aloud to the rest of the class.
- Remind students that at this stage they do not need to understand all of the vocabulary as items will be covered in the **WORD BOX** section.
- Elicit answers from a few students as to whether they feel any sympathy for Carl Maxwell and why or why not.

Background information

- *'QC' stands for Queen's Counsel and means that someone is a lawyer of high status.*

2

Aim: to scan for specific information

- In order to check your students' ability to scan for specific information from the passage, elicit the answers to the questions orally.
- Remind students that they don't have to reread large parts of the passage but should look for clues or key words that might help them find the answer.

1 six months
2 July last year
3 four months
4 She lives alone apart from her two cats.
5 She knew that Maxwell had been in prison before. When she searched his car she found a mask and a torch.
6 ten years

3

Aim: to practise an exam-type task

- First, remind students of the best way to approach it so that they become familiar with exam technique.

- Remind them of the importance of looking for key words or phrases which are synonymous or similar in meaning to the words in the sentences.
- Remind them, too, of the importance of underlining where they found the answer within the passage, as this makes it much quicker and easier for them to be able to justify their answers in class and check their work in the exam.
- Finally, remind them that the people may be chosen more than once and that some questions have more than one answer.
- Ask students to work individually or with a partner to do the exercise.
- Elicit answers, asking for justification from the passage.

1 D: *'Prison isn't a perfect solution …'*
2 C: *'Most burglars are just out looking for an opportunity …'*
3 A: *'I've never hurt anyone, so I think it's unfair that I'm in here.'*
4 A: *'… if people are so stupid that they leave their windows unlocked …'*
5 B: *'You can always replace … in your own home again.'*
6 C: *'When Mrs Norton reported the crime …'*
7 D: *'Most burglars are young men, often unemployed …'*
8–10 (in any order)
A: *'… I realised I could get things easily just by stealing them.'*
C: *'I knew he'd been in prison before …'*
D: *'It wasn't his first offence …'*
11 B: *'The crime rate around here is increasing …'*

Additional task

- Ask students to write a short paragraph of 50 words explaining whether they think that Carl Maxwell should have gone to prison and why or why not.

WORD BOX

4

Aim: to introduce new vocabulary

- First, ask students to read the definitions.
- Remind them of the importance of deciding whether they need to look for a noun, adjective, verb or adverb in the passage.
- Ask students to work individually or with a partner to do the exercise.
- Elicit answers.
- Ask students if there were any other words in the passage which they didn't know the meaning of.
- Remind them to make a note of the words and to look them up in a dictionary before the start of the next lesson.
- Ask students if they enjoyed reading the article and whether they learned anything from it or not and get them to justify their answers.

1 sentence	5 guilty
2 innocent	6 fingerprints
3 burglary	7 court
4 crime rate	

Additional task

- Ask students to choose five words from the **WORD BOX** and to jumble up the letters to create an anagram.
- Students then swap their anagrams with a partner who must try to find the word.

Have your say!

Aim: to give students the opportunity to express their own opinions

- Put the students in pairs and get them to ask each other the questions. Ask them to make brief notes on their partner's answers. When they have finished, invite various students to tell the whole class what they discussed.
- Alternatively, you may like to do the activity as a whole class. Invite various students to give their opinions, encouraging them to agree or disagree with what other students have said. Encourage them to give reasons for their opinions.

Suggested homework

Assign Ex. 1 – Workbook, p.110–111
Ex. 1 – Workbook, p.110

G Grammar clinic

1

Aim: to review the third conditional

- Before students do the exercises on this page, ask them to study page 196 of the **Grammar database**, either in class or at home before the lesson starts.
- The first exercise refers back to the reading passage so that students can see the grammar in question being used in context.
- Read the sentence and ask students to tell you which conditional is being used (third).
- Ask students to decide if the statements are true or false.
- Elicit answers.
- Ask students to look through the article again and find other examples of the third conditional and underline them.

1 T: The third conditional is used when we want to imagine the past being different.
2 T: Because it refers to the past and we can't change what has already happened or not happened.
3 F: The result did not happen in the example.

Other examples of the third conditional are:
'If I'd known what was going to happen, I'd have been more careful, but you never know, do you?'
'If I'd decided to turn to crime, I could have got lots of things for free.' 'Even if I hadn't known who he was, I would have searched his car…'
'If Mrs Norton had locked all her windows, Maxwell would have found another house.'

2

Aim: to practise identifying what the third conditional expresses

- Before students do the exercise go through the first sentence together.
- Ask: *Was I caught?* (yes)
- Ask: *Was I sentenced to prison?* (yes)
- Elicit the correct answer.
- Remind students that instead of *would, might* and *could* can also be used in the third conditional,
- Ask students to work individually or with a partner to do the rest of the exercise.
- Elicit answers, asking for students to justify their answers with grammatical rules.

1 b 2 a 3 a 4 a

3

Aim: to practise using the third conditional

- Before students correct the mistakes, go through the first one together.
- Elicit the correct form of the third conditional.
- Elicit the answer to number 1.
- Ask students to work individually or with a partner to do the exercise.
- Elicit answers, asking students to tell you which sentence is correct.

1 I would have escaped if I <u>had had</u> a faster car. / I <u>wouldn't</u> have escaped if I hadn't had a fast car.
2 I <u>wouldn't have</u> been sent to prison if I <u>hadn't</u> committed a burglary.
3 He wouldn't have become a thief if he <u>had had</u> more money when he was a child.
4 If there <u>had been</u> more police officers, the crime rate wouldn't have been so high.
Sentence 5 is correct.

4

Aim: to practise using the third conditional

- Before students do the exercise go through the first sentence together.
- Write this sentence on the board: *If Barbara ________ ________ a diamond ring, she ________ ________ been arrested.*
- Ask students to complete the sentence based on what they have learned about the third conditional in exercises 1, 2 and 3.
- Ask students to work with a partner to do the exercise.
- Elicit answers.

1 Barbara wouldn't have been arrested if she hadn't stolen a diamond ring.
2 If Joe hadn't attacked someone in the street, he wouldn't have ended up in prison.
3 If the criminal hadn't been guilty, I wouldn't have sentenced him to six months in prison.
4 If the evidence hadn't been very clear, the jury wouldn't have taken only a few minutes to decide.
5 If you had locked your car, it wouldn't have been stolen.
6 If my father hadn't been a police officer, I wouldn't have become one.

ON THE BOARD

If Barbara ____________ ____________ a diamond ring, she ____________ ____________ been arrested.

5

Aim: to practise using the third conditional

- Ask students to write five third conditional sentences in their notebooks which are true about their past.
- Ask a few students to read out their sentences to the rest of the class.
- Students then compare their sentences with other students.

Suggested homework

Assign Ex. 1 and 2 – Workbook, p.112

V Vocabulary builder

1

Aim: to focus on vocabulary connected to crime

- This exercise is probably best done as a whole class. If time allows however, divide the class into small groups and encourage them to use a dictionary in order to find the meaning of any unknown words.
- Before students attempt this exercise, ask them to read through the sentences 1–6 and underline any words which might act as clues.
- Elicit the clues and ask if there were any which they could do given the clues in the definition.
- As an example of this you could direct students' attention to number 3.The word *shops* corresponds to the word *shoplifting.* Even if students don't know the words, searching for clues can sometimes help them to make an educated guess.
- Elicit answers.

1 murder	4 assault
2 arson	5 robbery
3 shoplifting	6 blackmail

2

Aim: to focus on vocabulary connected to crime

- Explain to students that there are different ways of punishing criminals depending on the crime they have committed.
- Ask students to look at the four different means of punishment and to speculate on what they might involve.
- Divide the class into pairs.
- Students then work together to match the punishment to its definition.
- Elicit answers.

1 d 2 b 3 c 4 a

Additional task

- Have a class discussion about which punishments the students think are suitable for which crimes and why.

3

Aim: to practise irregular word formation

- First, remind students that there are verbs, adjectives, adverbs and nouns which are irregular and which don't take regular suffixes or prefixes. They need to learn each of these carefully.
- Go through the first one together.
- Ask students to read the first sentence and tell you whether they need to complete it with a noun, adjective, verb or adverb (a person noun).
- Elicit the person noun from the noun *crime* (*criminal*).
- Elicit whether the word should be in the singular or plural (plural).
- Emphasise that spelling is extremely important and that words which are spelled incorrectly will be marked as wrong.
- Ask students to work individually or with a partner to do the rest of the exercise.
- Elicit answers.

1 criminals
2 failure
3 description
4 poverty
5 proof
6 lower

Additional task

- After students have completed the exercise draw a four-column table on the board with the following headings: *verb, noun, adjective* and *adverb.*
- Ask students to look at the words from exercise 3 and brainstorm any other forms of the words which they might know already and write them on the board in the appropriate column.
- Encourage students to copy the table into their notebooks. Remind them that these tables will help them when doing word formation exercises.

4

Aim: to focus on lexico-grammatical word patterns

- Before students attempt this task, write on the board:

Charlie Lawson was sentenced with/to ten years in prison.

- Elicit from students the correct preposition (*to*).
- Ask students to look at the words in the box.
- Ask students to underline the prepositions in each of the phrases and to see if they can match each of the prepositions to one of the verbs.
- Students work individually or with a partner to complete the exercise.
- Elicit answers.

1 charge somebody with a crime
2 let somebody off with a warning
3 accuse/suspect somebody of (doing) something
4 accuse/suspect somebody of (doing) something
5 get away with a crime
6 blame somebody for a crime
7 sentence somebody to time in prison
8 apologise for (doing) something

ON THE BOARD

Charlie Lawson was sentenced with/to ten years in prison.

5

Aim: to practise word patterns connected to crime

- Explain to students that they are going to use the word patterns from exercise 4 to complete a short text.
- Ask students to quickly read the text, ignoring the gaps, and to say what it's about (what the police do when they suspect someone of committing a crime).
- Ask students to read the text again, this time using a word pattern from exercise 4 in each gap. You might get students to do this in pairs.
- Give students some time to complete the task and then elicit the answers.

1 get away with
2 suspect someone / a person of
3 let the person / them / him/her / him or her off
4 charge the person / them / him/her / him or her
5 sentence the person / them / him/her / him or her to

Suggested homework

Assign Ex. 1 – Workbook, p.112
Ex. 2 and 3 – Workbook, p.113

Listening

Warm up!

Aim: to introduce the topic and warm students up

- Ask students if they or anyone they know has ever been the victim of a crime. Ask them to describe what happened.
- Ask students what people can do to help prevent crime (make sure they lock doors, report suspicious people to

the police, watch neighbours' houses when they're on holiday, etc).

1

Aim: to practise listening for purpose

- Students are now going to listen to a man being interviewed about crime.
- Before students listen ask them to read the questions.
- Ask students to speculate about possible answers for question 1 (he may be a criminal/a police expert/a victim of crime/etc).
- Play the listening text.
- Elicit answers, asking students to justify their answers by paraphrasing what they heard.

CD2, Track 25

1 because he's a local police officer: *'We've asked Robert onto the show because he's a local police officer.'*
2 Neighbour Power: *'That's one of the reasons for Neighbour Power, the new scheme we're starting in this area.'*

Additional task

- In order to check your students' understanding, ask them if they can tell you the answers to the following questions.

1 What cause of poverty does Robert White mention? (unemployment)
2 What's the name of the new crime prevention scheme the police are starting in this area? (Neighbour Power)
3 Who do the police believe is the best protection against burglary? (neighbours)

2

Aim: to practise listening for specific information and to practise an exam-type task

- Tell students that they are going to listen to the interview again.
- Before the students do this exercise, remind them of the best way to approach it so that they become familiar with exam technique.
- Remind them of the importance of listening for key words or phrases which could fit the gaps.
- Encourage students to complete all of the gaps. If they are not certain of an answer, they should make an educated guess.
- Finally, remind students that they only need to write a word or a short phrase.
- Play the listening text.
- Walk around the class monitoring the students.
- Play the listening text again if necessary.
- Elicit answers, asking students to justify their answers by paraphrasing what they heard.

CD2, Track 25

1 the whole country: *'The crime rate is increasing across the whole country, so we shouldn't be surprised if we also see an increase at the local level.'*
2 unemployment: *'There's a lot of unemployment, which means people, especially young people, have more time on their hands and it's easy for them to get involved in crime.'*
3 their neighbours: *'We live in suburbs and travel to other areas to work or to see our friends. Most people today don't really know their neighbours.'*
4 burglary: *'... burglary, which is the biggest crime problem in the area.'*
5 technology / alarms and immobilisers: *'One reason is that new cars are much harder to steal than older cars because of alarms and immobilisers.'*
6 local police station: *'First of all, contact your local police station, to see if Neighbour Power has already started in your area. They'll tell you how to get involved.'*

Soundbite

Aim: to practise weak forms

- Tell students that they will hear some words being said in their weak forms in the context of sentences.
- Ask them to listen carefully to the difference in pronunciation.
- Play the listening text.
- Invite students to practise saying the sentences in the same way as they heard in the listening text to their partner or, if you prefer, to the whole class.
- Go round the class monitoring and helping, where necessary.
- Play the listening text again, if necessary.

CD2, Track 26

Speaking

1

Aim: to practise seeking clarification

- Remind your students that they might not understand everything the examiner or the other candidate asks them but that it is perfectly acceptable to ask for something to be repeated, as long as this is done politely.
- Ask students to look at the phrases given and to cross out those which are not polite.
- Elicit answers. Emphasise to students that they should learn these polite phrases to use in the classroom and in the exam interview.

I'm not sure I completely understand.
~~Repeat, please.~~
~~What?~~
Could you ask me that again, please?
Could you explain what X means?
Would you mind repeating the question?
~~Tell me what that means.~~
Do you think you could explain that again, please?

2

Aim: to further practise seeking clarification and an exam-type task

- Before students do this exercise, ask them to study the **Speaking database** on page 165.
- Students now work in pairs to discuss their opinions.
- Ask students to choose four or more of the questions from the list and to discuss their ideas with their partner.
- Remind them to use the phrases from exercise 1 when they need to check anything they don't understand and to use the prompts given to start their answers.
- Go round the class monitoring and helping, where necessary.
- Get students to report back to the whole class on what they have discussed.

Use of English

1

Aim: to focus on wishes and regrets

- Before students do the exercises on this page, ask them to study page 196 of the **Grammar database**, either in class or at home before the lesson starts.
- Before students attempt this task, write this sentence on the board: *I wish we weren't burgled while we were away on holiday.*
- Ask students to explain to you what is wrong with the sentence (when we are talking about wishes about the past (regrets) we need to use *wish* + past perfect).
- Elicit the correct answer (*I wish we hadn't been burgled while we were away on holiday.*).
- Before students correct the mistakes, go through the first one together.
- Ask: *Does the sentence refer to the past or the present?* (the past)
- Ask: *Which tense is used for regrets in the past?* (*past perfect*)
- Elicit the answer to number 1.
- Remind students to go through this process of asking themselves questions about the sentence before they correct it.
- Ask students to work individually or with a partner to do the exercise.
- Elicit answers.

1 I wish my new watch hadn't been stolen from my bag yesterday.
2 Don't you wish now you had locked your windows last night?
3 I'm sure everybody wishes they could prevent crime in their area.
4 I hope we don't get burgled when we go on holiday this summer.
5 I wish I hadn't mentioned the fact that Kelly's dad's in prison when I saw her last week.

ON THE BOARD

I wish we weren't burgled while we were away on holiday.

2

Aim: to practise rewriting sentences using *wish* or *If only*

- Remind students that *If only* is an emphatic form of *I wish.*
- Before students rewrite the sentences, go through the first one together.
- Based on what they have learned, ask them to tell you what must follow *I* (wish).
- Ask: *Does the first sentence refer to the present or the past?* (the present)
- Ask: *What follows 'wish' when you are talking about the present?* (*wish + past simple/continuous* or past modal)
- Elicit the answer to number 1.
- Remind students that when they want to talk about something that annoys or irritates them about someone's behaviour they should use *wish + would.*
- Remind students that when they have completed the sentences they should read them through again to make sure they make sense.
- Students then work individually to complete the exercise.
- Elicit answers.

1 'I wish I were/was tall enough to become a police officer!'
2 'If only I hadn't stolen sweets from my local shop!'
3 'If only I'd been more careful, I wouldn't have got caught.'
4 'I wish I didn't have to take a law exam next week.'
5 'If only I could afford to go to the cinema to see the crime thriller!'

3

Aim: to practise changing parts of speech

- Ask students to work alone or in pairs to complete each phrase with a verb from the box.
- Elicit answers.

1 have difficulty in doing
2 find something worrying
3 have no regrets about
4 make a complaint about
5 pay someone a visit
6 make a suggestion

4

Aim: to practise sentence transformations

- Students now do sentence transformations which are designed to practise what they have learned from exercises 1, 2 and 3.
- Ask students to look at the word in bold in number 2.
- Based on what they have learned from exercise 3, ask them to tell you which word in the first sentence they might need to replace (*complained*).
- Ask: *Which phrase from exercise 3 could replace 'complained'?* (*made a complaint about*)
- Elicit the answer to number 2.
- Remind them that they will need to rewrite the first sentence using the word in bold so that the second sentence means exactly the same thing. They shouldn't change the word given and they will need to use between two and five words.
- Remind students that they should write the missing words in capital letters.
- Remind them that contractions such as *don't, doesn't, hasn't,* etc count as two words. The exception to this is *can't* which counts as one word (because it comes from *cannot*).
- Remind students that when they have completed the sentences they should read them through again to make sure they have followed the instructions properly.
- Students then work individually to complete the exercise.
- Elicit answers.

1 Larry WISHED HE HAD TOLD the police about it sooner.
2 I MADE A COMPLAINT ABOUT my noisy neighbours to the police.
3 Alex WISHED HE HADN'T COMMITTED arson.
4 Mack HAS NO REGRETS ABOUT robbing the bank.
5 Mum suggested PAYING OUR UNCLE A VISIT in prison the following day.

Suggested homework

Assign Ex. 1 and 2 – Workbook, p.113
Ex. 1 and 2 – Workbook, p.114

Writing

1

Aim: to review stories

- Before students do the exercises on this page, ask them to study page 152 of the **Writing database**, either in class or at home before the lesson starts.
- Remind students that they have written a number of stories before and so they should be familiar with the form of stories.
- Put them in pairs and ask them to decide which statements about stories are true and which are not true. Ask them to tick the statements which are true.
- Give students some time to complete the task and then elicit the answers.

3 ✓ 4 ✓ 5 ✓ 6 ✓

2

Aim: to focus on the appropriate style for a story

- Ask one student to read the writing task aloud while the other students follow along in their books. Check comprehension by asking: *Why are you writing the story?* (for a competition) *Who is running the competition?* (a website for young people) *What are the rules of the competition?* (all stories must have the title given)
- Elicit from students what different styles of writing they know. They will probably be able to suggest 'formal' and 'informal', but may need prompting for other styles: informative, descriptive, conversational, business-like, entertaining, etc.
- Elicit what style(s) would be appropriate for a story to enter the competiton.

An appropriate style would be one that is neither too formal nor too informal, with good descriptive language.

3

Aim: to provide a model and to focus on paragraphs

- Ask students to read the model answer. You may like to ask one student to read it aloud while the other students follow along in their books.
- Ask students to paraphrase the story in their own words. Ask them to say what happens at the beginning, in the middle and at the end of the story.
- Ask students if (apart from the lack of paragraphs) this would be a good story to enter into the competition (Yes, it would.). Ask them to comment on the good aspects of the story (it has a simple plot / it uses good descriptive language / it has few characters / it has a surprise ending).
- Ask students to read the story again and to mark where they think paragraph breaks should be. Give them some time to complete the task and then ask them to compare their ideas with a partner's. Elicit answers from different students and point out that there is more than one correct answer.

There may be more than one way to divide the story into paragraphs. One good way is:

The Missing Diamonds!

Jake Johnson, the detective, was at a party being given by Mrs Spender, the richest woman in the area. It was a gorgeous evening and the guests were chatting in the garden. Suddenly, there was a scream and Mrs Spender rushed out of the house.

"My diamonds have been stolen!" she cried.

Jake immediately took control. He ordered the guests not to leave and he took Mrs Spender inside. He asked her what exactly had been stolen.

"My diamond necklace," she replied. "I placed it on the table while I fed the cat. And the next time I looked, it was gone!"

Jake told her to rest and then he questioned all the guests. It seemed that everyone had been in the garden at the time the crime was committed.

Jake suddenly heard a sound like glass. He looked up and outside the window was Mrs Spender's cat, with a diamond necklace around its neck! He picked up the cat and went into Mrs Spender's room.

"I think I've solved the mystery of the missing diamonds!" he said, laughing.

Additional task

- Ask students to look at the tenses the writer has used in the story. Put students in pairs and ask them to make notes on why the writer has used the different tenses.
- Give them some time to complete the task and then elicit answers.

The writer has used past simple for the main action of the story. He/She has also used past continuous for background actions in progress at the start of the story (*were chatting*). He/She has also used the past perfect for actions that happened before the main action of the story (*had been in the garden*).

He/She has also used the present perfect in direct speech for recent actions where the present result is important (*I've solved*).

4

Aim: to focus on descriptive language

- Explain to students that we use descriptive language in stories. This means that we use interesting, precise words instead of ordinary, general words.
- Draw students' attention to the first item and ask them to look for a word in the story that means the same as 'nice'. Tell them that they will find the answer in the first four lines of the story. Elicit that the answer is 'gorgeous'. Elicit that 'nice' is a general, ordinary word, whereas 'gorgeous' is a more descriptive word.
- Ask students to complete the task in the same way. Give them some time and then elicit the answers.

1 gorgeous	4 rushed	7 replied
2 chatting	5 cried	8 placed
3 scream	6 ordered	

5

Aim: to encourage students to plan their writing

- This exercise is designed to ensure that all students have enough ideas before they start writing, and to ensure that they understand how to organise those ideas.
- Ask students to look at the questions and to make notes in their notebooks.
- Remind them that they should answer the questions with one or two sentences. You might also tell them that, since this is a plan, it's not necessary to write in complete sentences at this stage.
- Give students some time to complete the task, and go round the class monitoring or helping where necessary.
- At the end of the exercise, ask individual students to read out their ideas.

1–9 students' own answers

- Ask students to turn to **Writing Planner 16** on page 162. Explain that each Writing Planner gives them a simple table to complete which helps them to put the right content in the right place in their piece of writing.
- Point out to students that each row of the table refers to a different part of their piece of writing and gives its purpose, together with useful expressions. Explain to students that they should complete the 'notes' column using their own ideas.
- Give students some time to complete the table. Invite a number of students to say what they have put in the 'notes' column for each part of the piece of writing. If possible, you may like to check the notes made by all students to ensure they have enough content to base their piece of writing on. Ask students to refer to the Writing Planner as they do their piece of writing.

6

Aim: to give students the opportunity to produce a story

- This exercise can be done in class or set for homework.
- Remind students of the importance of using descriptive language and of using paragraphs.

7

Aim: to encourage students to check their written work

- Draw students' attention to the checklist.
- When they have finished writing, ask them to read each statement and to tick each one that is true for them.
- Ask them to make sure that they have ticked all of the boxes before handing their story in to be marked.
- You might consider refusing to mark any story that does not meet all of the criteria in the checklist and asking the student to rewrite.

Additional task

- In order to monitor whether students have checked their work carefully, you could ask them to underline in pencil on their stories places where they have used 'good descriptive language', for example.
- Alternatively, invite individual students to read their stories to the rest of the class and get the whole class to comment on the good aspects of each story they hear.

Look Back

Aim: to review the unit and to practise scanning for specific information

- Students now have the opportunity to go back through the unit to check what they have learned.
- Ask the whole class the questions from **Look Back**.
- Elicit answers from different students.
- Encourage students to scan the unit to find any information they can't remember.

1 guilty
2 the past
3 shoplifting
4 poverty
5 Any of the following:
I'm not sure I completely understand.
Could you ask me that again, please?
Could you explain what X means?
Would you mind repeating the question?
Do you think you could explain that again, please?

Suggested homework

Assign Ex. 1, 2, 3 and 4 – Workbook, p.115

Webquest

- Ask students to complete the **Webquest** on page 201 of the Student's Book. You might ask students to work on this together in class if you have internet access, or you might assign it for homework.
- Explain to students that the answers to the questions are not in the Student's Book but that they need to find the answers online.
- Check the answers together and ask students to explain where they found the answers and how they found them (eg by typing terms into a search engine).

1 orchard
2 chlorofluorocarbon
3 environs/environmentalist
4 green
5 precipitation
6 (Sir) Robert Peel
7 gaol
8 (HMP) Slade (Prison)
9 spend time in prison / serve a prison sentence / go to prison, etc
10 copse

Further material

- For further practice and consolidation, ask students to complete the Unit 16 tasks on the Student's CD-ROM.
- To test students' understanding of the material in Unit 16, you may like to administer the Unit 16 Test, Term Test 3 and the FCE Lite Practice Test, which are in the Tests section of the Teacher's DVD-ROM. You may also like to construct your own test using the Test Generator material for Unit 16.

Revision Units 15-16

1

1 A	3 B	5 B	7 C	9 C
2 C	4 C	6 D	8 A	10 D

2

1 shoplifting
2 arson
3 murder
4 (bank) robbery
5 assault
6 burglary
7 blackmail

3

1 C	3 C	5 A	7 B
2 B	4 B	6 C	

4

1 to	3 with	5 of	7 with
2 of	4 for	6 for	

5

(2 marks for each correct answer)

1 politicians
2 scientists
3 protesters
4 director
5 survivors
6 inspectors

6

(2 marks for each correct answer)

1 I've got your school report here and I <u>find it a little worrying</u>, George.
2 We could go and <u>pay Hilary a visit</u> this weekend, if you like.
3 I'd like to <u>make a suggestion</u>, if you'd let me.
4 My dad says he <u>has no regrets about</u> giving up his career to look after us kids.
5 As I left, two hotel guests who <u>wanted to make a complaint</u> were demanding to see the manager.

7

1 f	3 a	5 b	7 e
2 g	4 d	6 c	

Audioscripts

Unit 1

Listening 2

1
Oh, you know what Dad's like. He's so hot-tempered! Well, he usually comes home late from work on Friday evenings. He's always in a bad mood as well, because of the traffic. This time, though, he decided to come home early. He thinks I study as soon as I get home on Friday, but I normally go into his office and have a game of 'Net Killer' on the computer. He caught me and went mad. I have to stay in for two weeks!

2
Even now, we are both very competitive. I think twin sisters are often like that, you know. I always wanted to be a doctor, so, of course, my sister did too. It takes a long time to realise that you both have very different talents. In a way, we both build things now. I think that I help my students to build their own characters, and she helps her clients to build whatever they want to build. We're very close, but it can be difficult sometimes, like all relationships.

3
Speaker 1: It's about six weeks since he left. I really miss him.
Speaker 2: It must be difficult. What does your dad say?
Speaker 1: Oh, you know. He doesn't show it. He says it's only two hours away.
Speaker 2: Doesn't your uncle live there?
Speaker 1: That's right. He helped Josh move into his new flat. Josh says that he's having a great time, but the work is quite hard. He says I can go and visit during the holidays. I can't wait.

4
It's so unfair! … Yeah, that's right. She's always doing it. Mum and Dad don't listen. She does it when I'm not there … A what? … Oh, a lock. Well, I could. You know me, though. I'd lose the key. It's not expensive make-up, but that's not the point. It's really annoying when I'm going out and I can't find it … It's all right for you. Your brother's not like that. That reminds me. Is he coming to Rose's party on Friday?

5
So, listen. About this party. It's happening on Saturday, at about nine o'clock. My mum's really excited about it because she hasn't seen them for a few months. She said that we don't need to take presents, but I was thinking of getting one anyway. Do you remember my brother's? When so many people came? That was so much fun. Well, this party's even bigger. My uncle's house is huge. Come round to mine at about eight and we'll get ready. Is that all right?

Soundbite

7 beat	9 peel	2 pill
6 mill	8 still	0 bit
4 seat	7 beat	
0 bit	4 seat	

Unit 2

Listening 2 & 3

Conversation 1
Woman: Can I help you?
Man: I'd like a first class return ticket to York, please.
Woman: You'll need to change at Manchester. You arrive at Platform 3 at 10:30 and you need to get to Platform 7 to catch the 10:45.
Man: Okay, I'll do that. And what time does it get to the station at York?
Woman: It takes two hours. And it'll be £77, please.

Conversation 2
Man: Have you been to France before?
Woman: Only once. I'm really looking forward to it. Do you know how long the voyage is?
Man: I think it's about six hours from here. It looks like we'll have good weather.
Woman: Oh, good. I think I'll go down to my cabin and make sure I haven't forgotten anything!
Man: Okay. Perhaps I'll see you later.

Conversation 3
Woman: Excuse me, driver. How long do you think it's going to take?
Man: It depends on which way you want to go. If we go over the bridge, it'll be faster because we'll avoid all the traffic in the city centre.
Woman: But that's further, isn't it? So the fare will be higher.
Man: Yes. It's up to you. We can go through the city centre if you like, but it'll be very slow at this time of day.
Woman: No, you're probably right. Let's go the long way.

Soundbite

1 thank bed thirty cat
2 head had said paid
3 apple ant ape arm
4 pet hut pat send

Unit 3

Listening 1

Speaker 1
I suppose I've been doing it for about four years now. The thing with karate is that you have to practise constantly. I found that quite hard at first because I wasn't used to it, but now I quite enjoy doing my exercises these days.

Speaker 2
I don't know if you'd call it a hobby exactly, but I do watch a lot of TV. I find it entertains me when I haven't got anything better to do. I'll watch whatever's on, really, although I'm not so interested in sports. I know some people think it's a waste of time, but I'm not embarrassed.

Listening 2

Speaker 1
I suppose I've been doing it for about four years now. The thing with karate is that you have to practise constantly. I found that quite hard at first because I wasn't used to it, but now I quite enjoy doing my exercises these days. A lot of it is in the mind. You have to be able to concentrate and to stay calm. The end result should be perfect harmony between mind and body. It can be difficult to stay calm, though, when you're trying to get the next belt. There's a lot of pressure on you to do all the moves perfectly.

Speaker 2
Basketball is a wonderful game. My uncle got me my first basketball and I've been playing ever since. From the moment I picked it up, I loved the game. I joined a team when I was old enough and now I play matches every weekend and train about three times a week. It's a sport that teaches you a lot about teamwork – you have to learn how to cooperate well with other people. Some people don't like that, but I think it's what sport is all about.

Speaker 3
I don't know if you'd call it a hobby exactly, but I do watch a lot of TV. I find it entertains me when I haven't got anything better to do. I'll watch whatever's on, really, although I'm not so interested in sports. I know some people think it's a waste of time, but I'm not embarrassed. I think I've learned a huge amount from television, and not just watching documentaries. Watching foreign programmes can help your English, and you learn about how people live in other countries much better than you can from a book. That's where you'll find me most weekends, in front of the TV.

Speaker 4
I like spending time on my own, so drawing is the ideal hobby for me. I started drawing when I was very young, like most people, and I found that I was quite good at it. I don't know. I can just look at something and I know how to put it onto paper. Mostly, I draw things that I see around me, but sometimes I just make things up from my imagination. I can escape from my everyday problems that way. And the good thing is that when you've finished you've got a work of art that you can hang on your wall, or give to somebody.

Soundbite

1 come though luck put
2 ran run won rule
3 fun far full fuss
4 truck trust track true

Unit 4

Listening 1

Interviewer: Today on 'World of Work' I'm joined by Craig Philips and Susan Walker, careers officers. Craig and Susan, welcome to the show.
Craig & Susan: Thank you.
Interviewer: Could I start by asking, just what does a careers officer do, exactly? Craig?
Craig: A number of different things, and over the 17 years I've been doing the job it hasn't changed much. My main role is still to go into schools and speak to teenagers to find out what kind of work they're thinking of doing and then I give them whatever advice I can. My area includes around 50 schools and I visit each one about once a year.
Susan: My area is similar, with around 5,000 pupils aged 17 to 18.That's a lot of interviews, and a lot of advice to give out. Unfortunately, we can only speak to each person for about 10 minutes, but I know that most of them find even such a short time quite useful.

Listening 2

Interviewer: Today on 'World of Work', I'm joined by Craig Philips and Susan Walker, careers officers. Craig and Susan, welcome to the show.
Craig & Susan: Thank you.
Interviewer: Could I start by asking, just what does a careers officer do, exactly? Craig?
Craig: A number of different things, and over the 17 years I've been doing the job it hasn't changed much. My main role is still to go into schools and speak to teenagers to find out what kind of work

they're thinking of doing and then I give them whatever advice I can. My area includes around 50 schools and I visit each one about once a year.

Susan: My area is similar, with around 5,000 pupils aged 17 to 18.That's a lot of interviews, and a lot of advice to give out. Unfortunately, we can only speak to each person for about 10 minutes, but I know that most of them find even such a short time quite useful.

Interviewer: I suppose that lots of youngsters must come to you with the same ambition.

Susan: Well, we do get a lot of people who want to follow a career as a doctor or a lawyer. Unfortunately, only about 10% of them will actually make it. Some of the people I speak to, though, do have quite different ambitions. Undertakers, politicians, pop stars, actors. Young people want to do all kinds of job.

Craig: I remember one young man who said to me that he wanted to be an astronaut. I really wasn't certain what advice would be best, so in the end I suggested he join the air force. I didn't think about it for years after that and then one day I saw a photo of him in a newspaper and he had become part of the European space programme. You never know.

Interviewer: What advice would you give to young people listening to the show?

Craig: First of all, my favourite piece of advice is: you can change your mind. Don't feel that saying 'I want to be an architect' means that you can't become a doctor if you want to. People's lives go in all kinds of direction. Try to have a clear idea of what you want, but be prepared to change.

Susan: I would say that there's nothing like experience.You can't really want to do a job unless you know something about it first. For example, some people say that they want to be a lawyer because they like helping people. Fine. But there are hundreds of different ways in which you can help people. Are you sure that working in the law is for you? Visit a local lawyer, ask them about their work. Are you still interested? Good, because now you know what you want.

Interviewer: Finally, are there any jobs you would like to do?

Susan: Oh, hundreds. Vet, nurse, writer, farmer … I can see a part of me in lots of different jobs. Having said that, I'm quite happy doing what I'm doing.

Craig: Me, too. There was a time when I thought that I might make a good actor, but I'm happy to be helping other people realise their ambitions now.

Interviewer: Craig and Susan, thank you for speaking to us today.

Soundbite

listen
plumber
lamb
climber
comb
tomb
pneumonia
knight

Unit 5

Listening 1

Extract 1

Now, Amy, your two thousand euros is safe – that's yours to take back home with you to Manchester whatever happens. Not nervous are you? Well, don't be, because tonight, Amy, you've got the chance to take away with you a brand-new sports car. Are you ready? Well, let's go play Super Money!

Extract 2

My next guest has been called a genius, a failure, a supermum and the wife from hell. Since her first days in action films, when she was known as 'the blonde James Bond', her career has never been easy. Currently starring in the hit show 'Girls and Guns' at the Grand Theatre, London, would you please welcome…Billie Davenport!

Extract 3

Listen to me. Sit down. I have to tell you something. It's important. It's about Brad. No, don't interrupt. I know it must've been hard for you since the divorce, but there are some things that you should know. Your father said not to tell you, but I think it's time. You see, Brad isn't really your cousin at all. I know you'll find this hard to believe, but … he's your brother. Brad is my son.

Extract 4

Dog: Woof!

Woman: Now, whatever happens, Chris mustn't know that you're here. He said no dogs in the flat, and that means you. Oh, my god, it's him. Quick, where can I put you. No, don't open the door. Here, get in the cupboard. That's it. Ah, Chris, you're back.

Chris: Sorry, dear. I forgot my passport. It's in the cupboard I think.

Woman: No! … er … I mean, no … need to worry about it. I'll get it for you.

Chris: What was that?

Woman: What was what?

Chris: That woofing sound.

Woman: Erm … oh, that was me.

Extract 5

Unemployment: fact or fiction? Tonight on *Global Focus*, we investigate the government's claims that the unemployment figures have fallen every month for the last three years. In the last three years, around a hundred businesses have closed. We ask, what has happened to the missing unemployed and why does the government keep changing the way it counts the number of people out of work?

Listening 2

[As above, but in this order: Extract 3, Extract 5, Extract 4, Extract 2, Extract 1.]

Soundbite

1	word	sorry	fear	bird
2	hard	heard	murder	bread
3	fair	fur	first	far
4	mean	meant	learn	burn
5	sir	occur	part	sour

Unit 6

Listening 1

Interviewer: Hello, and welcome to 'Tell Me Why', the programme that answers questions that *you* have about science. I'm going to jump straight in with the first question today. It's from Nicola in Derby and she says, 'Dear Tell Me Why, what is a rainbow? I've seen lots of them near where I live, but could you tell me exactly what a rainbow is?' Well, to answer your question, Nicola, I've got with me in the studio Dr Kate Williams of the Science Museum. Now, Kate, that's a good question, isn't it?

Listening 2

Interviewer: Hello, and welcome to 'Tell Me Why', the programme that answers questions that *you* have about science. I'm going to jump straight in with the first question today. It's from Nicola in Derby and she says, 'Dear Tell Me Why, what is a rainbow? I've seen lots of them near where I live, but could you tell me exactly what a rainbow is?' Well, to answer your question, Nicola, I've got with me in the studio Dr. Kate Williams of the Science Museum. Now, Kate, that's a good question, isn't it?

Kate: Yes, Mark, it certainly is. I'm sure we've all looked at rainbows and wondered about them. But let me ask you another question. Why is the sky blue?

Interviewer: Erm … I've got no idea.

Kate: Well, the energy from the sun is actually made up of radio waves, microwaves and light of lots of different colours. All this energy is travelling towards the Earth every minute of every day. When it reaches the Earth, dust in the atmosphere bends the light. Now, blue light bends more than red light so when you look up, you're seeing just the blue part of the light from the sun.

Interviewer: Okay … but what does that have to do with rainbows?

Kate: Let me ask you another question. When do you see a rainbow?

Interviewer: I think I usually see one when it's raining and the sun's shining at the same time.

Kate: That's right. It's all caused by raindrops. Next time you're out in the rain, look closely at a raindrop on a leaf. As you move your head, you'll see all the colours of the rainbow. You see, the light is bent as it passes through the raindrop. In a shower, there are millions of raindrops, all bending the sun's light.
Different colours are bent in different ways, so we see them in different places. That's what makes a rainbow.

Interviewer: Right. Now, rainbows always seem to happen in summer and never in winter. Why's that?

Kate: Simple. In winter, at high altitudes, the raindrops are frozen so they don't bend light in the same way. Even so, on a mild winter's day, you might see a rainbow if the conditions are right. Did you know, by the way, that you can even get a faint rainbow if the Moon is behind you and it rains?

Interviewer: Really? That's interesting. I'll look out for that. Finally, the last time you were on the programme you had a great experiment that our listeners could try at home. Is there any way we can explore rainbows at home?

Kate: Yes, there are a couple of things you could do at home. For example, you can often create your own rainbow. If you've got a garden hose, try spraying water into the air. The tiny drops work like rain. There's another good way to see the colours of the rainbow. You'll need the sun, of course. And you'll need a bowl, a small mirror and a piece of card. What you do is put the bowl where the sun is shining directly onto it, with the mirror under the water. Put the piece of card so that it gets the reflection from the mirror. If you move things around a bit, you'll soon see the seven colours of the rainbow.

Interviewer: Thanks, Kate, for that information. Moving on to the next question, this comes from Alison in Bolton. Alison wants to know what causes lightning. Well, thanks for that question, Alison, and to answer it we visited the Science Museum in London …

Soundbite

and I get a bit scared when there's lots of thunder and lightning.
an Don't forget to take an umbrella.
as It's not as cold as yesterday, is it?
at It started snowing at 10 o'clock and didn't stop.
can If it's warm, we can go to the beach.
for It seems like it's been raining for days.

Unit 7

Listening 1 & 2

Conversation 1

Woman: And what about the menu for this month?

Man: Well, I'd like to include some fresh, seasonal dishes on the menu. Perhaps we could have some interesting salads, even though it's winter.

Woman: I'll have a word with the chef. Carrots and leeks are in season, and I'm sure he'll have some ideas.

Man: Good. Let me know what he comes up with. Now, let's think about what we need to order for this month.

Conversation 2

Woman: I'd like you to try the new chicken dish and see what you think.

Man: It's delicious. So are we putting it on the menu this month?

Woman: Yes. Now that you know what it's like, you'll know what you're talking about when customers ask about it. We'll be serving it with spinach and rice.

Man: I'll make sure I recommend it. Now what new desserts are we planning to have?

Conversation 3

Woman: The beef is served with broccoli, cauliflower and a pepper sauce.

Man: Right. That sounds interesting. And how do you cook the potatoes?

Woman: However you want, although we suggest boiled.

Man: Okay, that sounds fine. Now, I'm not sure about the soup. Can you tell me what the ingredients are?

Woman: It's vegetable soup, with leeks, carrots, potato and onion. It's cooked very simply, like all our dishes.

Man: Okay, I'll give it a go. And we'll see about dessert later.

Conversation 4

Woman: Could you recommend something to go with the lamb?

Man: Well, it's quite spicy, so you might want to consider something simple like a selection of seasonal vegetables and mashed potatoes.

Woman: Could you do the potatoes with mustard? And cheese?

Man: I'm sure we can manage that. I'll pass the message on.

Woman: And please make sure you don't add any salt. I'm on a salt-free diet.

Man: Ah, okay. That's not a problem.

Soundbite

bag bang back bank

1	thick	think	thing
2	sank	sag	sang
3	sing	sick	sink
4	bring	brink	brick

Unit 8

Listening 1 & 2

Interviewer: Excuse me.

Woman: Yes?

Interviewer: Sorry to bother you. I work for a holiday company, and I'm doing market research on holidays. Would you mind answering a few questions?

Woman: Er … yes, okay. I've just come back from holiday, actually.

Interviewer: Okay … Can I start by asking where you went on holiday?

Woman: Originally, we were planning to go to Rome, but in the end we decided to stay in the United Kingdom and we flew up to Glasgow, in Scotland.

Interviewer: Right. And where did you stay?

Woman: The Bellevue Hotel. It's a large hotel in the centre. We arrived on the 17th and we were there for 10 days. It was full of other tourists, which was quite nice because it meant that there were people to chat to when we couldn't go out. That was quite often because I don't think it stopped raining the whole time we were there! The hotel staff did their best to make it as pleasant as possible, suggesting indoor places to visit, but still, it made life very difficult.

Interviewer: And what about the city itself?

Woman: Well, what we saw of it was very nice. We managed to get to some of the places in our guidebook, and they were very interesting. We were particularly impressed by the museums and art galleries. The thing we didn't like was the atmosphere. There are a large number of cars in the city centre, and my husband has a problem with his breathing and all the fumes made it worse. I really think they should do something about that.

Interviewer: What do you think they should do?

Woman: There's only one way to deal with it, and that's to make public transport easier to use. We found it quite confusing to get around the city, and we travel fairly regularly. I think clearer instructions and more trains would make a big difference.

Interviewer: Did you feel you learned about local culture?

Woman: Oh, yes. We went to a few different cultural events. We went to a very interesting display of traditional Scottish dancing, which made me think of another recent holiday, to India, where we also saw some very interesting dances. And then there were nights in local restaurants. I'm afraid we found those rather disappointing. It was a relief to get home and finally cook something for ourselves.

Interviewer: Finally, what did you think of your journey to and from your destination?

Woman: On the plane, you mean? Well, going was fine, but coming back was a bit of a nightmare. The first thing was that our plane was cancelled. We couldn't believe it! I know these things happen sometimes, but more information would have been a help. There were 150 of us in the airport, not knowing what was happening. The airline finally put us on another flight. With the delay, though, our luggage got lost! At least we were going home, so it wasn't such a big problem. We finally got it back a week later.

Interviewer: Right. Well, thank you very much for your time. That's very helpful.

Woman: You're welcome. Goodbye.

Soundbite

1 My brother says he wants to go to Spain.
2 I'd advise you to speak to a travel agent.
3 You need a holiday, if you're under so much stress at work.
4 I'm not really interested in travelling abroad, to be honest.
5 My dad doesn't like foreign food.
6 I'd like chicken, chips and peas, please.
7 There's been a huge increase in tourism this year.

Unit 9

Listening 1 & 2

Speaker 1
I've played lots of different computer games, so it takes a lot to surprise me. If you're looking for a lot of action, *Cave Warrior* is great. What you're trying to do is find the lost treasure of the Incas. I like the adventure element of it, much more than, say, *Cup Final*. It can be a bit predictable, though, so I'd rather play something like *Mad Driver City*, you know, the kind of game where you have to really plan what you want to do if you're to have any chance of success.

Speaker 2
It was the first time I'd tried these video game consoles, so I wasn't really sure what to expect. It all seemed to be happening a bit fast for me. I think you probably need really good reflexes for most of these games, especially sports games or driving games. *Mad Driver City* was just crazy. Something like *Night Thief* is probably more my style, not that I like stealing things in real life, or anything. Yeah, definitely. *Cup Final* started off okay, but I couldn't really control the players, so I lost interest in it quite quickly.

Speaker 3
Cave Warrior is a great game, although it's not perfect. If I wrote a video game, I'd put more action in it and make the whole thing a bit faster. Still, it's a lot faster than something like *Cup Final*, or *Tower of Evil*. My brother loves *Tower of Evil* because it's got such good graphics, which is true. I've also tried *Night Thief*, but it's a bit too much like being at criminal school for me – you have to solve mathematical problems to open safes and turn off alarms, that kind of thing. If I wanted that, I would do my maths homework.

Speaker 4
People say that computer games are a bit anti-social and that you spend time on your computer when you should be seeing your friends. It's not like that with me because my best friend plays computer games as well. We like games where we can play against each other, rather than go off on an adventure, like you have to in *Cave Warrior*. *Mad Driver City* would probably be the best if you could both drive at the same time but you have to take it in turns and then compare scores, which spoils it for us. We are always looking out for something where we can compete against each other. You can imagine how we felt when *Cup Final* came out.

Speaker 5
If you're thinking about buying a new game, you have to be a bit careful because they're quite expensive. I've made some expensive mistakes in the past. I hardly ever get *Cup Final* out of the box, for example. You have to think about what you like. If it's great graphics you like, then something like *Tower of Evil* would suit you, or if you like driving games then *Mad Driver City*. You have to play quite a few to find out what your tastes are,

otherwise you could waste money on a puzzle game, like *Night Thief*, when you don't really like puzzles. Personally, I like beautiful games, where you look at the screen and it's just all so real. You might be able to find a better look than *Tower of Evil*, but I doubt it.

Soundbite

1 Only half of the people were saved.
2 Could you get me a sheet from the office, please?
3 Did you show all of them?
4 They have lots of different sorts.

Unit 10

Listening 2

Carl: I'm joined now in the studio by Liz Hogan, and we're going to be talking about a fun and creative thing for you and your friends to try. Liz, welcome.

Liz: Thanks for inviting me on the show, Carl!

Carl: Glad you could come. And of course the reason we invited you on is because a couple of weeks ago we asked listeners to email us with their ideas for fun, constructive things for teenagers to do in their free time. And your idea really appealed to all of us. So, maybe you'd like to start by telling us your suggestion.

Liz: Sure! Well, this is something that I've done with my friends on several occasions and it's really satisfying – and great fun. The basic idea is to make a short film and then upload it to YouTube® or Vimeo© or a site like that.

Carl: Now, that sounds very simple, but it takes quite a lot of planning, doesn't it?

Liz: If you want to do it properly, then yes, it does. Of course, you could just all sit around and film yourselves without any preparation at all, but the chances are that won't be very interesting for the viewer! No, what I'm talking about is some kind of scripted or semi-scripted drama that you act out.

Carl: Okay, so – what tips do you have for people who want to do something like this?

Liz: Firstly, the good news is that you don't need expensive equipment. Most smartphones these days have video cameras, and they're pretty good quality – certainly good enough for these purposes. You might have problems with picking up sound outdoors sometimes, so you do have to be a bit careful where and how you film.

Carl: But before you film, you have to have an idea of what you're going to film, right?

Liz: That's right. You probably don't want too many people – five or six is perfect. You should all get together first of all and decide what kind of film you want to make. You know, a comedy, a thriller, a social drama, a ghost story, whatever.

Carl: Okay.

Liz: Then you need to decide on characters, come up with some kind of plot, and either write the full script or a rough outline of the script.

Carl: Can you just explain that, because earlier you mentioned it maybe being 'semi-scripted'.

Liz: Yes, what I mean by that is that you might just put in the script, for example, 'Adam and Justine argue about whether to go to the party or not' and then leave the actual dialogue up to the actors when you film it.

Carl: I see. Any other tips?

Liz: It's probably best that the person filming it doesn't actually appear in the film. You could take turns filming, of course, but we've found it's better if there's just one cameraperson, who also serves as the director. Apart from that, my other major piece of advice would be to set it in your own surroundings in the present day. That way, you don't have to worry about buying costumes or finding unusual backgrounds and buildings, etc. It's much easier if the actors can wear their own clothes, and you can film right where you live.

Carl: Really good advice there, Liz. Many thanks.

Liz: You're welcome.

Carl: And if any of you do decide to make your own film – and I really hope you do –send us the link in an email and we'll mention it on the show.

Soundbite

(Part 1)
There's a new theatre across the road from me.

(Part 2)

letter	leisure
about	exercise
entertain	occur
teacher	

Unit 11

Listening 2

Speaker 1
Well, it's not a bad job, and I've been here for 20 years now. I don't mind the kids. In fact, some of them can be quite funny, but I never really have a chance to speak to the teachers, apart from when they send for me when something is broken. The biggest problem here at St George's is probably graffiti. I seem to spend half my life cleaning graffiti off the walls. Apart from that, I spend a lot of time repairing doors and windows.

Speaker 2
St George's has really achieved some excellent academic results this year. We do try to encourage students to be involved in other things as well, and I don't just mean sports teams. I'm very pleased to say that the school play was a great success this year. Unfortunately, the

head of English, Mrs Drinkwater, is retiring this year so I'll have to find someone to replace her. It can be a real problem finding qualified teachers, you know.

Speaker 3
I've been in a number of schools, and none of them are quite as good as St George's. It has a really good atmosphere and everyone cares about the students. Mine all work hard and do everything I ask them to, which is all you can expect, really. The only problem is the hours. There's a lot of work to be done at home, so sometimes I don't finish until midnight, and then I'm here at eight-thirty the next morning.

Speaker 4
When Simon started at St George's, I was quite worried because he hadn't really enjoyed the last one. It turned out to be a really nice place in the end. The teachers are quite understanding and the students don't get hours and hours of homework, which is good. They still get good results, so we're keeping our fingers crossed for Simon. The staff keep the parents informed about their child's progress, and everything seems fine so far.

Speaker 5
It's quite a traditional school, so we do things like Latin and we don't really do computers very much. Everybody likes the teachers, although some of them are a bit strict. We get about an hour's homework each day, which isn't bad, but Mrs Atwood always gives us more than the others. The only day I don't really like is Thursday because we've got double German followed by double maths. Generally, I'd give St George's top marks.

Soundbite

As far as **I'm** concerned, home education is a great idea.
In **my** opinion, home education is a great idea.
If you ask **me**, home education is a great idea.
To **my** mind, home education is a great idea.
From **my** point of view, home education is a great idea.

Unit 12

Listening 1 & 2

Darren: Now, as you all know we've got Body Health Week coming up soon, and everyone who works on this show – including me – has promised to do something to get a little fitter. So what we're doing over the next few days is talking to all the production crew, and seeing what they're doing. And today it's Judy. Hi Judy.
Judy: Hi Darren!
Darren: Now, Judy, you're a production assistant here on the show. What are you doing in preparation for Body Health Week?
Judy: Well, I started a new diet last week.
Darren: A diet? What do you mean? Look at you. You don't need to lose weight! Let me just explain to the listeners that Judy is already extremely slim.
Judy: Ha! Thank you! Well, it's actually not that kind of diet at all. It's just to get healthy, really. I've been feeling a bit down recently, so I thought I'd try to get a bit fitter. I joined a gym and started working out and I just felt like I didn't have any energy. I saw something about this diet on the internet and I decided to try it.
Darren: So, tell us about it.
Judy: The first thing is that you can eat whatever you want.
Darren: That sounds like my kind of diet! What, you can even eat junk food and cakes and that sort of stuff?
Judy: Yes. It's called the 5-Point Plan. The first thing you have to do is learn a lot about how healthy different kinds of food are and why.
Darren: Don't we know that already? Isn't is just 'salads good, burger and chips bad'?
Judy: No, it doesn't really work like that. Ask yourself this: why do we think burgers and chips are bad for us?
Darren: Because it's junk food.
Judy: Yes, but why do we think junk food is bad for us?
Darren: Well, it's got a lot of fat in it.
Judy: Okay. So, which is better: to only eat fruit and vegetables or to only eat fast food?
Darren: To only eat fruit and vegetables, of course.
Judy: No, because then you're not getting the fat you need. The idea is that you have to have a balanced diet, you know, with a bit of everything in it, even fast food.
Darren: So how do you do it?
Judy: Well, there are five basic kinds of food. That's why it's called the 5-Point Plan.
Darren: Don't tell me. Erm ... fruit and vegetables, that's one. Rice and pasta and bread, things like that. That must be another. Let me think. Meat. I suppose meat must be one of them. So, what are the other two?
Judy: Dairy products. You know, eggs, milk, cheese, yoghurt, cream. And then there's everything else. They call that group the 'Enjoyment' group, because it's got things like cakes and sweets and chocolate in it. When you eat something from each group, that's one point, and you have to count your points each day. You have to have two points from each group, apart from the 'Enjoyment' group, where you can have one point. So, today I've had toast for breakfast and a sandwich for lunch – 2 bread points. A glass of milk for breakfast, and there was cheese on my sandwich – 2 dairy points. And I'm going out for dinner, so I'll have my meat and fruit points then.
Darren: There's just one problem.
Judy: What's that?
Darren: How do you decide what you're going to have from the 'Enjoyment' group?
Judy: Oh, that's easy. I'll just have one dessert. A great big one!

Darren: Well, best of luck with the diet, Judy. We'll be talking to Judy again – and everyone else on the show who's trying to get a little bit healthier – during Body Health Week. If you'd like more information on Judy's 5-Point Plan, go to our website or call …

Soundbite

1	car	fat	father	can't
2	word	sword	court	bored
3	boot	look	too	shoot

Unit 13

Listening 1 & 2

Conversation 1

Guide: As I said earlier, the art world went through some dramatic changes in the first quarter of the twentieth century, led by Pablo Picasso. This painting here is typical of his early work. Picasso was influenced by …

Visitor: Sorry, but when would that have been?

Guide: This particular piece was completed in 1905 and the other pieces you see here were all completed between 1905 and 1906.

Visitor: They all seem to be quite similar.

Guide: This period in Picasso's work is known as the 'Rose period' and he tended to use light colours and became interested in painting circus performers. If you look at this particular example more closely, you'll see that Picasso …

Conversation 2

Man: Oh, we've been in this room before, haven't we?

Woman: No, I don't think so. You must be thinking of the one where we saw the Rembrandts. Oh, look! Now, I really like this one. Look at the colours.

Man: What is it?

Woman: Well, it's abstract. I love this orange here. That'd look great in the office, wouldn't it?

Man: I'm not sure the manager would like it. You've seen what he's got in his office, all that old-fashioned stuff. Talking of the office, isn't it about time we were getting back?

Woman: I suppose so. We'll have to come back when we've got more time to look around.

Conversation 3

Woman 1: What about this one? Who's that by?

Woman 2: Let me just look in the catalogue. Oh, it's George Harding. Ah, yes. I can see it now. It's definitely his style.

Woman 1: Hmm. I'm not sure. I liked his other stuff, but this one …

Woman 2: It's a bit depressing, isn't it? I find that with all his works. I don't want works of art in my house that depress me every time I look at them. Where would you put it?

Woman 1: In the hallway?

Woman 2: Oh, no. We don't want that to be the first thing that our guests see when they visit us. No. Let's see if we can find something else. Oh, and we wanted one for the living room, as well.

Woman 1: Okay. Well, what about something more abstract?

Woman 2: As long as it's bright and colourful. Come on. Let's see what's in this section, through here.

Conversation 4

Man 1: Oh, look, Simon. Posters. That's a bit like the one . . . er . . .

Man 2: Oh, yes, but it's a bit smaller, isn't it? And it's got a few more . . . er . . . It would look great in my living room, because my furniture's, you know, a bit like that.

Man 1: Good idea. But we're wasting time. What about ideas for your project? It's due on Monday, at least that's what they said in the lecture last week. Are you going to do what I did or …

Man 2: Oh, with the colours and that? No, I don't think so. We don't want to do the same thing, do we? No, I just need to get a few ideas. What about that one over by the thing over there?

Man 1: Er … mmm. I suppose so. Let's have a closer look.

Conversation 5

Gallery owner: So we moved the exhibition of Great Masters into the large room so that we could hold the modern exhibition in here.

Artist: I see. Yes, good idea. Lots of light in here. I see you've got me next to Linda Ponting.

Gallery owner: Yes, I hope you don't mind. We thought there was a good contrast, you know. She's so, well … so bright and confident, whereas your work is a little quieter, more understated, isn't it? A little less … erm … it demands a bit more of the viewer, don't you think?

Artist: Oh, yes. I can see what you mean. Yes. And I like Linda's work. Quite different to my … oh, did I tell you I've started a new piece?

Gallery owner: Really? Let's go up to the cafeteria and get a coffee and you can tell me all about it.

Artist: It's an idea I've had for some time …

Soundbite

1 hour
2 hello
3 himself
4 heir

5 handkerchief
6 honour
7 heel
8 humour

Unit 14

Listening 1

Welcome back to another edition of *Women In Sport*. Today, I'm joined in the studio by Angela Oliver, who's 15 years old and has been playing snooker since she was six. Last month, Angela became the first teenage girl ever to win the Lancashire Amateur Snooker Championship, and she hopes when she's older to become a professional player.

Listening 2

Elaine: Welcome back to another edition of *Women In Sport*. Today, I'm joined in the studio by Angela Oliver, who's 15 years old and has been playing snooker since she was six. Last month, Angela became the first teenage girl ever to win the Lancashire Amateur Snooker Championship, and she hopes when she's older to become a professional player. Angela, welcome.
Angela: Hi.
Elaine: First of all, congratulations on your incredible victory last month!
Angela: Thank you!
Elaine: How did you feel when you'd realised you'd won?
Angela: It was an amazing feeling! I still can't really believe it.
Elaine: Your dad must have felt very proud, too.
Angela: Yes, very! I think he was more excited than I was! He introduced me to snooker, of course, and taught me how to play, and he's always supported me, so it was wonderful to share it with him.
Elaine: Now, I know many of our listeners don't live in Britain and so don't know much about snooker, so maybe you could start by explaining the basic rules to them.
Angela: Sure. Well, the main aim is to get more points than your opponent. You get points by 'potting' balls – that means knocking them into one of the pockets in the corners and on the long sides of the snooker table. There are 15 red balls, and six balls of different colours. And the white ball, of course. That's the ball you hit with your snooker cue. The red balls are worth one point each, and if you pot one, it stays in the pocket.
Elaine: In other words, it doesn't get put back on the table.
Angela: Right. Once you've potted a red ball, you can try to pot one of the coloured balls. They're worth different points. Yellow's worth two points, green three points, then brown, blue, pink and black, each going up by one point each time.
Elaine: So black's worth seven points?
Angela: That's right.
Elaine: And what happens if you successfully pot one of the coloured balls?
Angela: You get the points, the coloured ball gets put back on the table, and you can then try for another red ball.
Elaine: Now, you said the red balls don't get put back on the table. What happens when there are no more red balls?
Angela: Then you try to pot the coloured balls in order of points, so you start with the lowest first, and finish with the black.
Elaine: There's a couple of other important things to know, aren't there? For example, what happens if you pot the black by mistake during the game?
Angela: If you pot any of the colours at the wrong time the points go to your opponent. So if you incorrectly pot the black, that's seven to the other side!
Elaine: It's best not to do that, then.
Angela: Definitely!
Elaine: And, the game's called snooker, of course, but what is a 'snooker'?
Angela: It's a situation which happens in the game sometimes. If you can't directly hit the ball you need to hit because there's another ball in the way, that's a 'snooker', or, as we usually say, you're snookered. You have to try to hit the ball by bouncing the white ball off one of the cushions…
Elaine: The cushion is what we call the inside side of the table, right?
Angela: That's right. Or by curving the white ball around the ball that's in the way.
Elaine: Okay, that's a pretty good introduction to the game, Angela. When we come back after the break, I'll be asking Angela what it's like to…

Soundbite

1 photograph photographer photographic
2 athlete athletic
3 victory victorious
4 famous infamous
5 science scientific
6 concentrate concentration

Unit 15

Listening 1

Speaker 1
Let me try to make this a little clearer. What happens is that factories and cars release chemicals into the atmosphere. Now, those chemicals don't just disappear.

Just because you can't see the smoke once the wind has blown it away doesn't mean that it isn't still there. And high in the atmosphere these chemicals combine with other chemicals to form acid. As a cloud forms, this acid is dissolved in the water until eventually it returns to the ground, where it enters the soil and affects plants. It can even affect animal and human health. Moving on now to the …

Speaker 2
So there we were, deep in the Amazonian rainforest, and we'd heard about this tribe of people who lived there, the Matacaxu, who apparently had only met white people once before. So we had to fight our way through the forest, you know, with all the bushes and plants, and there were no paths because no-one ever goes in that direction. Finally, we saw a clearing and there, in the middle of nowhere, was a village. The people came out to meet us and, you'll never guess. One of them was wearing a Coca-Cola® T-shirt and they were all smoking cigarettes. Seems like the Western world got there before we did.

Speaker 3
Look at the local park, for example. Every time you go there, there's litter all over the place. It's not that people don't care, although that's probably true for some of them. There just aren't enough litterbins. And that's the council's responsibility. What they need to do is put more bins there. They should employ a park keeper as well, you know, someone whose job it is to go round and make sure people don't just drop their rubbish where they feel like it. It's just not good enough, really.

Speaker 4
What the Tropical Rainforest Campaign needs more than ever is your help. You can start by recycling as much of your paper and plastic as possible and by writing to your local MP about the problems facing the rainforests. Why not join the campaign and start raising money to help protect this valuable natural resource? With a little time and effort, we can make a real difference to our world. Those of you under 18 might like to join our Forest Friends club, especially for young people.

Speaker 5
The idea that this government is responsible for the levels of pollution in this country is just not true. Since we took power, levels of air pollution have actually fallen by around 4%. It was the previous government that caused this situation by introducing new regulations that allowed factories to pump chemicals into our rivers and our atmosphere. That was why they lost three years ago, and that's why they are going to lose again in two years' time. This government is proud of its environmental achievements.

Listening 2

[As above but in this order: Speaker 4; Speaker 2; Speaker 1; Speaker 5; Speaker 3.]

Soundbite

hotel
shopping
stop
not
lock
hole
woke
boat
bomb
forgotten
wrote
comb

Unit 16

Listening 1 & 2

Presenter: With crime on the increase, many local people are asking what is being done to prevent it. With me in the studio I have Robert White. We've asked Robert onto the show because he's a local police officer. Robert, welcome to the show.

Robert: It's good to be here.

Presenter: Now, Robert, if I could start by asking you, why is the crime rate increasing in our area?

Robert: That's a very complicated question. In many ways, the local situation is a mirror of the national situation. The crime rate is increasing across the whole country, so we shouldn't be surprised if we also see an increase at the local level. Another thing we have to look at is poverty. Some people with very little money will steal because they feel they have to to survive. We understand that it can seem like the only way sometimes, but I want to emphasise that theft is always illegal. You know, you have to look at the causes of poverty, really. There's a lot of unemployment, which means people, especially young people, have more time on their hands and it's easy for them to get involved in crime.

Presenter: So what other causes do you see?

Robert: Part of it is the way we live today. We live in suburbs and travel to other areas to work or to see our friends. Most people today don't really know their neighbours. That's one of the reasons for Neighbour Power, the new scheme we're starting in this area. We hope that it'll make a big difference to crime.

Presenter: Tell us more about that idea.

Robert: We believe that crime prevention is very important. What we want to see happening is people helping their neighbours, you know, checking if everything is all right, looking after the house when the neighbour's on holiday, that sort of thing. We believe that the person next door is your best protection against burglary, which is the biggest crime problem in the area.

Presenter: What about other crimes? Car theft, for instance.

Robert: Well, statistics show that that's actually falling in our area, so we need to think about why that is. One reason is that new cars are much harder to steal than older cars because of alarms and immobilisers. We think that technology has an important part to play in crime prevention.

Presenter: So, if you had to give our listeners some simple crime prevention advice, what would it be?

Robert: Get to know your neighbour. We can only really start to deal with crime by helping each other. And remember that most burglars are out looking for an easy chance. Don't give it to them. Simply remembering to lock all your doors and windows at night can keep you and the things you own safe.

Presenter: What should listeners do if they want more information on Neighbour Power?

Robert: First of all, contact your local police station, to see if Neighbour Power has already started in your area. They'll tell you how to get involved. If there isn't a scheme in your area, then they'll advise you on starting one.

Presenter: Robert White, thank you. I hope you'll come back to speak to us in the future on what effect the scheme has had.

Robert: It would be a pleasure.

Presenter: Now we'll go over to Vanessa who has the latest national and international news for us.

Soundbite

do: **Do** you always lock your doors and windows at night?
from: My purse has been stolen **from** my bag!
some: I think we need **some** advice about crime prevention.
than: The crime rate has increased by more **than** 10 per cent.